This is the first full-length study to explore Simone de Beauvoir's autobiographical and biographical writings in the context of ideas on selfhood formulated in *Le Deuxième Sexe* and her other philosophical essays of the 1940s. Drawing on recent work in autobiographical studies and working within a broadly Foucauldian framework, Ursula Tidd offers a detailed analysis of Beauvoir's auto/biographical strategy as a woman writer seeking to write herself into the male-constructed autobiographical canon. Tidd first analyses Beauvoir's notions of selfhood in her philosophical essays, and then discusses her four autobiographical and two biographical volumes, along with some of her unpublished diaries, in an attempt to explore notions of selectivity, and the politics of truth-production and reception. The study concludes that Beauvoir's vast auto/biographical project, situated in specific personal and historical contexts, can be read as shaped by a testimonial obligation rooted in a productive consciousness of the Other.

Ursula Tidd is Lecturer in French at the University of Salford. She has published on Beauvoir in a number of journals. This is her first full-length book.

CAMBRIDGE STUDIES IN FRENCH 61

# SIMONE DE BEAUVOIR
# GENDER AND TESTIMONY

# CAMBRIDGE STUDIES IN FRENCH

GENERAL EDITOR: Michael Sheringham (*Royal Holloway, London*)
EDITORIAL BOARD: R. Howard Bloch (*Columbia University*),
Malcolm Bowie (*All Souls College, Oxford*), Terence Cave (*St John's College,
Oxford*), Ross Chambers (*University of Michigan*), Antoine Compagnon
(*Columbia University*), Peter France (*University of Edinburgh*),
Christie McDonald (*Harvard University*), Toril Moi (*Duke University*),
Naomi Schor (*Harvard University*)

*Recent titles in the series include*

ELZA ADAMOWICZ
*Surrealist Collage in Text and Image: Dissecting the Exquisite Corpse*

NICHOLAS WHITE
*The Family in Crisis in Late Nineteenth-Century French Fiction*

PAUL GIFFORD AND BRIAN STIMPSON (*eds.*)
*Reading Paul Valéry: Universe in Mind*

MICHAEL R. FINN
*Proust, the Body and Literary Form*

JULIE CANDLER HAYES
*Reading the French Enlightenment: System and Subversion*

A complete list of books in the series is given at the end of the volume.

# SIMONE DE BEAUVOIR
# GENDER AND TESTIMONY

URSULA TIDD

CAMBRIDGE
UNIVERSITY PRESS

PUBLISHED BY THE PRESS SYNDICATE OF THE UNIVERSITY OF CAMBRIDGE
The Pitt Building, Trumpington Street, Cambridge, United Kingdom

CAMBRIDGE UNIVERSITY PRESS
The Edinburgh Building, Cambridge CB2 2RU, UK   http://www.cup.cam.ac.uk
40 West 20th Street, New York, NY 10011–4211, USA   http://www.cup.org
10 Stamford Road, Oakleigh, Melbourne 3166, Australia

First published 1999

Printed in the United Kingdom at the University Press, Cambridge

Typeset in Baskerville 11/12.5pt (CE)

*A catalogue record for this book is available from the British Library*

*Library of Congress cataloguing in publication data*
Tidd, Ursula.
Simone de Beauvoir, gender and testimony / Ursula Tidd.
p.   cm. (*Cambridge studies in French*)
Includes bibliographical references.
ISBN 0 521 66130 7 (hardback)
1. Beauvoir, Simone de, 1908–   – Criticism and interpretation.
I. Title. II. Series.
pq2603.E362z887   1999
848'.91409 – dc21 99–11940 CIP

ISBN 0 521 66130 7 hardback

*For Harriet Lukens*

# Contents

# Acknowledgements

I would like to express my gratitude to the following people and organisations who have assisted me in the preparation of this study, originally based on my doctoral thesis. Firstly, I would like to thank Susan Heward who awakened my interest in feminist research when I was at Lancaster University in the early 1980s and has consistently supported me in my work. I would also like to thank Elizabeth Fallaize, who first suggested that I might do research on Beauvoir's autobiography and has always expressed interest in my work. My thanks also to former colleagues in the French Department at Birmingham University, particularly Alex Hughes for her advice and encouragement, Margaret Callander and Kate Ince. I owe an enormous debt of gratitude to my thesis supervisor, Professor Jennifer Birkett, whose incisive criticism and advice, intellectual rigour, support and patience were invaluable. I am also grateful to colleagues in the Departments of Modern Languages and English at Salford University for their encouragement during the final stages of the project. My thanks also to Linda Bree at Cambridge University Press for her advice during the process of publication.

Within Beauvoir studies, a number of other people have helped me in various ways. I would particularly like to thank Eva Lundgren-Gothlin, who read the original thesis and offered many useful comments. Margaret Crosland and Kate and Edward Fullbrook also sent me material related to their work on Beauvoir. I would also like to thank Margaret Simons and Yolanda Patterson for inviting me to present my research at conferences in the USA. I am grateful to Sylvie Le Bon de Beauvoir for kindly agreeing to be interviewed and for allowing me to quote from Beauvoir's unpublished diaries and published writing. I would like to thank Claudine Monteil who worked with Beauvoir in le mouvement de libération des femmes (MLF) and talked to me about her friendship with Beauvoir between 1970–86. In the wake of the publication of her book, *Mémoires d'une jeune fille dérangée*, Bianca Lamblin also kindly agreed to talk to me. I would like to thank Hélène de Beauvoir for agreeing to be interviewed and for her hospitality when I visited her in Alsace.

Additionally, I would like to thank several organisations who supported me financially by providing me with teaching work and/ or with various grants, bursaries and scholarships, thereby enabling me to conduct and publish this research, namely the University of Birmingham, the Sir Richard Stapley Educational Trust, the British Federation of Women Graduates and the European Studies Research Institute (*ESRI*) at the University of Salford.

A number of friends have supported me at various stages during this period of research. I would like to thank Ann Cronin, Judith Whyte, Professor Mary Fuller, Emma Tyler, Sabine Leschevin and Muriel Chiappelli. I would also like to thank my parents and the Lukens family who have consistently supported me.

Finally and most of all, I express my deepest gratitude to Harriet Lukens, with whom I have learned much about reciprocal self-other relations and whose support, advice and encouragement have always been unstinting.

Parts of this book have already been published and I am grateful to the following organisations for permission to draw on this earlier material here. Material from Chapter Four has appeared in 'Telling the Truth in Simone de Beauvoir's Autobiography' in *New Readings* 2 (1996), published by the School of European Studies at the University of Wales, College of Cardiff. The same extract has also appeared as Literary and Cultural Studies Working Paper no.26, published in February 1996 by ESRI at The University of Salford. Material from the second half of Chapter Six formed the basis of a paper called 'The Function of Testimony in Simone de Beauvoir's Autobiography' at the *Women in French* 1996 biennial conference in Ilkley, Yorkshire, and has been published as 'From Disciplining the Self to an Autobiography of Praxis: Simone de Beauvoir's Cycle of Testimony' in Volume 5 of *Women In French Studies* (1997).

# Abbreviations

| | |
|---|---|
| *AJLJ* | *L'Amérique au jour le jour* |
| *BI* | *Les Belles Images* |
| *CDA* | *La Cérémonie des adieux* |
| *DSi* | *Le Deuxième Sexe i* |
| *DSii* | *Le Deuxième Sexe ii* |
| *EN* | *L'Etre et le néant* |
| *FA* | *La Force de l'âge* |
| *FCi* | *La Force des choses i* |
| *FCii* | *La Force des choses ii* |
| *FR* | *La Femme rompue* |
| *JG* | *Journal de guerre* |
| *LNA* | *Lettres à Nelson Algren, un amour transatlantique 1947–64* |
| *LSi* | *Lettres à Sartre 1930–9* |
| *LSii* | *Lettres à Sartre 1940–63* |
| *MJFR* | *Mémoires d'une jeune fille rangée* |
| *PC* | *Pyrrhus et Cinéas* |
| *PMA* | *Pour une morale de l'ambiguïté* |
| *QPLS* | *Quand prime le spirituel* |
| *SDA* | *Le Sang des autres* |
| *TCF* | *Tout compte fait* |
| *THSM* | *Tous les hommes sont mortels* |
| *UMTD* | *Une mort très douce* |

# Introduction

Simone de Beauvoir has been described as 'the emblematic intellectual woman of the twentieth century'.[1] The range of her contribution to twentieth-century cultural capital is certainly impressive: Goncourt prize winner and author of seven fictional works; a key theorist within French existentialism; author of *Le Deuxième Sexe* (1949),[2] which is arguably the most pioneering feminist text of the century; a significant figure in twentieth-century French autobiography; an important travel writer and contributor to the French epistolary tradition; a thinker and political activist, who addressed contentious issues such as the brutality of the French army during the Algerian War, attitudes to ageing and women's right to contraception and abortion within a patriarchal society.

Such an extensive contribution to twentieth-century culture has been the focus of a vast amount of critical and popular attention. In particular, since Beauvoir's death in 1986, the publication of the *Lettres à Sartre* and *Journal de guerre* in 1990 and recently, of her letters to Nelson Algren, critical interest in her oeuvre has assumed a renewed impetus.[3] These events have encouraged re-evaluations of her work, particularly in Britain and the United States. This has mainly taken the form of a re-assessment of Beauvoir's status as a philosopher, involving a recognition of her contribution to existential phenomenology and an increased awareness of the ethical concerns in her writing – a development itself resulting perhaps from a 'fin de siècle' and millennium anxiety to evaluate the significance of intellectual and philosophical traditions, an increased awareness of women's contribution to the production of philosophy and a related criticism of the assumptions of white, Western, patriarchal intellectual traditions and systems of thought.

Since 1990, in addition to two biographies of Beauvoir – Deirdre Bair's *Simone de Beauvoir, A Biography* (1990)[4] and Margaret Crosland's

*Simone de Beauvoir, The Woman and Her Work* (1992)[5] – there have been
significant new critical readings of her work. Perhaps the most
important of these, in terms of its originality, intellectual calibre and
range, is Toril Moi's *Simone de Beauvoir: The Making of an Intellectual
Woman* (1994). Some other recent contributions which have sought to
illuminate individual areas of Beauvoir's work include Eva
Lundgren-Gothlin's *Sex and Existence*, which offers new philosophical,
historical and feminist insights into *Le Deuxième Sexe*, by placing it in
the context of Hegelian philosophy, phenomenology and Marxist
theory.[6] Further contemporary re-assessments of *Le Deuxième Sexe* are
provided in a collection of interdisciplinary essays edited by Ruth
Evans – *Simone de Beauvoir's The Second Sex* (1998).[7] Kate and Edward
Fullbrook's controversial *Simone de Beauvoir and Jean-Paul Sartre, The
Remaking of a Twentieth-Century Legend* (1993),[8] argues that Beauvoir
was responsible for the philosophical framework of Sartre's *L'Etre et
le néant*. In *Philosophy as Passion, The Thinking of Simone de Beauvoir*, from
a Foucauldian critical perspective, Karen Vintges delineates a
Beauvoirian ethics drawing on a wide range of her writing.[9] In 1998,
the Fullbrooks' second book, *Simone de Beauvoir, A Critical Introduction*,
offered a philosophical reading of some of the fictional texts and
philosophical essays.[10] Joseph Mahon's *Existentialism, Feminism and
Simone de Beauvoir* provides a re-reading of her philosophical essays of
the 1940s, in defence of Beauvoirian existentialist feminism.[11]
Finally, ten years after her influential study of Beauvoir's fiction,
Elizabeth Fallaize's recent edited collection of key critical readings of
*Le Deuxième Sexe*, the autobiography and the fiction, published
between 1961 to the mid-1990s, demonstrates the diversity of critical
interest in Beauvoir's writing.[12]

   In the United States, there has been a relatively consistent interest
in Beauvoir's work in recent decades. She had been interested in
American literature since her student days, and, from 1947, developed a strong connection with the United States when she first
visited the country.[13] The American engagement with Beauvoir's
work gained impetus in the late 1960s, when key figures of the US
Women's Liberation Movement such as Shulamith Firestone and
Kate Millett became interested in the materialist analysis of women's
oppression in *Le Deuxième Sexe*. Since the early 1970s, The Society for
Women in Philosophy has acted as a forum for discussion of
Beauvoir's philosophy.[14] In 1983, the Simone de Beauvoir Society of
America was founded.[15] In 1986, an edition of *Yale French Studies*

devoted to Beauvoir was published,[16] with North American contributors such as Elaine Marks, Yolanda Patterson and Margaret A. Simons, who have all written books on Beauvoir. The social constructionist account of gender in *Le Deuxième Sexe* was also a starting point for Judith Butler, in her ground-breaking *Gender Trouble, Feminism and the Subversion of Identity* (1990).[17] The Simone de Beauvoir Circle, which seeks to explore Beauvoir's philosophical work, was also formed in North America. Moreover, articles on Beauvoirian philosophy have regularly appeared in the feminist philosophy journal, *Hypatia*, based in the United States.[18] Recently, Margaret Simons has edited a collection of philosophical essays, *Feminist Interpretations of Simone de Beauvoir* (1995) and written a book on Beauvoir and existentialism.[19] Debra B. Bergoffen's *The Philosophy of Simone de Beauvoir, Gendered Phenomenologies, Erotic Generosities* (1997) explores the original contribution of Beauvoirian ethics to the phenomenological tradition.[20]

In France, there appears to be less critical interest in the range of Beauvoir's work. This relative 'phénomène de rejet' may be explained by several factors: first, the prevailing masculinism of French intellectual life and of the construction of the French philosophical tradition, noted by Toril Moi.[21] Second, the predominance of psychoanalytically inspired feminism in France which, with its concern for psycho-sexual difference, is incompatible with Beauvoir's materialist and anti-essentialist approach to gendered identity in *Le Deuxième Sexe*.[22] The third factor is her lifelong partnership with Jean-Paul Sartre which has, until recently, obscured her independent contribution to twentieth-century French culture.

Since 1990, following the publication of the *Lettres à Sartre* and the *Journal de guerre*, controversial and popular first-hand accounts of episodes in Beauvoir's and Sartre's lives were published in France. Gilbert Joseph's sensationalist *Une si douce Occupation . . .: Simone de Beauvoir et Jean-Paul Sartre 1940–1944* (1991) attempted to demolish any notion that they had played an active role in the French Resistance.[23] In 1993, in response to the account of her relationship with Sartre and Beauvoir in the letters and war diary, Bianca Lamblin's *Mémoires d'une jeune fille dérangée* was published, which related her version of events.[24] The following year, Jean-Pierre Saccani's journalistic account, *Nelson et Simone* (1994), described Beauvoir's relationship with the American novelist, Nelson Algren.[25] To coincide with the ten-year anniversary of Beauvoir's death, another first-hand 'témoignage' was published: *Simone de Beauvoir, Le Mouvement des Femmes: Mémoires d'une jeune fille rebelle* (1996), by a member of Beauvoir's feminist circle, Claudine Monteil.[26]

Since 1990, there has been limited critical interest in Beauvoir in France. In addition to occasional articles on her work in academic journals, in *Les Temps modernes*, and in the French press, an edition of *Roman 20–50* was devoted to Beauvoir in 1992, comprising a previously unpublished fragment of *La Femme rompue*, 'Malentendu à Moscou', and several articles on *L'Invitée* and *Les Mandarins*.[27] In 1994, continuing her work begun in *L'Etude et le rouet* (1989) on the Sartre-Beauvoir philosophical collaboration,[28] Michèle Le Doeuff contributed an article to the *Magazine littéraire* for its special issue on existentialism.[29] In 1995, Mona Ozouf offered an appraisal of Beauvoir's life and writing project in *Les Mots des femmes*.[30] Fortunately for Beauvoir's status as an intellectual and writer in France, Toril Moi's 1994 study has been translated and published with a preface by Pierre Bourdieu.

The present study engages with two areas in Beauvoir studies: her philosophy of selfhood and her auto/biographical writings. It seeks to examine critically Beauvoir's auto/biographical project in the context of her notion of selfhood, as represented in her philosophy of the 1940s. In the early days of Beauvoir criticism (the first study of her writing was published in 1958),[31] two critics noted the theme of her relationship to existence, as it is evident in her project of self-representation in her autobiographical writing. In 1958, the psycho-analyst Octave Mannoni gave a lecture at the *Collège de philosophie* on *Mémoires d'une jeune fille rangée*, in which he argued that Beauvoir's autobiographical relationship with herself was manifest from a reading of the *Mémoires*.[32] Mannoni based his argument on the narrative organisation of the text, the role played by the unsaid and Beauvoir's notion of the autobiographical task (at the time of writing the *Mémoires*) as 'telling all'. In 1966, Francis Jeanson explained what he perceived as Beauvoir's perpetual 'autobiographisme' in his important study, *Simone de Beauvoir ou l'entreprise de vivre*:

Cet écrivain n'a guère entrepris, sous des formes diverses, que de se dire, de se décrire elle-même, de nous raconter sa vie, de ramener à soi tous les problèmes humains qu'elle a rencontrés dans ce monde. Presque tous ses livres peuvent être considérés comme autobiographiques.[33]

Jeanson rejected the charge of narcissism in Beauvoir's case, and argued that she demonstrates an attentiveness to her own temporally situated existence in the world with others. He maintained that because the Other plays a key role in Beauvoir's notion of literature, her concern to represent her own experience could not be viewed as motivated by narcissism and self-satisfaction.

Both these critics raised an issue central to this discussion: Beauvoir's concept of selfhood and the role played by narrative in the representation of selfhood in her auto/biographical writing. Both critics failed, however, to consider discourses of gender, class or sexuality as important in setting the parameters of Beauvoir's auto/ biographical self-representation. Similarly they did not consider the impact of her situation as a woman writer on her negotiation of auto/biographical representation.

Texts from Beauvoir's extensive auto/biographical corpus (memoirs, biography, letters and diaries) are frequently cited as sources of information on her life in discussions of her work. Yet relatively little critical attention has been paid to her auto/bio-graphical self-construction or her negotiation of auto/biography as an historically contingent discourse in the context of her notions of selfhood in her earlier philosophical writings.

There have been certain important, although brief, critical discussions of her autobiography. For example, in 1989, Jane Heath offered a Lacanian feminist reading of the memoirs in a single chapter in her book, *Simone de Beauvoir*.[34] In a feminist study of five French women autobiographers, *Autobiographical Tightropes* (1990), Leah Hewitt argues (also in a single chapter) that Beauvoir's memoirs can be viewed as texts problematically situated within the male auto-biographical tradition.[35] Hewitt says that Beauvoir refuses to engage with her marginalised status as a woman writer and that her notion of literature and her specific engagement with autobiography produce many tensions in the texts. Although this study adopts a different theoretical perspective, Heath's and Hewitt's discussions have been useful in developing the arguments in Part II concerning Beauvoir's autobiographical writings. In *Autobiography and the Existential Self* (1995), there are two interesting examinations of her letters and war diary within the context of the memoirs by Terry Keefe and Emma Wilson.[36] Keefe compares the different accounts of a brief wartime period given in the letters, war diary and memoirs. He argues that this type of comparative textual analysis enables us to identify omissions and thereby to determine the nature of autobiographical selectivity. Wilson's reading of the *Journal de guerre* sheds interesting light on Beauvoir's representation of her relationship with Nathalie Sorokine and of the female couple in her writing. More recently, in 1997, Valérie Baisnée has briefly analysed *Mémoires d'une jeune fille rangée* within a broader discussion of women's autobiographical writing as a strategy of resistance.[37]

The theoretical approach to Beauvoir's philosophy and auto/biography employed here has been influenced by feminist work in philosophy and autobiography studies. Michel Foucault's early work on the elaboration of the modern subject through discourses of truth, knowledge and power has also been valuable in shaping the theoretical perspective on Beauvoir's writing and on autobiography. Recent work on the viability of a Foucauldian feminism has proved helpful in this respect.[38] This has highlighted the limitations of Foucault's work for theorising female agency and collective action because of his relative silence on the systematic oppression of women by patriarchal societies. In his later work, notably in the three volumes of *L'Histoire de la sexualité*, Foucault's interests shifted away from the disciplined subject as the product of power relations to the ethical subject who fashions himself. Although this self-fashioning is (superficially) similar, as Karen Vintges has argued, to the Beauvoirian existentialist ethical concept of an anti-essentialist self, who fashions his or her life as a project, there are serious tensions between Beauvoir's ethical project and the late Foucauldian account of the subject, which Vintges seems to overlook.[39] It is necessary to expose some of these tensions here in order to clarify my own methodological use of Foucault's work.

Many feminist commentators have noted Foucault's masculinist perspective,which is particularly evident in *L'Usage des plaisirs* and *Le Souci de soi*, the second and third volumes of *Histoire de la sexualité* respectively, in which he explores the treatment of sexuality and the aesthetics of subjectivity in Greek, Graeco-Roman and early Christian ethics.[40] Seductive as Foucault's rhetoric and notions of self-stylisation and actualisation may be for the critic of autobiography, as Kate Soper has argued, his account is 'systematically abstracted not only from the female but from any relational conception of the person' and is concerned only with how societal changes affect a 'masculine ethics of self-comportment'.[41] Although Beauvoir was never a keen proponent of sexual difference, she recognised that the social construction of the subject entailed differentiated gender roles.

There are, then, serious tensions between Foucault's masculinist self-actualising subject and Beauvoir's notion of socially-constructed and socially-committed ethical selfhood.

Although Beauvoir did not advocate a universalist moral theory, she was nevertheless concerned throughout her life with moral questions which had a direct impact on self-Other relations of all kinds. Rooted in the real, the Beauvoirian self is confronted by moral questions and choices at both the day-to-day, micro-political level and the wider, collective level of his or her relations with the Other. From her philosophical essays of the 1940s onwards, Beauvoir articulates a concept of the agential self as situated in relation to other people, time, space and in relation to identity categories such as age, gender, class, sexuality and race. In Foucault's late work, however, as Soper argues: 'the ethical is . . . defined in terms of personal style, self-mastery and authorial creation' and this aestheti-cised self has minimal transgressive power.[42]

Moreover, as Terry Eagleton and Jean Grimshaw have argued, Foucault's notion of the subject is insubstantial in the later volumes of *Histoire de la sexualité*, as subjectivity is conflated with corporeality and the ethical is mistaken for the aesthetic.[43] Further, Grimshaw notes that Foucault's preoccupation with the male body and tech-niques of self-mastery leads him to disregard completely how women in patriarchal societies have been subject to the male gaze and attendant disciplinary techniques of corporeal self-mastery and mutilation, such as anorexia – areas which Beauvoir explores particularly in *Le Deuxième Sexe* and in her fiction.[44] Grimshaw argues that Foucault's espousal of an 'aesthetic' approach to morality as an alternative to a universal moral code overlooks the possibility of elaborating an ethics which respects difference, mutuality and collectivity. Such an ethics need not be either prescriptive and universalist or aestheticised, masculinist and solip-sistic in orientation, as Beauvoir's thought demonstrates. Similarly, Eagleton observes that Foucault's emphasis on the individual and his capacity for self-mastery disregards the effects of his actions on others:

Foucault's vigorously self-mastering individual remains wholly monadic. Society is just an assemblage of autonomous self-disciplining agents, with no sense that their self-realization might flourish within bonds of mutuality . . . What matters is one's control over and prudent distribution of one's powers and pleasures.[45]

For all these reasons, Beauvoir's practical ethics and notions of gendered subjectivity, rooted as they are in the real and always already in relation to the Other, are substantially removed from Foucault's aestheticised and somewhat narcissistic, solipsistic subject found in his later work.

In other respects, aspects of early Foucauldian theory have been productive in this discussion. His work on the disciplinary gaze, the discursive production of the 'corps docile' (the body as object and focus of power), his view of the truth of the subject as a product of historically and politically contingent discourses and his notion of power as operating generatively and locally have been fruitful in developing the methodology of this study of Beauvoir's auto/biographical writing.

Foucauldian theory has, therefore, opened up the possibility of reading Beauvoir's writing project and her collaboration with Sartre at times more productively than a psychoanalytic reading, for example. There is some degree of engagement with psychoanalytic theory in this study, although this approach similarly has its tensions. Firstly, psychoanalytical accounts of subjectivity give disproportionate and deterministic emphasis to early infancy, to the detriment of later elaborations of subjectivity, during which early childhood psycho-social scripts can be, and frequently are, reworked. Beauvoir's life is a good example of this reworking, as we will see in Part II. By attributing a necessary role to the past, psychoanalytical accounts of subjectivity neglect the present and future experience and potential of subjectivity, as a continuing synchronic and diachronic negotiation of the possibilities of agency. Secondly, a psychoanalytic critical methodology can be viewed as politically conservative because of its emphasis on the past and because it privileges the middle class, nuclear family of white, Western, heterosexual patriarchy as the locus of identity formation – which Beauvoir tried to escape throughout her life. A psychoanalytic reading of her work might act, consequently, as a bourgeois, heterosexist recovery of Beauvoir's literary and intellectual project. In their emphasis on the individual subject, psychoanalytical accounts largely neglect the impact of historical and political change on the elaboration of situated subjectivity, which, it will be argued, is relevant in a consideration of Beauvoir's notion of selfhood and her project of testimonial autobiography. Lastly, several critics have read her writing project psychoanalytically (as Beauvoir herself anticipated), and in this study of her auto/biographical writing, I have sought to explore the viability of a range of theoretical approaches.

Before outlining the structure of this study, further explanation is required with respect to the choice of texts to be examined. In Part I, theoretical texts published in the 1940s have been chosen in which Beauvoir elaborates a theory of selfhood. This notion of selfhood is then related in Part II to her auto/biographical self-representation. A central question for the discussion in Part II was to establish a working definition of autobiography. As Philippe Lejeune has noted in *Moi aussi* (1986), to define autobiography is to enter a vicious but necessary circle: 'impossible d'étudier l'objet avant de l'avoir délimité, impossible de le délimiter avant de l'avoir étudié'.[46] After much reflection, it seemed most productive to examine the four volumes of Beauvoir's memoirs with two biographical texts and some of her letters and diaries in order to consider how she negotiates auto/biographical self-Other representations as a woman writer, working within a tradition until recently constructed as predominantly male.

The issue of communicative strategy in auto/biography was also important to consider – both in terms of Beauvoir's writing project and, more generally, because of the allied issue of auto/biographical agency. Given that women auto/biographers have been marginalised until recently in auto/biography studies, it was important in this discussion to respect the specificity of Beauvoir's autobiographical agency and communicative strategy.

These considerations were paramount in deciding whether to include a sustained discussion of her letters and diaries. Diaries and letters are interesting aspects of a writer's *oeuvre*, but they are usually, and certainly in Beauvoir's case, less 'travaillés' than formal auto/biography. In an interview I conducted with Hélène de Beauvoir, she remarked that '[Simone] savait qu'elle n'était pas vraiment une épistolière. Elle ne s'applique pas du tout. Elle s'appliquait quand elle écrivait ses romans, elle ne s'appliquait pas pour ses lettres.'[47] Nevertheless, much of Beauvoir's correspondence is now in the public domain and offers the reader significant information about the context in which her writing was produced. The reader's desire for access to such information nevertheless has to be weighed against certain moral considerations, such as the ethics of the posthumous publication of writers' diaries and letters in the literary marketplace with or without the consent of their author and the related question of whether to respect auto/biographical privacy. Despite Sartre and Beauvoir's idealised and somewhat naïve notions of transparency, rooted in their respective views of language and their developing theories of the self-Other relation, diaries and letters are usually private documents, intended to be read by a specific individual at a specific time.[48] Beauvoir's letters and diaries are discussed on a limited basis here, as background to the composition of *Le Deuxième Sexe*, and in a brief discussion in Chapter 6, to illustrate the processes of textual (self-)construction involved in her auto/biographical project. Given that one of the aims of the discussion in Part II is to consider Beauvoir's negotiation of auto/biography as a discourse of truth-telling about the self, it was important to avoid a 'disciplinary' reading of her texts which played off different versions of auto-biographical truth against each other in an attempt to establish the 'right' one. Such a reading would attempt, erroneously, in my view, to eliminate inevitable autobiographical selectivity and construction in order to establish a hegemonic truth of Beauvoir's life, which would position her as an unreliable narrator and the critic as sole arbiter of 'truth'. Rather than policing her autobiographical writing for a disciplined truth, it is argued in Chapter 6 that several kinds of testimony operate in Beauvoir's auto/biography which construct her as 'witness to a century' within an 'age of testimony'.[49]

As a whole, the study seeks to explore Beauvoir's notions of the self in the context of her project of testimonial auto/biography. In Part I, Beauvoir's concept of selfhood is outlined. In Chapter 1, *Pyrrhus et Cinéas* (1944) and *Pour une morale de l'ambiguïté* (1947) are examined as the first theoretical texts in which Beauvoir elaborates a concept of the temporally situated self as a being-with-the-Other in the world.[50] In Chapter 2, *Le Deuxième Sexe* is then considered as a theoretical study of subjectivity, in which gender plays a key role. Beauvoir's correspondence with Nelson Algren provides useful back-ground to the composition of *Le Deuxième Sexe* and demonstrates her awareness of the connections between racial and sexual oppression in her developing concept of selfhood in the late 1940s. In Chapters 1 and 2, temporal and spatial situation, embodiment, gender, sexuality, race and class are viewed, then, as important facets of Beauvoir's notion of selfhood.

In Part II, this notion of the situated self is related to her negotiation of auto/biography and to her testimonial approach to auto/biographical self-representation. In Chapter 3, Beauvoir's approach to autobiography is examined within the context of her relationship to women's autobiographical writing more generally, to the role of the Other in autobiography and in terms of her project of 'telling all' in a narrative production of the temporally-situated self. In Chapter 4, her detailed negotiation of autobiographical self-representation with the reader is examined. In Chapter 5, the narrative construction of a disciplined 'self' is considered in *Mémoires d'une jeune fille rangée*. This self is rejected, and through her erotic attachment to Zaza, it is argued that Simone formulates a strategy to escape the patriarchal bourgeoisie. Beauvoir finished writing the *Mémoires* in the late 1950s. Remembering the deaths of Zaza in 1929 and of her cousin Jacques in the early 1950s, from the *Mémoires* onwards she assumes the role of surviving witness.[51] In Chapter 6, it is argued that Beauvoir's project of self-representation in testimonial autobiography works cyclically, from the disciplined self of the *Mémoires*, through a narrative of experience, to the politically committed autobiographical subject, as witness to both personal and collective history, a stance which is worked out in the subsequent volumes. In the final chapter, Beauvoir's negotiation of the bio-graphical is considered in an examination of *Une Mort très douce* and *La Cérémonie des adieux*.

PART I

*Becoming the self*

# CHAPTER I

# 'Pyrrhus et Cineas' *and* 'Pour une morale de l'ambiguïté'

*Pyrrhus et Cinéas* and *Pour une morale de l'ambiguïté* constitute Simone de Beauvoir's early philosophical works, prior to the publication of *Le Deuxième Sexe* in 1949. Yet, until relatively recently, most critics have tended to regard them as derivative of Sartre's *L'Etre et le néant*. Such a stance, which negates Beauvoir's independent contribution to the development of existential phenomenology, is increasingly hard to justify.[1] In this chapter, it will be evident that Beauvoir goes beyond slavish reproduction of ideas in *L'Etre et le néant*, not only displaying broad knowledge of the sources of existential phenomenology, but also distancing herself from certain Sartrian notions of freedom, action, corporeality and intersubjective relations. Space constraints preclude a complete analysis here of the divergences in Beauvoir's and Sartre's philosophical trajectories in the 1940s, let alone across the broader spectrum of their careers.[2] Instead, this chapter and Chapter 2 focus on Beauvoir's notion of selfhood in *Pyrrhus et Cinéas*, *Pour une morale de l'ambiguïté* and *Le Deuxième Sexe*, in the context of Sartre's *L'Etre et le néant* and Merleau-Ponty's *Phénoménologie de la perception* (1945) because, as Sonia Kruks and Toril Moi have noted, both these texts are important for Beauvoir's development of her own notion of subjectivity as a situated freedom in the world.[3]

It may be objected that by choosing to examine Beauvoir's essays for an account of her notion of selfhood, rather than her early fiction of the 1940s, this discussion is inattentive to political issues pertaining to the relationship between gender and genre. In contrast to Sartre, it can be argued that Beauvoir, as a woman writer and philosopher, might be positioned differently to the perceived generic identity of philosophy because of psycho-social interdictions which operate regarding women's production of philosophy in a traditionally patriarchal society. These interdictions have prevented women from fully participating in the production of philosophy in France and elsewhere, and have ensured that the philosophy produced by women has not been received as philosophy. An intertextual approach to women's philosophical writing would challenge masculinist definitions of philosophy and would maintain that Beauvoir's philosophy may be found in her fiction as well as in her philosophical essays.[4] She certainly drew upon her philosophical knowledge in her fiction, and texts such as *L'Invitée* or *Le Sang des autres* can be read as specific illustrations of certain existential issues, in particular, the parameters of the self-Other relation.[5] However, an intertextual approach to Beauvoir's philosophical writing is problematic for several reasons. First, she was, at times, strategic in her choice of genre and in the timing of her publications. Second, to read her fiction as disguised philosophy dismisses the literary craft of her writing and overlooks the complex issue of using the medium of literary discourse to communicate philosophical theory. Third, it can be argued that her choice of literature over philosophy is not entirely explained by gendered power relations which govern the production of intellectual and creative work. If this were the case, how and why did Beauvoir produce philosophy at all?

Beauvoir has often defended her choice of genre, asserting that different genres fulfil different functions for her. In *La Force des choses*, distinguishing between her use of the novel and essay forms, she says:

Mes essais reflètent mes options pratiques et mes certitudes intellectuelles; mes romans, l'étonnement où me jette, en gros et dans ses détails, notre condition humaine. Ils correspondent à deux ordres d'expérience qu'on ne saurait communiquer de la même manière. [. . .] Si je me suis exprimée sur deux registres, c'est que cette diversité m'était nécessaire.[6]

In her explanation in *La Force de l'âge* of how she came to write *Pyrrhus et Cinéas*, Beauvoir says that 'sur certaines choses que j'avais abordées dans *Le Sang des autres* il me restait des choses à dire, en particulier sur le rapport de l'expérience individuelle à la réalité universelle'.[7] Beauvoir has described the early 1940s as 'la "période morale" de ma vie littéraire', during which she began to articulate what she had learned since 1939 about solidarity, personal responsibility towards others and the significance of death.[8] She explains in *La Force de l'âge* that her purpose in *Pyrrhus et Cinéas* was to 'fournir à la morale existentialiste un contenu matériel'.[9] To a certain extent, the complex narrative construction of *Le Sang des autres* had enabled

Beauvoir to explore some of these issues. The narration of events by both central protagonists, Jean Blomart and Hélène Bertrand, in the first and third person, and in flashback,[10] enabled Beauvoir to convey that 'our lives are lived both as subject and object, as personal experience and yet inserted in a wider social and political perspective'.[11] The range of issues raised by our relationship to others, and the constraints upon our actions in the world, cannot, however, be adequately or easily addressed within the constraints of a fictional framework; in *Pyrrhus et Cinéas*, all these issues could be discussed more extensively.

## PYRRHUS ET CINÉAS

*Pyrrhus et Cinéas* is the first theoretical text in which Beauvoir outlines her notion of subjectivity as 'situated' and 'practical'.[12] She raises two related questions: what is the purpose of human existence and what is the nature of our relationship to the world and to others?[13]

The focus on 'autrui' is established at the beginning of Beauvoir's discussion, when she relates a number of daily incidents, in which we choose whether or not to become involved in other people's concerns. She gives the example of the bourgeois sitting at home reading about an ascent in the Himalayas, who identifies himself with human achievement. In Beauvoir's view such an identification is erroneous:

> En s'identifiant à son sexe, à son pays, à sa classe, à l'humanité entière, un homme peut agrandir son jardin; mais il ne l'agrandit qu'en paroles; cette identification n'est qu'une prétention vide.[14]

We can identify with others' projects, but if this is not accompanied on our part by active involvement, it remains empty self-deception. Here she argues that language plays an active part in the formulation of a project, but it cannot substitute for action. This is later reiterated at the end of the essay when she argues that there is no 'outside' to the human condition, which is always already saturated in language:

> Nous pouvons toujours nous échapper vers un "ailleurs", mais cet ailleurs est encore quelque part, au sein de notre condition humaine; nous ne lui échappons jamais et nous n'avons aucun moyen de l'envisager du dehors pour la juger. Elle seule rend possible la parole. C'est avec elle que se définissent le bien et le mal; les mots d'utilité, de progrès, de crainte n'ont

de sens que dans un monde où le projet a fait apparaître des points de vue et des fins.[15]

Here language takes on a crucial role as the means to found a project. Language is a feature of the human condition, and immediately involves the existence of others. This point is likely to derive from Beauvoir's reading of Hegel, who argues in the *Phenomenology of Spirit* that 'in speech, self-consciousness qua independent separate individuality, comes as such into existence, so that it exists for others'.[16] Language is thus a crucial feature of our situation as being-with and for-others.

Beauvoir describes subjectivity here using the Sartrian terminology 'transcendance', although she uses it differently to Sartre. In *L'Etre et le néant*, Sartre uses the term 'transcendance' (derived from Husserlian phenomenology) at times as a synonym for 'le Pour-soi' and at other times to indicate a process of being. In both cases it represents consciousness as 'un jaillissement', moving towards the realisation of its own possibilities *by means of* the Other. While Sartre acknowledges in *L'Etre et le néant* that we exist in a world of others, he describes self-Other relations in the following (rather pessimistic) way:

Pendant que je tente de me libérer de l'emprise d'autrui, autrui tente de se libérer de la mienne; pendant que je cherche à asservir autrui, autrui cherche à m'asservir. [. . .] Le conflit est le sens originel de l'être-pour-autrui.[17]

Although Beauvoir refers to consciousness as 'un jaillissement', she appears to discard this definition quite quickly. She argues for a notion of the Other as reciprocally equal, as a being who is always already included in this movement of consciousness towards its own perpetual self-construction. Although Beauvoir and Sartre are working within the same philosophical framework – drawing on Husserlian phenomenology, Hegel, Kant and Heidegger – there is already an emphasis on reciprocity in self-Other relations in Beauvoir's argument. This is not evident in Sartre's account of *L'Etre et le néant*, where the emphasis is rather on the conflictual aspects of self-Other relations.[18]

Later in the first part of her essay, Beauvoir explains that although we may believe that we act according to our own specific concerns at a particular time, our actions inevitably take on a collective (and potentially different) significance in the future, which is beyond our control. Our actions are therefore temporally situated and situated in relation to others. She argues, using Sartre's vocabulary in *L'Etre et le néant* (although using a revised notion of transcendence), that we are transcendent beings constantly striving to make ourselves exist.[19] At the end of the first part of *Pyrrhus et Cinéas* she refutes solipsism, as she would two years later in *Tous les hommes sont mortels*:

Un homme seul au monde serait paralysé par la vision manifeste de la vanité de tous ses buts; il ne pourrait sans doute supporter de vivre. Mais l'homme n'est pas seul au monde.[20]

In the second part, Beauvoir begins by alluding to her auto-biographical project. She reasons that it is pointless to relate one's lifestory to oneself or to look at oneself in a mirror in order to authenticate one's existence because one can only experience oneself in isolation as a lack. For Beauvoir, this lack is effectively a lack of the Other, for only the Other can act as a guarantor of my actions and existence.[21] Any 'culte du moi', such as that proposed by Maurice Barrès, which, as a philosophy, had tempted Beauvoir during her late teens, is therefore impossible. We need the Other to act as witness to our actions, as receiver of our testimonies. This is a crucial point in relation to Beauvoir's testimonial auto/biographical project and will be developed in Chapter 6.

Beauvoir then focuses on self-sacrifice, because through this type of behaviour, some individuals try to assume others' projects as their own. Self-sacrifice is at the far end of the continuum of being-for-others and is also explored in 'L'Amoureuse' in the second volume of *Le Deuxième Sexe* and in Beauvoir's fiction, notably in *Les Mandarins* and *La Femme rompue*. If one were to interpret this section biographically, one might view her as working out the philosophical implications of her collaboration and partnership with Sartre.

In her discussion of self-sacrifice, Beauvoir examines the self-deception which is often involved in attempting to exist for the Other, and in mistakenly viewing oneself as the means to the Other's self-fulfilment. She argues that 'nous ne créons jamais pour autrui que des points de départ'.[22] Nevertheless, the Other is a crucial element of one's experience of subjectivity and the world:

Je ne peux rien ni pour autrui, ni contre autrui [. . .] Car quoi que je fasse, j'existe devant lui. Je suis là, confondu pour lui avec la scandaleuse existence de tout ce qui n'est pas lui, je suis la facticité de sa situation.[23]

To describe self-Other relations as constituting reciprocally the

facticity of my situation, or the given features of my existence in the
world which I have not chosen, signifies that, for Beauvoir, the
Other assumes the same importance for me as other elements of my
facticity, such as my class, my body, my past, my birth. I did not
choose these features of my existence and cannot choose to exist
without them, although I can choose *how* to live them. We cannot
use the Other or retreat to collective identity as a means to avoid the
burden of individual responsibility for our existence. The existential
irreducibility of the Other represents a form of given as far as each
individual is concerned. Citing the Dostoievskian epigraph to *Le
Sang des autres*, 'chacun est responsable de tout, devant tous',
Beauvoir explains that my individual freedom is always enmeshed
with another's freedom, so that the limit of my freedom is the
beginning of another's freedom. Freedom is therefore a collective
responsibility.

Beauvoir continues to grapple with the nature of our relationship
with others in the next section, and effectively, running in autobiographical parallel, her own relationship to Sartre's philosophy.
She argues that 'chacun n'est sujet que pour soi', which appears very
Sartrian, for according to his conflictual account of self-Other
relations in *L'Etre et le néant*, I am either subject or object for the
Other and vice-versa. Yet as Laurie Spurling notes, this notion of
self-Other relations is limited:

There are for Sartre only two paradigmatically authentic emotions:
arrogance (myself as subject) or shame (myself as object). Now this
framework for understanding relations between people can certainly be
illuminating for certain emotions or behavioural ploys – but it is sometimes
too dualistic and dogmatic. There are, for example, cases where I can
experience the Other as a subject for me – when I experience him as a
centre of orientation for objects around him, or as the agent of his actions –
without, as a correlate, experiencing myself as an object for him, which
should be impossible, if we stick strictly to Sartre's ontology.[24]

While Beauvoir similarly advocates that each person's experience of
subjectivity is unique to him or herself, we can nevertheless attempt
to communicate that experience of subjectivity to each other. She
argues that we need others, as free beings – and that involves them
acting as subjects – in order to escape the contingency of our
existence: 'nous avons besoin d'autrui pour que notre existence
devienne fondée et nécessaire'.[25] Although given that we are in
perpetual process of self-construction, no project can express the

totality of our individual existences. Although we may receive occasional validation for a particular action, a single instance of validation by the Other cannot 'save' our entire existence, for we are always condemned to reconstruct ourselves if we are to live authentically. This individual desire to be recognised for the totality of one's being is not valid for Beauvoir, because the totalisation of individual existence or the ultimate determination of the significance of individual existence cannot take place until death. Nevertheless, the desire for totalisation is strong and appears to motivate her to write autobiography, as will be argued in Chapter 4.

Beauvoir makes a significant point here in terms of her autobiographical project about the use of name and the production of identity:

Ainsi nous imaginons que la louange accordée à un de nos actes justifie tout notre être: c'est pourquoi nous nous soucions d'être nommés; le nom, c'est ma présence totale rassemblée magiquement dans l'objet.[26]

She expresses a patriarchal view of naming here, according to which name is deemed to contain identity unproblematically. Yet, only a year later, in 1945, Beauvoir had to confront the gendered significance of name, when she wrote some articles for *Combat* on the Liberation of Paris, which appeared under Sartre's byline.[27] In terms of her autobiographical project which she was to undertake ten years later, it is significant that Beauvoir specifically indicates the importance of name in *Pyrrhus et Cinéas* as a means of being present to the Other and as a talismanic symbol of identity.

Beauvoir continues by asserting that we are obliged to recognise others as free agents who implement their freedom in different ways. She substantiates her point by an autobiographical example of a disagreement between her father and Zaza, an incident which later appears in *Mémoires d'une jeune fille rangée*.[28] In *Pyrrhus et Cinéas*, Beauvoir describes this episode as an existential 'scandale' because it demonstrated to her the relative aspect of her world. Similarly, in the *Mémoires*, the incident revealed, according to the narrator, that 'on pouvait avoir un autre avis que mon père'.[29]

In *Pyrrhus et Cinéas* and, later, in *Pour une morale de l'ambiguïté*, Beauvoir's emphasis is less on the conflictual character of relationships with others, and more on the need for reciprocity, although she acknowledges that the latter may not always be possible. Beauvoir concedes that, at times, violence may be necessary against those who wish to oppress me, although recourse to violence is undesirable because it destroys equality, and equality is necessary for reciprocal relations between people.[30]

In summary, Beauvoir argues in *Pyrrhus et Cinéas* that there is no pre-determined purpose to life, but it is our responsibility to construct ourselves constantly. Subjectivity is therefore an ethical self-fashioning always within the context of our relationship with the Other. We are transcendent beings, who are intrinsically nothing but our projects. There is no recourse to God, an abstract notion of humanity or to any form of the absolute because, as individuals, we need to have our own sense of purpose which is individually relevant to us. Subject to the constraints of our situation, we can choose how to live our relationship with the Other, just as we can choose what significance we give to our past – for our subjectivity is temporally-situated. The notion of choosing our past is highly relevant to Beauvoir's autobiographical self-representation and will be analysed further in Part II.

In *La Force de l'âge*, Beauvoir offers a commentary on *Pyrrhus et Cinéas*, published sixteen years earlier. She explains that in this text she had attempted to reconcile her differences with Sartre over the issue of 'la situation'. The notion of 'situation' or the unavoidable fact of being positioned in time, space and in relation to others (among other factors) was introduced by Sartre in *L'Etre et le néant*. Beauvoir argues in *La Force de l'âge* that as far as freedom is concerned, 'les possibilités concrètes qui s'ouvrent aux gens sont inégales'.[31] This crucial recognition of a hierarchy of different situations with different material consequences which impinge on an individual's possibilities of freedom is introduced in *Pyrrhus et Cinéas* and developed in her subsequent essay, *Pour une morale de l'ambiguïté*. In *La Force de l'âge*, Beauvoir explains that in *Pyrrhus et Cinéas* she still appeared committed to the primary existence of the individual, who is then obliged to negotiate the limits of freedom with the Other. She claims that her view at the time of writing *Pyrrhus et Cinéas* was rather that 'l'individu ne reçoit une dimension humaine que par la reconnaissance d'autrui'. She explains that 'en vérité, la société m'investit dès ma naissance; c'est en son sein et dans ma liaison avec elle que je décide de moi'.[32]

It remains puzzling why Beauvoir appears to have deliberately articulated views which were effectively more Sartrian than her own, or played down her own notions of freedom and subjectivity as always already interdependent. In *La Force de l'âge*, Beauvoir claims that in mid-April, 1940,[33] when Sartre returned to Paris on leave and discussed his ideas in *L'Etre et le néant*, she disagreed with him about his notion of 'situation'. She says:

Nous discutâmes certains problèmes particuliers et surtout le rapport de la situation et de la liberté. Je soutenais que, du point de vue de la liberté, telle que Sartre la définissait – non pas résignation stoïcienne mais dépassement actif du donné – les situations ne sont pas équivalentes: quel dépassement est possible à la femme enfermée dans un harem? Même cette claustration, il y a différentes manières de la vivre, me disait Sartre. Je m'obstinai longtemps et je ne cédai que du bout du lèvres. Au fond, j'avais raison. Mais pour défendre ma position, il m'aurait fallu abandonner le terrain de la morale individualiste, donc idéaliste, sur lequel nous nous placions.[34]

As Sonia Kruks has noted, Beauvoir 'was never willing to challenge Sartre's conception of freedom head-on' but instead 'was quietly to subvert it'.[35] Furthermore, Toril Moi, in her discussion of the intellectual collaboration between Sartre and Beauvoir, has offered many convincing reasons why Beauvoir remained intellectually and affectively loyal to her 'significant Other', such as her precarious position as a female intellectual, her determination to forge an innovative relationship with Sartre, her admiration for his intellect and 'superior' philosophical gifts and her view of Sartre as her lifelong project.[36]

It was only in the late 1940s, with the publication of *Pour une morale de l'ambiguïté*, that Beauvoir was to develop further her own notion of the importance of the Other in 'situation'. Her different notion of 'situation' was not acknowledged, however, as she was already perceived as espousing Sartre's philosophy of *L'Etre et le néant*. Furthermore, as Sonia Kruks and Terry Keefe have argued, from the mid-1940s, Sartre had already begun to understand the limitations of the conflictual system of self-Other relations in *L'Etre et le néant*.[37] Keefe argues that although there is clear evidence in *L'Etre et le néant* that Sartre does accept the role of others within our 'situation', he is constrained by his own subject/object dualism – either I am a subject or object for the Other and vice versa. The range of different ways I can exist for-Others thus remains largely untheorised. Keefe notes that in *Cahiers pour une morale* (which although written between 1947–48 remained unpublished until 1983) Sartre develops a third attitude towards the Other – reciprocity.[38] As already noted, Beauvoir had already advocated the reciprocity of self-Other relations in *Pyrrhus et Cinéas* and its fictional counterpart, *Le Sang des autres*, which she had begun in October 1941. Furthermore, as will be argued below, Maurice Merleau-Ponty, who was also working within a phenomenological framework, had argued (in opposition to Sartre) for the existence of incarnate intersubjective relations in his *Phénoménologie de la perception* (1945).

*Pyrrhus et Cinéas*, however, is the first theoretical text in which Beauvoir began to outline her notion of subjectivity as 'situated' and 'practical'.

### POUR UNE MORALE DE L'AMBIGUÏTÉ

Beauvoir developed her notion of subjectivity further in her second essay on ethics, *Pour une morale de l'ambiguïté* which, after being serialised in *Les Temps modernes*, was published integrally in November 1947.[39] It is longer than *Pyrrhus et Cinéas* and is rather badly constructed because of repetitiveness and lack of clarity, which may be a result of its initial serialised publication. These stylistic flaws have probably not encouraged positive reception of Beauvoir's philosophy.

In *Pour une morale de l'ambiguïté* Beauvoir begins by arguing that the human condition is ambiguous, by which she means that the meaning of human existence is not fixed, but must be constantly created. We are embodied consciousnesses who are condemned to mortality. For Beauvoir, the majority of philosophers have failed to deal with the ambiguity of existence. They either lapse into dualism, which establishes a hierarchy between mind and body and fails to integrate both elements into human existence, or theories of immortality, which deny the reality of death, or the subordination of life to spirituality, which denies the material reality of life. Existentialism, according to Beauvoir, deals with the ambiguity of the human condition. In the first of several references to the post-Second World War situation, she argues that now more than ever, following a world war which involved multiple forms of genocide, people are forced to address this ambiguity. Part of the first section is a defence of Sartrian existentialism, conceived much in the same manner as her essay, 'L'Existentialisme et la sagesse des nations', first published in *Les Temps modernes* at the end of 1945. She addresses herself particularly to the charge that existentialism is a subjective if not a solipsistic philosophy. Comparing existentialism with Marxism, she argues that the existentialist's focus on the individual's assumption of his or her own freedom is a moral act, and one that involves others' freedom.

In the introductory section, Beauvoir tries to distinguish between different ways of conceptualising the relationship between freedom and existence. She cites Sartre's proposition that everyone is free because it is not possible for us not to be free, and that we can always escape our fate because we are free. However, Beauvoir distinguishes between the subject's natural freedom, which is the spontaneous, contingent freedom of coming into existence, and moral freedom, grounded by a project. This latter type of freedom implies the need to consider other people. As moral freedom needs a future dimension in order to have a purpose, it is automatically temporally-situated.

In the second section, anticipating her autobiographical self-representation, Beauvoir begins with a philosophical discussion of childhood, certain features of which are represented in the specific case study constituted by *Mémoires d'une jeune fille rangée.* In *Pour une morale de l'ambiguïté,* she says that the child finds him or herself in a given world, which appears absolute. The child is happily irresponsible because parents play the role of divine beings to which she or he is subject. Yet the child's world is metaphysically privileged because he or she escapes the anguish of freedom as a result of the existential unimportance of his or her actions.[40] This brief description of the childhood 'situation' is significant for, as Margaret Simons has noted, Beauvoir's philosophical interest in the experience of childhood is a feature which distinguishes her work from Sartre's prior to 1950.[41] It is also an aspect of this essay which has received little critical attention.[42]

Beauvoir continues her discussion by challenging indirectly Sartre's views on freedom in *L'Etre et le néant.* She argues that there are certain groups of people who are obliged to live in an infantile world, because they have been kept in a state of slavery and ignorance, such as black slaves in the Southern American states or women in patriarchal societies. She notes:

Même aujourd'hui, dans les pays d'Occident, il y a encore beaucoup de femmes, parmi celles qui n'ont pas fait dans le travail l'apprentissage de leur liberté, qui s'abritent dans l'ombre des hommes; elles adoptent sans discussion les opinions et valeurs reconnues par leur mari ou leur amant, et cela leur permet de développer des qualités enfantines interdites aux adultes parce qu'elles reposent sur un sentiment d'irresponsabilité.[43]

There is evidently a degree of irony in Beauvoir's observation here because her comments form part of her own subversion of Sartre's philosophy. She points out that whereas the child's situation is imposed upon him or her, (Western) women choose or at least consent to their situation. This contrasts with the situation of a black slave in the eighteenth century or a Muslim woman forced to remain in a harem, who have no means of challenging their oppression. Their position has to be judged according to their relative possibilities of action. Once the possibility of freedom exists, however, it is remiss not to seize the chance to act.

Returning to the situation of the child and adolescent, Beauvoir characterises adolescence as a time when one discovers one's own subjectivity and the subjectivity of others. The adolescent discovers that he or she is obliged to participate in the adult world by assuming his or her subjectivity and this is a source of existential crisis and moral choice. The experience of being 'irresponsibly' free during childhood produces a lifelong nostalgia for that time. For Beauvoir, unsurprisingly, the child does not contain the future adult, although it is always on the basis of the past that an adult makes choices regarding future behaviour:

C'est toujours à partir de ce qu'il a été qu'un homme décide de ce qu'il veut être: dans le caractère qu'il s'est donné, dans l'univers qui en est corrélatif, il puise les motivations de son attitude morale; or, ce caractère, cet univers, l'enfant les a constitués peu à peu sans en prévoir le développement.[44]

Although the 'choix originel' made by an individual can be reversed or remade, it is not without significance because the world reflects back to us our earlier choices, which means that it is increasingly difficult for us to escape the consequences of such temporally-situated choices. The importance of childhood in the construction of the self is also emphasised in Beauvoir's memoirs, as we shall see in Part II.

## *POUR UNE MORALE DE L'AMBIGUÏTÉ*: FREEDOM AND OTHERS

In the second part of *Pour une morale de l'ambiguïté*, Beauvoir resumes the discussion begun in *Pyrrhus et Cinéas* about the issue of freedom and the role of Others. Here she offers a series of portraits, or case studies, of types of individuals who exhibit different forms of self-deception. This is a technique she also uses both in the second volume of *Le Deuxième Sexe* and in her memoirs, in micro-biographical sketches of people in her entourage, and can be viewed as evidence of Beauvoir's interest in psychology and psychoanalysis. Robert Cottrell has likened these portraits to La Bruyère's *Caractères* (1688); but perhaps a more useful comparison is to the various portraits of the absurd man in *Le Mythe de Sisyphe* (1942), particularly since Beauvoir and Camus use similar categories on occasions, albeit for different purposes.[45] In his essay on the absurd, Camus offers the examples of Don Juan, the actor, the conqueror and the artist, as illustrations of life lived in the recognition and rationalisation of absurdity. Beauvoir, however, uses the categories of the sub-man, the serious man, the nihilist, the adventurer and the passionate man as demonstrations of various types of 'mauvaise foi' through which such people attempt to avoid their freedom. At the end of *Pour une morale de l'ambiguïté*, differentiating her position from that of Camus, she explains the difference between an absurd existence (which she rejects) and an ambiguous one (which she endorses):

Déclarer l'existence absurde, c'est nier qu'elle puisse se donner un sens; dire qu'elle est ambiguë, c'est poser que le sens n'en est jamais fixé, qu'il doit sans cesse se conquérir. L'absurdité récuse toute morale; mais aussi la rationalisation achevée du réel ne laisserait pas de place à la morale; c'est parce que la condition de l'homme est ambiguë qu'à travers l'échec et le scandale il cherche à sauver son existence.[46]

Towards the end of Part II, Beauvoir agains rejects a conflictual model of self-Other relations, derived from Hegel and employed by Sartre in *L'Etre et le néant*. She cites the epigraph which she used for *L'Invitée* from Hegel's *Phenomenology of Spirit*, 'chaque conscience pour-suit la mort de l'autre', and notes that this hatred can only be a naïve, preliminary reaction to the Other, because the Other simul-taneously takes and *gives* the world to me. Without the Other my world is meaningless:

S'il est vrai que tout projet émane d'une subjectivité, il est vrai aussi que ce mouvement subjectif pose de soi-même un dépassement de la subjectivité. L'homme ne peut trouver que dans l'existence des autres hommes une justification de sa propre existence.[47]

While we might need others, however, our relationships with them are nonetheless problematic, and in the final part of *Pour une morale de l'ambiguïté*, Beauvoir examines various factors relating to oppressive relationships.

She initially condemns the 'aesthetic attitude' vis-à-vis others, which involves regarding others with detached contemplation, because if we are all free in all circumstances, why do we need to bother to struggle to preserve freedom? Beauvoir gives the example of the French accepting the German Occupation in 1940, and the indifference of certain intellectuals, which constituted 'une manière de fuir la vérité du présent'.[48] Anticipating again her subsequent testimonial autobiographical project, Beauvoir concludes here that because we cannot undo the atrocities of the past, 'tout ce que nous pouvons faire, c'est d'empêcher leur histoire de retomber dans la nuit indistincte de l'être, c'est de la dévoiler, de l'intégrer au patrimoine humain'.[49]

In her discussion of oppression, Beauvoir observes that it is the mutual dependence within our relationships with others which explains how oppression exists at all, and why it is unacceptable. Oppression creates two classes of people – those who parasitically depend on the oppression of the Other, and who force humanity to forge ahead in spite of itself, and

Ceux qui sont condamnés à piétiner sans espoir, pour entretenir seulement la collectivité; leur vie est pure répétition de gestes mécaniques, leur loisir suffit tout juste à la récupération de leurs forces.[50]

Significantly, Beauvoir demonstrates here the effect of oppression on the material reality of people's lives and its power to crush their physical, psychological and emotional capacity for resistance.

As Sonia Kruks has noted, this analysis of oppression is distinct from Sartre's voluntaristic account in *L'Etre et le néant*.[51] Sartre describes freedom here as an 'all or nothing' phenomenon:

La liberté n'est pas *un* être: elle est l'être de l'homme, c'est-à-dire son néant d'être. Si l'on concevait d'abord l'homme comme un plein, il serait absurde de chercher en lui, par après, des moments ou des régions psychiques où il serait libre; autant chercher du vide dans un récipient qu'on a préalablement rempli jusqu'aux bords. L'homme ne saurait être tantôt libre et tantôt esclave: il est tout entier et toujours libre ou il n'est pas.[52]

Sartre at no point denies the existence of obstacles to freedom. He argues however that we choose how to interpret such obstacles:

La réalité-humaine rencontre partout des résistances et des obstacles qu'elle n'a pas créés; mais ces résistances et ces obstacles n'ont de sens que dans et par le libre choix que la réalité-humaine *est*.[53]

Sartre's overestimation of individual will power and choice when faced with crushing oppression leads him to the unhumanitarian and naïvely abstract position from which he argues that those who submit under torture do so freely, and that a Jew is free to choose whether to accept his or her oppression at the hands of anti-Semitic people.[54] As Sonia Kruks has also noted, it is astonishing that Sartre is able to make the latter point in the middle of the Second World War.[55]

Beauvoir, on the other hand, discusses the mechanisms of oppression at some length in *Pour une morale de l'ambiguïté*, addressing how we can struggle for the freedom of others – by assisting others to reach a position where they might assume their freedom – yet acknowledging that acting for some people in certain circumstances is often to act simultaneously against others. There are privileged courses of action in struggling for freedom from oppression: for example, Beauvoir acknowledges that it is more appropriate that black people struggle for other black people, Jews for Jews, and so on. To belong to an oppressed group is to have a 'privileged' *experience* of oppression that cannot be shared by an individual who merely wishes to express solidarity with the struggle of another oppressed individual.

In her conclusion, Beauvoir reverts to defending existentialism against the charge of solipsism, arguing that individuals can only be defined by their relationship to the world and to others. We must therefore assume our existence both as individuals and as members of society, and existentialism's focus on 'la vérité de la vie' helps us to do this.

Despite this focus, Terry Keefe notes that Beauvoir makes few concessions to the average reader in her references to Hegelian philosophy and Marxist theory.[56] On the other hand, she draws extensively on relevant and comprehensible examples from the Second World War and its aftermath, such as the Nuremberg Trials which were taking place as Beauvoir wrote her essay. This contrasts with Sartre's abstract condemnation of anti-Semitism, *Réflexions sur la question juive* (1946), which, as Claude Lanzmann has noted, failed to mention the Holocaust.[57]

*Pour une morale de l'ambiguïté* nevertheless makes a significant contribution to the development of Beauvoir's notion of selfhood, on several counts. Firstly, it develops the notion of reciprocity introduced in *Pyrrhus et Cinéas*, according to which I assume my subjectivity by assuming a relationship to the Other. Secondly, it briefly examines childhood and adolescence as important stages during which we assume subjectivity. Thirdly, Beauvoir addresses some of the mechanisms of oppression and makes connections between types of oppression, especially anti-Semitism, sexism and racism. Lastly, Beauvoir develops further the notion of temporally situated subjectivity first outlined in *Pyrrhus et Cinéas*, which will be particularly important in her project of testimonial autobiography. All of these features will shortly be developed in *Le Deuxième Sexe* in the context of an analysis of gendered subjectivity.

A notable absence in *Pour une morale de l'ambiguïté*, which *Le Deuxième Sexe* will remedy, is any extended discussion of the body and its role in subjectivity. Although Beauvoir acknowledges that our physicality plays a role in our relations with others, if, for example, we use violence to resist oppression or if it is used against us, the body does not have any determining role at this stage:

Sans doute est-ce à partir de ses possibilités physiologiques que chacun s'y jette [dans le monde], mais le corps même n'est pas un fait brut, il exprime notre rapport au monde et c'est pourquoi il est lui-même objet de sympathie ou de répulsion, et d'autre part il ne *détermine* aucune conduite.[58]

For all their flaws, *Pyrrhus et Cinéas* and *Pour une morale de l'ambiguïté* constitute an important stage in Beauvoir's development of her notion of subjectivity. They are also important because they establish that, although she is working within the same philosophical framework as Sartre, Beauvoir gives a different emphasis to the manner in which individual subjects acquire a notion of selfhood in relation to others. The next chapter, which concludes this examination of Beauvoir's notion of selfhood, will examine the text for which she is possibly best-known: *Le Deuxième Sexe*.

CHAPTER 2

# Le Deuxième Sexe

In the previous chapter it was argued that in *Pyrrhus et Cinéas* and *Pour une morale de l'ambiguïté* Beauvoir explored how subjectivity is always already situated from childhood. She focused on the role of the Other in the self's situation and examined specific ways of relating to others, through relationships of oppression, reciprocity or solidarity. She also had begun to draw parallels between different forms of oppression, such as anti-Semitism, sexism and racism. In *Le Deuxième Sexe* she develops this earlier work in the context of gender relations and offers an explanation of female (and to a limited extent, male) subjectivity. She analyses the mechanisms of oppression which can operate within gender relations to construct woman's subjectivity as relative to the universal (male) subject. In this chapter, *Le Deuxième Sexe* will be examined particularly for its account of female subjectivity, focusing on Beauvoir's description of power relations, gender construction and sexuality. The text will initially be briefly positioned within the various intersecting histories of the situation of French women in the twentieth century, the Second World War and its aftermath and Beauvoir's personal trajectory in the late 1940s.

In terms of its role within Western feminism, *Le Deuxième Sexe* is a groundbreaking text. It was published in 1949, five years after women gained the right to vote in France. It has been described as 'the most important feminist book of this century'.[1] Perhaps the principal reasons for its continuing relevance to debates on gender and sexuality in the 1990s are its broad scope of analysis, its exploration of the operation of power in the construction of subjectivity and its focus on the materiality of women's situation. In the 1990s, *Le Deuxième Sexe* remains a key text in the development of Western feminism and in the understanding of gendered identity.

In what ways can the changing notions of subjectivity evident in

*Le Deuxième Sexe* be viewed as informed by the Second World War and its aftermath? Critics such as Elizabeth Houlding, Dorothy Kaufmann, Toril Moi and Eva Lundgren-Gothlin have argued that in order to appreciate the radicalism of Beauvoir's text, *Le Deuxième Sexe* must be read 'en situation' or within its immediate historical, political, philosophical and social context.[2] Lundgren-Gothlin has also demonstrated convincingly that, in addition to her own existentialist philosophy, Beauvoir drew extensively on Hegel, Heidegger and Marxist theory – sources which have been previously overlooked in Sartrian readings of *Le Deuxième Sexe*.

Elizabeth Houlding has argued that the Occupation is crucial to an understanding of *Le Deuxième Sexe* because of the public discourses aimed at women during and immediately after the war and because, according to Houlding, 'Beauvoir herself lived more "like a woman" during the Occupation than at any other time in her life.'[3] Houlding's conflation of biography with the theoretical analysis of *Le Deuxième Sexe* is typical of many who read the text alongside Beauvoir's memoirs, seeking points of convergence between the political and the personal.[4] Before looking at some of the discourses which aimed to circumscribe the parameters of female subjectivity, for they are clearly relevant to this discussion of *Le Deuxième Sexe*, it is first necessary to probe Houlding's assertion that Beauvoir's personal wartime experience informed the analysis of *Le Deuxième Sexe*.

Houlding argues that:

For Simone de Beauvoir, who had scrupulously rebelled against the life of a dutiful French daughter until this point, the Occupation provided an obvious working example of the social and historical construction of gender. Through her exposure to the nature of women's everyday lives during the Occupation, Beauvoir first began to perceive the active construction of femininity. Writing daily letters to Sartre (who was absent from Paris on military duty and then in prison camp until March 1941), waiting in food lines, preparing meals, and attempting to secure the continuity of life for those within her care, Beauvoir herself lived more "like a woman" during the Occupation than at any other time in her life.[5]

In *La Force de l'âge*, written ten years later, Beauvoir does indeed claim that before the war she had not been aware of the existence of 'une condition féminine' and says that her acquaintance with older women in her milieu alerted her to it.[6] However, if we pursue this problematic biographical reading of *Le Deuxième Sexe* by considering accounts of Beauvoir's life in *La Force de l'âge*, her *Journal de Guerre*,

*Lettres à Sartre* and her letters to Nelson Algren, it is difficult to accept Houlding's argument completely. For it can be argued, as Mary Evans has done, that it is precisely because Beauvoir's lifestyle was so removed from that of the average Frenchwoman that she was able to research and write *Le Deuxième Sexe*.[7] Clearly one biographical reading of the text which positions the life as 'origin' can be played off against another biographical reading in search of 'true sources' of the text – although unless they acknowledge the constructionism involved in autobiographical self-representation, such readings unintentionally only demonstrate the plurality of truths in autobiographical discourse. Throughout the war, Beauvoir was teaching (until 1943), writing, reading, socialising and conducting various relationships with Sartre, Jacques Bost, Bianca Lamblin and Nathalie Sorokine. It is reasonable to accept that *Le Deuxième Sexe* is informed by her experience of the predominantly bourgeois 'milieu féminin' in which she moved during the early years of the war. However, the economic, social and sexual freedom which Beauvoir enjoyed was clearly removed from the lack of freedom experienced by – for example – a working class Frenchwoman, with no knowledge of contraception (which was illegal), who was married with several children and perhaps had lost her job as a result of Vichy legislation prohibiting women from working or because her husband did not allow her to work.[8] Eva Lundgren-Gothlin notes that this bourgeois bias evident in *Le Deuxième Sexe* was condemned by the Communists in 1950–51.[9] Criticism focusing on the bourgeois bias of *Le Deuxième Sexe* does not invalidate Beauvoir's arguments but rather helps us to understand the way in which, as she shows, subjectivity is contextualised within various bourgeois discourses – literature and philosophy – and within middle-class career options and middle-class domesticity.

### DISCURSIVE PRODUCTIONS OF DESIRABLE WOMEN

In *Le Deuxième Sexe*, Beauvoir engages with various discourses such as biology, psychoanalysis and Marxism which, she argues, often had the effect of controlling maternity, women's juridical status, sexuality and the (desirable) parameters of their psycho-sexual difference.

In terms of maternity and sexuality, it is significant that for most of the first half of the twentieth century, as Eva Lundgren-Gothlin has noted, a pronatalist policy was pursued in France, despite the

efforts of the suffragists and the activities of movements such as the
Neo-Malthusians, who advocated birth control as a means to
improve the lot of the working class, rather than out of concern for
women's autonomy. These groups effectively saw women's bodies as
*a means* to tackle inequality arising from social class.[10] This prioritisa-
tion of the struggle for social equality over sexual equality was not
unusual. Both the Socialist and the Communist Parties throughout
the first part of the twentieth century subordinated women's issues to
the struggle for socialism. In 1920, legislation was passed which
prohibited all information on birth control and the sale of contra-
ceptives, and in 1923 this legislation was tightened up with respect to
the prosecution of women who had abortions. Contraception was
illegal until 1967 and abortion illegal until 1974.

In the first half of the twentieth century, women's sexuality was
mainly contained within marriage for heterosexual women, particularly since the birth rate was a highly political issue and contraception was illegal. In the 1930s and 1940s, the French Communist
Party spoke out against divorce and sex outside marriage, which is
significant because, following the Second World War, this was the
party with the highest numbers of women members and women in
positions of influence. Predictably, the Vichy government tightened
up the divorce laws in 1941 to delay the whole process of divorce and
to narrow the definition of 'injures graves' under which divorce
could be obtained.[11]

As far as lesbians were concerned, there was no specific legislation
aimed at them at this time. In 1800, there had been an edict passed
which restricted cross-dressing in public which affected some women
(and men). This was enforced with greater stringency at the turn of
the century in Paris by Lépine, the Préfet de police, and had a
significant impact on women who cross-dressed in order to gain
access to masculine spheres.[12] As Christopher Robinson has observed, although the Napoleonic Code of 1810 ignored the issue of
homosexuality it introduced two offences which were later used
against lesbians and gay men.[13] These were the offences of affronts
to public decency (article 330), which clearly has a fluid definition
according to currently accepted notions of socio-sexual behaviour at
any particular time, and incitement to debauchery and corruption of
young persons under the age of twenty-one (article 334). This latter
article was made more stringent in 1903. In 1942, the Vichy regime
specified the 'offence' of homosexual sex as coming under the terms

of article 334. On 8 February, 1945 this particular feature of Vichy legislation was confirmed by De Gaulle's provisional government, and reclassified as article 331. This homophobic legislation was not definitively removed from the statute book until 1982.

This repressive attitude towards homosexuality and lesbianism is significant in terms of Simone de Beauvoir and in terms of her representation of lesbianism in *Le Deuxième Sexe*, in her fiction and autobiographical writing. From late 1941 until June 1943, when she lost her teaching job, Beauvoir was the subject of an investigation by the education authorities which became a police investigation because Nathalie Sorokine's mother had filed a complaint against Beauvoir, on the grounds of 'excitation de mineure à la débauche' relating to her daughter Nathalie.[14] At the beginning of the investigation, Nathalie Sorokine was twenty, that is, under age in terms of article 334.[15] This also involved an investigation of Sartre by the head of the Lycée Pasteur, and interviews with Beauvoir's friends and ex-pupils. Beauvoir was therefore personally affected by this legislative climate, although she was reinstated in 1945.[16] The charge did not result in prosecution because the police were unable to prove their case. Nevertheless, this incident is significant because it effectively constituted, as far as Beauvoir was concerned, a juridical intervention to circumscribe her sexuality which may, to some degree, explain her lifelong disavowal of her sexual relationships with women. This disavowal is at odds, as we shall see, with the relatively positive stance on lesbianism (for its time) in *Le Deuxième Sexe*. It is nevertheless surprising that in the critical reception of Beauvoir's lesbian experiences, which varies from neglect to inclusiveness, no critic, to my knowledge, considers the 'disciplinary effect' of this judicial investigation into Beauvoir's sexuality, which is likely to have produced her silence on this issue.[17]

Lesbian sexuality did not legally exist in its own right at the time of *Le Deuxième Sexe*, even though, according to Shari Benstock, 'by 1900 [Paris] had an international reputation as the capital of same-sex love among women and was designated "Paris-Lesbos"'.[18] Literary representations of lesbians were relatively common, either as figures of male fantasy, as in the work of Baudelaire or Zola in the nineteenth century, or later in work by women writers at the turn of the twentieth century such as Colette, Nathalie Barney and Renée Vivien, whose work Beauvoir cites in her chapter on lesbianism.[19]

In terms of discourses concerned with women's sexuality prior to

1949, it is useful to note Michel Foucault's account of the deployment of sexuality in *La Volonté de savoir* (1976). Foucault argues that the female body was constituted as the locus of sexuality in the eighteenth century as one of several strategies to produce knowledge and (patriarchal) power in relation to sex.[20] He argues that the result of these strategies was to produce sexuality.[21] The family had an important role in the deployment of sexuality:

Il ne faut pas comprendre la famille sous sa forme contemporaine comme une structure sociale, économique et politique d'alliance qui exclut la sexualité ou du moins la bride [. . .] Elle a pour rôle au contraire de l'ancrer et d'en constituer le support permanent.[22]

Within the bourgeois family, the sexuality of children and adolescents was constituted as problematic and female sexuality was medicalised.[23] Foucault claims that the first figure to be sexualised was 'la femme oisive' who became the hysterical bourgeoise. The purpose of this hystericisation of women was to confine their role within the family and to determine their role in society:

L'hystérisation des femmes, qui a appelé une médicalisation minutieuse de leurs corps et de leur sexe, s'est faite au nom de la responsabilité qu'elles auraient à l'égard de la santé de leurs enfants, de la solidité de l'institution familiale et du salut de la société.[24]

As far as lesbians were concerned, the rise of sexology in the West in the nineteenth century similarly produced a proliferation of medical discourses to 'explain' lesbian sexuality, amid attempts to explain and catalogue other forms of sexuality. The German sexologists, such as Richard von Krafft-Ebing, Karl Ulrichs, Carl Westphal and Magnus Hirschfeld, Charcot and Chevalier in France and Havelock Ellis in Britain, all published theories of homosexuality from the latter part of the nineteenth century until the early 1930s, as part of their work on sexuality.[25] Moreover, in 1905 Freud had outlined a theory of female homosexuality in *Three Essays on the Theory of Sexuality* and in his case history, 'The Psychogenesis of a Case of Homosexuality' in 1920, as well as formulating an ongoing theory of female heterosexuality. After Freud, Helene Deutsch and Ernest Jones were the principal psychoanalysts to consider female homosexuality in detail, while others referred to it within general discussions of female sexuality.[26] Beauvoir read the work of these theorists of sexuality and of psychologists such as Pierre Janet (Freud's main French rival) during her research for *Le Deuxième Sexe*. Her critique of psychoanalysis will be examined in the context of her account of lesbianism and female heterosexuality. However, before considering the notions of gender, sexuality, the body and power relations proposed in *Le Deuxième Sexe*, a brief glance at Beauvoir's personal trajectory is useful to contextualise her interest in developing these notions in the late 1940s. It also enables us to consider how Beauvoir represents herself in her autobiographical writing in relation to *Le Deuxième Sexe*.

BEAUVOIR IN THE LATE 1940S: AUTOBIOGRAPHICAL
SUB-TEXTS

Beauvoir began working on *Le Deuxième Sexe* in mid-1946. In her discussion of the genesis of the text in *La Force des choses* she claims that she had wanted initially to write about herself. Beauvoir seemed to view *Le Deuxième Sexe* as a preparatory task to writing her autobiography. In an interview in 1984 with Hélène V. Wenzel, she agreed with the view of the text as 'an embryonic autobiography', commenting that 'it was in order to understand myself, and to do so I had to understand the nature of women's lives in general'.[27] Judith Okely has argued that 'the hidden use of herself as a case study' is one of the strengths of Beauvoir's text.[28] However, this covert self-representation in *Le Deuxième Sexe* had certain consequences for her self-representation in autobiography, for example in her portrayal of sexuality, which is largely excised from the memoirs. In 1978, in an interview with Alice Schwarzer, Beauvoir commented that she would have liked to have given 'a frank and balanced account' of her own sexuality in her memoirs.[29] She claimed that she did not 'appreciate the importance of this question, nor the need for personal honesty' when she wrote them.

In *La Force des choses*, Sartre is credited with alerting Beauvoir to the social construction of her femininity. It is worth looking at Sartre's role in more detail in terms of *Le Deuxième Sexe* because there are certain inconsistencies in Beauvoir's portrayal of his role in her autobiography.[30] In true 'Road to Damascus' fashion, she describes how she experienced through him the revelation that 'ce monde était un monde masculin, mon enfance avait été nourrie de mythes forgés par les hommes et je n'y avais pas du tout réagi de la même manière que si j'avais été un garçon'.[31]

This 'revelation' provoked by Sartre appears, for several reasons, to be an autobiographical device. It implies that Beauvoir was

unaware of the role of gender in the constitution of situation, which
is incorrect. In *Pour une morale de l'ambiguïté*, as noted earlier, she had
already made connections between different forms of oppression,
including oppression on the grounds of gender. Furthermore, in the
early 1930s, Beauvoir had talked with Colette Audry about Audry's
plan to write a book about women.[32] By the late 1940s, Beauvoir
had an established literary reputation in her own right, and had
published some philosophical work. She had also realised the
importance of 'situation' both during the war, through her acquaintance with older women who lived a more traditional lifestyle than
her own as noted above, with Jewish friends such as Bianca
Bienenfeld and 'Bourla', and after the war with politically-aware
friends such as Richard Wright and Nelson Algren. In addition to
his consistent interest in black identity politics, back in 1939–40
Wright had begun working on a novel, which was never completed,
entitled 'Little Sister' about 'the status of women in modern American society'.[33] Finally, there was a certain emotional distance
between Beauvoir and Sartre in the late 1940s which may have
contributed to the production of *Le Deuxième Sexe*. During this period
they were both in love with other people, Sartre with Dolores
Ehrenreich and Beauvoir with Algren.[34] These factors considered,
Beauvoir's apparent 'revelation' of the social construction of gender
in the late 1940s, recounted in *La Force des choses*, appears to be an
autobiographical technique which indicates her desire to represent
Sartre as saviour and creative genius, as at the end of the *Mémoires*,
as we will see in Part II.

In terms of the composition of *Le Deuxième Sexe*, this positioning of
Sartre as its source of inspiration also appears exaggerated when one
looks more closely at Beauvoir's use of philosophical sources in the
text. Eva Lundgren-Gothlin has argued that Hegel (mediated by
Kojève), Heidegger, Marx and Engels, among others, are crucially
important sources for the text, as well as Sartre's *L'Etre et le néant*.
Merleau-Ponty's *Phénoménologie de la perception* (1945) is also an important (although barely acknowledged) source for the text.

Furthermore, Beauvoir's knowledge of the work of Algren and
Richard Wright is significant.[35] These social realist writers had first-
hand experience and knowledge of the material aspects of racial,
political and class oppression upon which they drew extensively in
their writing. Like Beauvoir, they were interested in representing
how oppression shaped individual lives on psychological, physical

and emotional levels; hence, their work seems more relevant to Beauvoir's materialist analysis of gender than Sartre's philosophical and rather abstract interest in oppression.[36] Yet Sartre has been accorded a pivotal role as provider of the initial inspiration and of the philosophical framework by critics who read Beauvoir's memoirs as the authoritative 'explanation' of all of her writing. The philosophical originality of *Le Deuxième Sexe* has, as a result, been underestimated until relatively recently.

To close this discussion, and before examining the account of subjectivity offered in *Le Deuxième Sexe*, it will be helpful to consider briefly Beauvoir's correspondence with Algren, which has so far received little attention within Beauvoir studies. These letters offer useful information about the text's composition and indicate how, in the late 1940s, Beauvoir was developing her notion of the subject as a product of his or her situation.

## THE ALGREN CORRESPONDENCE AND *LE DEUXIÈME SEXE*

Beauvoir maintained a correspondence with Nelson Algren from 1947 until the mid-1960s.[37] These letters are a significant source of information about *Le Deuxième Sexe* because they were written contemporaneously with its composition. In addition, as a form of self-expression, Beauvoir's letters are less 'travaillées' and thus more spontaneous than her formal autobiography so that on this occasion they offer, perhaps, a more vivid, additional account of the composition of *Le Deuxième Sexe*.[38]

Beauvoir met Algren in February 1947, when she first visited America on a lecture tour. She had by this time begun working on *Le Deuxième Sexe*, although she was to take some time off to write *L'Amérique au jour le jour* (1948). From her correspondence with Algren, a number of useful points can be noted. On 28 June, 1947, for example, Beauvoir writes that she had begun working on *Le Deuxième Sexe* again because a New York magazine had offered her $500 which could be used to finance their trip to New Orleans.[39]

Her growing awareness of black identity politics is evident from these letters. On 1 December, Beauvoir wrote to Algren that she was reading Gunnar Myrdal's *An American Dilemma* (1944), a pioneering work on racism in the USA, and that she wanted to write a book about women which would be just as important:

Tout en avançant le gros *Dilemme américain*, comme ma propre petite *Amérique* va vers sa fin, je me remets à réfléchir à l'essai que j'ai commencé sur la condition des femmes. J'aimerais réussir quelque chose d'aussi important que le Myrdal; il souligne d'ailleurs quantité de très suggestives analogies entre le statut des Noirs et celui des femmes, que j'avais déjà pressenties.[40]

As Margaret Simons has noted, Alva Myrdal's essay, 'A Parallel to the Negro Problem', which drew parallels between the situations of the US black population and women, was included as an appendix to *An American Dilemma*, and this essay is likely to have encouraged Beauvoir to make further connections between the mechanisms of racial and sexual oppression.[41] Some of the terms in which she describes the social construction of black identity in *L'Amérique au jour le jour*, for example:

Mais beaucoup de racistes, passant outre les rigueurs de la science, s'entêtent à déclarer que même si on n'en a pas établi les raisons psychologiques, le fait est que les noirs *sont* inférieurs aux blancs. [. . .] Mais que signifie le verbe *être*: définit-il une nature immuable comme celle de l'oxygène? Ou décrit-il le moment d'une situation qui *est devenue*, comme toute situation humaine?[42]

are exactly the same as those used to describe gender ontology in *Le Deuxième Sexe*:

quand un individu ou un groupe d'individus est maintenu en situation d'infériorité, le fait est qu'il *est* inférieur; mais c'est sur la portée du mot *être* qu'il faut s'entendre; la mauvaise foi consiste à lui donner une valeur substantielle alors qu'il a le sens dynamique hégelien: *être* c'est être devenu, c'est avoir été fait tel qu'on se manifeste.[43]

As Margaret Atack has argued, in *Le Deuxième Sexe* a dynamic vision of the subject/Other gender relation is presented, although it is frequently mistaken by men and women as a permanent state – a mistake that Beauvoir is concerned to expose:

The subject/other dynamic is precisely that, a dynamic which is in constant flux, demands constant reaffirmation both collectively and individually, has to to be continually reinvented because it can ultimately never satisfy, never be established once and for all [. . .] what Beauvoir is writing against is the way gender socialisation gives the illusion of permanency and security, falsely naturalising a hierarchichal difference, effectively offering a belief in the (illusory) metanarrative of gender as security to both sexes.[44]

In *L'Amérique au jour le jour*, Beauvoir wrote about Gunnar Myrdal's work as part of her longer discussion of race politics in America in the late 1940s.[45] According to Beauvoir, Myrdal approached black oppression as a white problem. He argued that the effects of racial oppression permeated white American society, which, although it profited economically and politically from oppressing the black minority, experienced guilt and anguish on a collective and individual level – hence its 'dilemma'. Black culture was 'une réaction secondaire à la situation créée par la majorité blanche'.[46] Myrdal assumed that the US black population wished to be assimilated into white US society, and he therefore advocated that it was most practical for blacks to adopt cultural characteristics which were valued positively in white society – a position reminiscent of Beauvoir's arguments concerning gender in Le Deuxième Sexe.[47] Like Myrdal, she was challenged for ignoring the specificity of the oppressed group under consideration.

On 2 January 1948, Beauvoir wrote to Algren that she was beginning to plan Le Deuxième Sexe, and on 6 February that she had finished re-reading Richard Wright's Native Son (1940) and Black Boy, A Record of Childhood and Youth (1945).[48] Beauvoir first met Wright in 1946 when he visited Paris from May to December 1946, and was close friends with him and Ellen Wright from 1947 onwards in New York and Paris.[49] She refers to Wright's Black Boy and Native Son in L'Amérique au jour le jour and Le Deuxième Sexe.[50] These texts by Wright explore the collective bad faith and oppression which racism involves and the construction of the oppressed personality, which Beauvoir would also explore in the context of gender in the second volume of Le Deuxième Sexe and in her later fiction.[51]

Throughout Beauvoir's correspondence with Algren there is a tension deriving from the paradoxical situation in which she found herself – working on Le Deuxième Sexe, perhaps the most important feminist text of the century, while conducting the most highly charged sexual relationship of her life with a man who was no feminist. On 23 February, 1948 she writes that she was working in the public library learning about how men like Algren oppress women like her.[52] In a letter written on 17 July, after Beauvoir had visited Algren again, she notes that, re-reading her manuscript on women, she cannot recognise it as hers and cannot imagine how she will finish it as he has upset her routine so much.[53] On 26 July, Beauvoir refers to her research at the Bibliothèque Nationale on human conception for Le Deuxième Sexe and to her practice of asking every woman she meets to tell her the story of her life for her research.[54] This collating of women's lifestories was important not only for the empirical content of *Le Deuxième Sexe* but also for Beauvoir's own long-standing autobiographical project, for it exposed her to other (predominantly middle-class) women's lives and, perhaps more importantly, to how those women conceptualised their lives.

Many critics have rightly noted the importance of Beauvoir's visits to the USA in terms of *Le Deuxième Sexe*, which enabled her to see how American women lived and also gave her crucial insights into the material and psychological mechanisms of racial and sexual oppression in the US. However, her knowledge of and interest in women's status in other cultures was also significant, and her correspondence with Algren offers some evidence of how this was growing. In early September 1948, Beauvoir visited Algeria with Sartre and Jacques Bost – a visit to which she refers in her correspondence with Algren. She continued to work on *Le Deuxième Sexe* during this time in Algeria, and became aware of the situation of Algerian women.[55] There are several references in her letters to the plight of Algerian women as well as to the French colonial presence. She relates for example on 9 September how she had been sexually harassed in a bar and concludes, 'pays dangereux pour les femmes'.[56] On 20 September she notes that there were no women in the market as they rarely leave their homes.[57] On 8 October she writes about a desert tribe which 'allows' women to earn money for their marriage by prostitution.[58] Approximately ten years later and rather more politically aware of the situation of Algerian women than she had been in her letters to Algren, Beauvoir would take up the case of Djamila Boupacha, an Algerian woman who was raped and tortured by French soldiers during the Algerian war.

On 31 December, she writes that she is reading the very recently published *Sexual Behaviour in the Human Male* (1948) by Alfred Kinsey,[59] and regrets that the same work has not already been done for women.[60] Although it is difficult to estimate how Kinsey's later report on female sexuality might have changed *Le Deuxième Sexe*, Kinsey's positive stance towards sex and sexuality and his recognition of cultural and religious factors in the expression of female sexuality are clearly germane to Beauvoir's arguments in her study of gender. It might also have positively influenced the representation of female sexuality in her writing more generally. The recognition of the difference and scope of female sexuality evident in the 1953

Kinsey report may also have modified Beauvoir's somewhat deterministic account of female biology and sexuality in *Le Deuxième Sexe* (for
which she has received much feminist criticism), which will be
examined next.

## OTHERNESS, BIOLOGY, THE BODY AND SEXUALITY

In *Le Deuxième Sexe*, before tackling the biological, psychoanalytical
and Marxist analyses of women's position, Beauvoir initially establishes her theoretical framework, namely, existential ethics. Referring
to Emmanuel Lévinas's argument that 'l'altérité s'accomplit dans le
féminin', she observes that although woman may be obliged to
assume a position as an 'être relatif', she is a (self-)consciousness and
potentially able to live authentically.[61] Beauvoir says that Lévinas
does not register the reciprocity which exists between man as subject
and woman as Other: that in exchange for recognising man as a
sovereign subject, woman gains the 'advantage' of living as 'être
relatif'. Seeking an explanation for the origins of woman's oppression, Beauvoir argues that historical 'evidence' is not conclusive
because it is produced by men to justify their oppression of women.
Instead she proposes that, following Hegel, we might interpret
woman's position as Other as the result of an earlier process. She
argues, as noted above, that 'être, c'est être devenu'.[62] Although
conflict between men and women may have been at the source of
this positioning of woman, Beauvoir says there has also always been
a Heideggerian 'Mitsein' or 'being-with' in the relationship between
women and men, which explains how women have never been
consistently positioned as Other.

A brief explanation of Hegel's theory of self-consciousness and
recognition is useful here because Beauvoir adapts it in *Le Deuxième
Sexe* as a philosophical model for oppressive power relations. Yet, she
focuses on different aspects of Hegel's account of self-consciousness
to Sartre in *L'Etre et le néant*. Michèle Le Doeuff has noted that
Beauvoir read Hegel before Sartre during the summer of 1940.[63] In
a letter she advised him that it would be relevant to his work on
*L'Etre et le néant*:

Vous savez, c'est horriblement difficile, Hegel, mais c'est extrêmement
intéressant et vous devez le connaître, ça s'apparente à votre propre
philosophie du néant. Je me réjouis de le lire en pensant précisément à vous
l'exposer.[64]

In *The Phenomenology of Mind*, Hegel argues that self-consciousness does not exist in isolation but needs an external object against which to define itself.[65] This external object is the Other, who is similarly aware of himself as a material subject, and reciprocally dependent on an external, material Other for his existence. To assert his independence from his own materiality and to show independence from the Other, the self has to engage in a life or death struggle to prove that he does not value the materiality of being. The self seeks to become a pure or disembodied self-consciousness. This struggle is doomed to failure as the Other must not be entirely destroyed because the self needs the Other to recognise him. Thus the 'master' spares 'the slave': what was a temporary state of equality is replaced by a situation of oppression. In this situation, the master, although in a position of domination, has lost consciousness of the Other as an equal being, and is fixed in the static position of receiving the advantages of being dominant. Significantly he has lost the recognition formerly given to him by the Other as a free being, since the Other is now oppressed. Meanwhile the slave gains a certain satisfaction from his work, and gains consciousness of himself and of his oppression.[66]

Sonia Kruks has argued that in Sartre's use of the Hegelian master-slave scenario, 'the question of material or political inequality between master and slave is simply irrelevant to their relation as two freedoms, as two absolute subjects'.[67] Yet, as noted above, it was the self's acknowledgement of the materiality of existence and his desire to deny that materiality which triggered the struggle between master and slave in the first place; furthermore it is in the material world that the master 'enjoys' the fruits of domination and the slave gains consciousness of his oppression through his work. Although Beauvoir used this Hegelian model of oppressive self-Other relations in *Le Deuxième Sexe* to a limited degree, she was far more interested in exploring the crucial *recognition* which takes place between individuals and the reciprocal dimension of self-Other relations.

In her detailed reading of *Le Deuxième Sexe*, Eva Lundgren-Gothlin argues convincingly that Beauvoir does not position man as master and woman as slave in her use of the master-slave dialectic, which was influenced by Alexandre Kojève's interpretation of Hegel.[68] Unlike Sartre in *L'Etre et le néant* and following Kojève, Beauvoir privileges reciprocal recognition as the means to overcome the potential, perpetual conflict between self and Other:

Le drame peut être surmonté par la libre reconnaissance de chaque individu en l'autre, chacun posant à la fois soi et l'autre comme objet et comme sujet dans un mouvement réciproque. Mais l'amitié, la générosité, qui réalisent concrètement cette reconnaissance des libertés, ne sont pas des vertus faciles; elles sont assurément le plus haut accomplissement de l'homme, c'est par là qu'il se trouve dans sa vérité: mais cette vérité est celle d'une lutte sans cesse ébauchée, sans cesse abolie; elle exige que l'homme à chaque instant se surmonte.[69]

The key concepts here for Beauvoir's notion of selfhood and her later self-representation in autobiography are the free recognition between self and Other and the ethical self-mastery and fashioning which are necessary to create that recognition.

As Lundgren-Gothlin notes, women do not participate in the Hegelian struggle for recognition, which takes place between men. Beauvoir is working here with two different notions of 'altérité': the master-slave conflict which seeks to establish self and Other among men, and the non-dialectical relationship of self and absolute Other between men and women, a relationship rooted in their biological and psychological dependence on each other.[70] This dependence is the result of sexually differentiated roles, which find their origins in female and male biology.[71]

Beauvoir tackles discourses of biological and sexual determinism in the first chapter of Le Deuxième Sexe. Yet, as we will see, she does not offer an empowering account of the role played by female biology and fails to integrate lesbian experience into her account of biology and sexuality. She therefore appears to endorse, to some extent, the deterministic arguments circumscribing female biology and sexuality which she attempts to dismantle.

In the 1940s the female body was, as it remains today, a chief area of focus for discourses on sexual oppression. As noted earlier in this chapter, the pronatalist policies pursued in France in the first half of the twentieth century meant that women's reproductive capacity was constituted as a reason for arguing for their relative subjectivity. Women acceded to this relative subjectivity through their enforced dependence on male desire (which entailed women's enforced heterosexuality and controlled fertility) and on male hegemony (because of women's conditional access to power). As Elaine Baruch notes:

Perhaps because The Second Sex was written before the legalisation of contraception and abortion in France, for [Beauvoir], the main sexual differentiator lies in woman's subordination to the species, her enslavement by reproduction.[72]

In her discussion of female biology in *Le Deuxième Sexe*, Beauvoir also tackles the issue of the embodied subject. Although she argues that self-Other relations are interdependent, she appears unable to develop the corporeal implications of reciprocity in her concept of self-Other relations. Her central argument concerning women's biology is that women have been obliged to experience their body as facticity rather than contingency: women do not choose how they experience their body because their relationship to their own embodiment has been pre-defined by the patriarchal society in which they find themselves. Woman's relationship to her body is culturally produced. In a strikingly Foucauldian formulation of the disciplined body as locus and focus of power, Beauvoir asserts: 'ce n'est pas en tant que corps, c'est en tant que corps assujetti à des tabous, à des lois, que le sujet prend conscience de lui-même et s'accomplit'.[73]

Beauvoir's view of embodied existence in *Le Deuxième Sexe* is situated between Sartre's account of the body as 'le dépassé' in *L'Etre et le néant* and Merleau-Ponty's description of the incarnate subject in *Phénoménologie de la perception*, although closer to the latter, as will be argued.[74] As Sonia Kruks, Toril Moi and others have observed, Beauvoir's relationship to these different philosophies of the subject is evident from her positive review of *Phénoménologie de la perception* in *Les Temps modernes* in 1945.[75] Beauvoir signals her enthusiasm for Merleau-Ponty's view of subjectivity as always already incarnate. She says:

Notre corps n'est pas d'abord posé dans le monde à la manière d'un arbre ou d'une pierre; il l'habite, il est notre manière générale d'avoir un monde; c'est lui qui exprime notre existence, ce qui signifie non qu'il en est un accompagnement extérieur, mais qu'elle se réalise en lui.[76]

Again, Beauvoir refrains from explicitly signalling her disagreement with Sartre's view of the embodied subject as effectively striving towards its own perpetual self-disembodiment.[77] For Sartre argues that the body is the physical evidence of what I have been or transcended:

Avoir un corps, c'est être le fondement de son propre néant et ne pas être le fondement de son être; je *suis* mon corps dans la mesure où je *suis*; je ne le *suis* pas dans la mesure où je ne suis pas ce que je suis; c'est par ma néantisation que je lui échappe.[78]

The verb 'être' is used transitively by Sartre so that consciousness is not consciousness *of* one's body (that is, the body as object in the world) but rather consciousness *exists* the body. This means that according to Sartre we have non-thetic consciousness of our bodies or that the body is not an object of consciousness. Although this notion of the body is useful to Beauvoir's argument that biology is not destiny, it raises a number of problems. Some of these are addressed by Beauvoir in *Le Deuxième Sexe* and by Merleau-Ponty in *Phénoménologie de la perception.*

The first problem is that Sartre's view of the body is unhelpfully abstract in that it does not correspond to the material realities of how we live and are forced to live our bodies. For example, being a black, disabled woman in a white supremacist patriarchy which privileges the able-bodied has a number of oppressive implications on material, psychological and social levels. The body cannot simply function as 'un dépassé' because this stance fails to take into account the material consequences (which we are often forced to endure) of assuming a particular gender identity, race or sexuality.

The second related problem is that Sartre's view is too voluntaristic and dualistic. It does not account for some of the sophisticated ways in which we experience our bodies, which Merleau-Ponty explores in *Phénoménologie de la perception.* For example in 'Le Corps comme objet et la physiologie mécaniste', he cites the case of an amputee who continues to move as if his or her limb had not been amputated, which suggests that we can remember the corporeal style of our experience of existence. Later, in 'La Spatialité du corps propre et la motricité', Merleau-Ponty cites the case of Schneider, who had become brain-damaged and was unable to perform spontaneous, abstract actions on demand, although he could perform actions which had been learned in a particular context. His actions were triggered by the situation in which he found himself. This is evidently germane to Beauvoir's argument that how women exist their bodies can be viewed as a learned corporeal style. Merleau-Ponty argues that there are two layers to bodily reality, the habitual body and the present body.[79] The habitual body is the mode of existing our bodies based on past experience – gestures learned within a spatial and temporal context, and importantly, within an intersubjective context. The present body is the way in which we exist corporeally according to the demands of present and future contexts, which may require a reworking of our learned physical identity. For Merleau-Ponty, the body is always already anchored in space, time and in relation to others, and constitutes the point at which we assume our subjectivity in the world:

Il ne faut donc pas dire que notre corps est *dans* l'espace ni d'ailleurs qu'il est *dans* le temps. Il *habite* l'espace et le temps.[80]

In her review of the *Phénoménologie*, Beauvoir demonstrates her intellectual sympathy with Merleau-Ponty's view of the subject as always already embodied within space and time, and 'geared into' the experience of intersubjective relations in the world. She develops this and his distinction between the lived body and the represented body in the context of gender in *Le Deuxième Sexe* and in her autobiographical self-representation. However, she does not explicitly signal her theoretical proximity to Merleau-Ponty's view of embodied subjectivity, and since Beauvoir's work has, until relatively recently, been read through Sartrian philosophy, this proximity has been largely overlooked.[81] In addition, Beauvoir helped to promote the view that her philosophy was closer to Sartre's than Merleau-Ponty's – for reasons of intellectual and emotional loyalty and because, until after the publication of *Mémoires d'une jeune fille rangée*, she had viewed Merleau-Ponty as someone who had contributed to the death of her friend Zaza.[82]

In terms of the account of female biology in *Le Deuxième Sexe*, Beauvoir adapts Merleau-Ponty's argument within the context of gender: 'La femme, comme l'homme, est son corps: mais son corps est autre chose qu'elle.'[83] Woman's physicality is separated from her transcendence and she is rewarded for alienating (or reducing) her subjectivity to her physicality. While Beauvoir makes it clear in *Le Deuxième Sexe* that woman's alienation in her body is not inevitable, her lurid portrayal of female biology nevertheless might appear rather deterministic. As Moi notes, 'for Beauvoir, women are the slaves of the species. Every biological process in the female body is a "crisis" or a "trial", and the result is always alienation.'[84]

What is the explanation for this biological pessimism? Beauvoir sees the 'données biologiques' as being crucial to an understanding of woman's situation. Charlene Haddock Seigfried argues that Beauvoir is a prisoner of the scientific discourses of her time, and slides into biological essentialism in her 'description' of female biology.[85]

However, recent work encourages a more positive reading of Beauvoir's position. Elizabeth Fallaize has argued that Beauvoir is not unconsciously replicating the masculinist bias of the scientific discourses of her time in the chapter on biology, she is concerned rather to dismantle certain biological myths and metaphors about the female in the natural world, which have prevented serious discussion of women's role in society. Beauvoir is therefore attempting to disentangle myth from reality in her assessment of biological discourses of sexual difference.[86] This reading is confirmed by Beauvoir's recognition of Merleau-Ponty's distinction between the representation of the body and the lived experience of the body, in her review of his *Phénoménologie* for, as Debra Bergoffen notes:

On the one hand, *The Second Sex* might be said to reject the idea that the represented body is superimposed on the lived body, if by superimposed we mean artificially appended. On the other hand, the liberating moment of *The Second Sex* may be said to be grounded in the hope that as superimposed, woman's represented body can be jettisoned as women's lived bodies are allowed to speak.[87]

The point can be made, however, that articulating the lived experience of the body is also to represent the body in some way and so, Merleau-Ponty's distinction is perhaps a moot one for just as we are always already embodied, we are always already immersed in linguistic representations of our experiences, including our corporeal experiences. A distinction needs therefore to be drawn between naturalising and dynamising forms of representation, and it seems that in *Le Deuxième Sexe*, Beauvoir is concerned to dismantle biological myths concerning women's corporeality which reify and naturalise women's relative status in society, and looks towards the possibility of alternative, dynamising representations of women's embodied existence, which enable them to assume their corporeal subjectivity.

Beauvoir addresses the issue of sexuality in the following chapter, 'Le Point de vue psychanalytique', and predominantly in the 'Formation' section of the second volume. She had a complex relationship to psychoanalysis, which will be briefly examined here because it is relevant to her notion of subjectivity and to her project of autobiographical self-representation.

What is striking about Beauvoir's use of psychoanalysis in *Le*

*Deuxième Sexe* is that, as Toril Moi has noted, despite her rejection of Freudian psychoanalysis in the psychoanalysis chapter, she regularly uses psychoanalytic references to support her argument.[88] In *Le Deuxième Sexe* Beauvoir outlines the various phases of psycho-sexual development according to Freud. Her main criticisms are the following: firstly, that his account of female sexuality is grafted onto a male model, so that the girl can only consider herself as a mutilated boy. Beauvoir does not accept this globalised view of female sexuality or that girls value the penis in the way Freud describes. Her reading of Adler against Freud explains why she came to this conclusion. Adler says that the girl's entire situation contributes to her sense of inferiority, not simply the fact that she does not have a penis. She envies instead the privileges brought by the possession of this appendage.[89] Secondly, Beauvoir criticises Freud because he does not account for the social construction of the father as a dominant figure, which would explain to some degree any attraction that the girl might feel towards her father.

Beauvoir argues here that all psychoanalysts allot the same destiny to woman – that of undergoing a conflict between her masculine and feminine tendencies – so that in asserting her independence within this binary she can only become virilised. As an existentialist, Beauvoir views psychoanalysis as suppressing the notions of choice and value, that is, as a deterministic system which internalises human reality rather than viewing existence as a material experience which is lived in 'the real' with other people.[90] As noted in the previous chapter and as will become evident in the later analysis of Beauvoir's project of testimonial autobiography, presence, self-presence, temporal situation and reciprocal relations with others are key factors in her notion of subjectivity. In Beauvoir's view, the psychoanalytic subject appears locked into a fixed pattern of development, without any choice, whose reality is perpetually explained in terms of a necessary past, regardless of present circumstances or future possibilities. This emphasis on the past in psychoanalysis conflicts with her notion of temporality, according to which the subject is simultaneously situated in *three* temporal dimensions (past, present and future). For Beauvoir, although we are radically separated from our past, subjectivity must be assumed within these three dimensions to formulate an authentic project in the world.

Some remarks made by Sartre about the relationship between his intellectual background and his views on psychoanalysis are also useful to consider in this context, for, on this occasion, they are equally pertinent in terms of Beauvoir who broadly shares that background. Sartre said:

Pour revenir à Freud, je dirai que j'étais incapable de le comprendre parce que j'étais un Français nourri de tradition cartésienne, imbu de rationa-lisme, que l'idée de l'inconscient choquait profondément.[91]

He explains further that he rejects the finalistic biologism of psycho-analytic vocabulary, and he criticises the syncretism of psychoana-lysis, which attempts to conflate the inconsistencies of a person's behaviour through the use of schematic explanations such as the Oedipus complex.[92]

This is especially relevant for Le Deuxième Sexe, where Beauvoir consistently focuses on the inherent inconsistencies of woman's psycho-sexual and social situation within a patriarchal society, while avoiding the simplistic explanation that women are exclusively victims of patriarchal control. Her view of human reality, like Sartre's, is dialectical and, therefore, is difficult to reconcile with Freudian psychoanalysis, which Beauvoir perceived as mechanistic and reductive.

She did however recognise Freud's 'discovery' of children's sexu-ality as highly significant, and she uses psychoanalytic theory in her description of sexual development in Le Deuxième Sexe. The influence of psychoanalytic theory can also be discerned in the portrayal of nascent subjectivity in Mémoires d'une jeune fille rangée. In an interview published in 1984, Beauvoir said:

La psychanalyse a eu raison d'indiquer l'importance de l'enfance pour le devenir de quelqu'un: on ne comprend bien une personne, on ne la comprend de près, que si on l'a connue enfant ou si on a connu de près son enfance. Mais je n'accorde pas beaucoup d'importance à la psychanalyse en tant que technique, métier, et manipulation des gens. [. . .] Il y a des tas de choses que je n'aime pas du tout chez Freud, mais je crois que sa découverte de la sexualité infantile, de l'importance de l'enfance, sont des choses essentielles.[93]

Beauvoir had argued in Pour une morale de l'ambiguïté that the child-hood situation is metaphysically privileged and that, during ado-lescence, we are forced to assume our subjectivity. In Le Deuxième Sexe, she continues to pay close attention to childhood and ado-lescence, specifically in the context of the assumption of gendered identity.

In her chapter on 'Enfance' in *Le Deuxième Sexe* Beauvoir draws on a wide range of psychoanalytic evidence to describe male and female psycho-sexual development (for example Lacan's *Les Complexes familiaux dans la formation de l'individu,* Havelock Ellis's *Studies in the Psychology of Sex* and Helene Deutsch's *The Psychology of Women*).[94] In her account of childhood development, Beauvoir stresses how initially both girls and boys have the same kinds of experiences, and how any different capacities identified at this stage are constructed by gender-differentiated treatment within their environment. Beauvoir argues that as little boys are encouraged to become 'little men', some reject this role and cling to femininity by, for example, lamenting the loss of their hair when it is cut (a direct reference by Beauvoir to an event in Sartre's childhood which features in *Les Mots*).[95] This indicates an awareness on her part of the social construction of masculinity as well as of femininity, a feature which has often been overlooked by critics and which makes Beauvoir's 1949 text an early (albeit limited) precursor to more recent debates on masculinity. Boys' rejection of masculinity in favour of femininity is cited by Beauvoir as evidence of 'une des manières de s'orienter vers l'homosexualité'.[96] This is a spurious claim, for it appears only to be based on an incident from Maurice Sachs' autobiography, *Le Sabbat,* and suggests an essentialism on Beauvoir's part which she rejects elsewhere.[97] This example also demonstrates her overdependence on literary sources in *Le Deuxième Sexe,* itself an indicator of Beauvoir's reluctance or inability to distinguish between the constructionism involved in autobiographical self-representation and the empirical, or the text and the life.

In *Le Deuxième Sexe,* spatiality is a key feature in the assumption of subjectivity. Before puberty transforms the girl's body, she is discouraged from assuming her physicality in the world; the assumption of gendered identity involves a gendered spatial experience. Beauvoir refers again here explicitly to Adler's observations on psycho-sexual development and spatiality, and implicitly to Merleau-Ponty's notion of the incarnate subject who is always already spatially situated.[98] Beauvoir notes:

Adler remarque que les notions de haut et de bas ont une grande importance, l'idée d'élévation spatiale impliquant une supériorité spirituelle, comme on voit à travers nombre de mythes héroïques; atteindre une cime, un sommet, c'est émerger par-delà le monde donné comme sujet souverain; c'est entre garçons un prétexte fréquent de défi. La fillette à qui ces exploits sont interdits et qui, assise au pied d'un arbre ou d'un rocher, voit au-dessus d'elle les garçons triomphants s'éprouve corps et âme comme inférieure.[99]

In *Phénoménologie de la perception*, Merleau-Ponty similarly argues that our experience of space is crucial to our experience as subjects in the world, because 'le corps exprime l'existence totale', and the body is always already situated in space.[100] Space is not 'out there' or a container for objects and human subjects; our experience of subjectivity is always already channelled through the body as a spatial field. He notes that space is not only a physical phenomenon but also a mental one:

Nous avons dit que l'espace est existentiel; nous aurions pu dire aussi bien que l'existence est spatiale, c'est à dire que, par une nécessité intérieure, elle s'ouvre sur un "dehors" au point que l'on peut parler d'un espace mental et d'un monde des significations et des objets de pensée qui se constituent en elles.[101]

The notion of space as an integral feature of the experience of subjectivity is important for Beauvoir's arguments about the assumption of female subjectivity in *Le Deuxième Sexe*. Yet it is not unique to this text, but is also evident in her fiction and memoirs.

In *L'Invitée*, *Le Sang des autres* and *Les Belles Images* for example, there are representations of the female subject assuming a vantage point over the city (from or looking towards Sacré-Coeur), which suggest an Adlerian influence because these are passages in which the female character's autonomous subjectivity is under threat.[102] In her autobiographical self-representation, Beauvoir again draws on the notion of the subject as spatially situated. In *La Force de l'âge*, for example, the character Simone assumes a vantage point on the hills of Saint-Cloud during a major disagreement with Sartre over the function of language and writing.[103] A more positive representation of the spatially-situated female protagonist in this text is Simone's arrival in Marseille. Pausing at the top of the stairs outside the station, she surveys the city, à la Rastignac, in which she is to pursue an autonomous lifestyle.[104] For Beauvoir, spatiality plays an important role, then, in the experience of subjectivity.

In her portrayal of sexual relationships in *Le Deuxième Sexe*, she offers a more positive account of lesbian sexuality than heterosexuality, although viewed together, the inconsistencies between the two accounts suggest that Beauvoir had not developed a coherent theory of female sexuality in her account of gendered subjectivity. The chapter on 'La Lesbienne' is positioned between 'L'Initiation sexuelle' and 'La Femme mariée', and interestingly, closes the 'Formation' section which suggests that Beauvoir did not envisage lesbianism as a long-term option for women. In her portrayal of heterosexual sex, Beauvoir represents the woman as passive while her male partner is predatory. The man expresses his active subjectivity in sex, whereas the woman is equated with passive viscosity, the object of desire rather than the sexual initiator or peer, a prisoner of either clitoral pleasure (which Beauvoir associates with 'l'indépendance juvénile') or vaginal pleasure (associated with men and motherhood).[105]

Many critics have taken Beauvoir to task for her over-valorization of male sexuality. More specifically, Eva Lundgren-Gothlin and Toril Moi have noted how Beauvoir reproduces Sartre's misogynist discourse describing female sexuality as 'le visqueux' in *L'Etre et le néant*.[106] This inability to offer an empowering account of female sexuality can be viewed as the result of a number of factors: firstly, Beauvoir's failure to problematise sufficiently the discourses which she is attempting to dismantle (psychoanalytical, biological and philosophical) which conceptualised female sexuality within a heterosexual binary according to which women's role was conditioned by male desire and motherhood.[107] Secondly, although Beauvoir's relatively positive account of lesbianism was groundbreaking, she fails largely to incorporate it with her account of female subjectivity, so that the description of lesbianism functions as 'other' to her own heterosexualised discourse. Beauvoir's discursive marginalisation of lesbianism apparent in *Le Deuxième Sexe* would be re-enacted in her memoirs as far as her own lesbian experiences were concerned because they are omitted.

Beauvoir's account of lesbianism is nevertheless surprisingly radical for its time, for she notes that within a patriarchal society, a lesbian relationship is at least as valid as any heterosexual relationship. She says 'l'homosexualité peut être pour la femme une manière de fuir sa condition ou une manière de l'assumer'.[108] Characteristically, Beauvoir argues here that one is neither irrevocably heterosexual nor homosexual, one chooses one's sexuality perpetually and what is more pertinent is the authenticity of the choice. She asserts:

Et si l'on invoque la nature, on peut dire que naturellement toute femme est homosexuelle. La lesbienne se caractérise en effet par son refus du mâle et son goût pour la chair féminine; mais toute adolescente redoute la pénétration, la domination masculine, elle éprouve à l'égard du corps de l'homme une certaine répulsion; en revanche le corps féminin est pour elle comme pour l'homme un objet de désir.[109]

Beauvoir appears to be challenging here the notion of 'the lesbian' as a discrete identity, arguing that all women are predisposed – in a somewhat 'adolescent' way – to have a physical affinity with women. This notion of a continuum of sexuality is quite radical for its time and had been used in Kinsey's studies of sexuality, as noted earlier.[110]

While Beauvoir gestures towards the notion of a 'lesbian continuum' in her chapter on 'La Lesbienne', she nevertheless marginalises lesbian experience in *Le Deuxième Sexe* as a whole by confining her discussion largely to this single chapter and a few pages in 'La Jeune Fille'. Furthermore there is no sustained attempt to address the issue of heterosexuality as a political institution in *Le Deuxième Sexe*. Beauvoir appears to assume here that most women are irrevocably heterosexual.

Nevertheless, Beauvoir's attempt to question the notion of 'the lesbian' as a discrete, marginalised figure challenges the discursive production of the pathologised figure of 'the lesbian' in psychoanalytic and sexological discourses, which had been in evidence since the mid-nineteenth century. Beauvoir was, in effect, challenging the discourse, identified by Michel Foucault, which had produced 'peripheral' sexualities in order to discipline them.[111]

There remain nevertheless certain problems relating to Beauvoir's representation of lesbian experience. As Toril Moi has noted, Beauvoir oscillates between arguing on the one hand for its authenticity and on the other, describing its narcissistic character.[112] Moi says:

True reciprocity, Beauvoir implies, presupposes difference: too much similarity reduces sexual interaction to a narcissistic mirroring of the Other: it is not a coincidence that she speaks of the "miracle of the mirror" precisely in the context of lesbian sexuality.[113]

But what does 'same' and 'different' mean in the context of sexuality? Same body, same experiences, same social positioning? The physical mirroring process which Beauvoir claims exists in lesbian sexuality is rooted in a recognition of corporeal similarity which is then deemed to determine sexual behaviour. Beauvoir appears to see lesbian sexuality both as a solipsistic attempt to recreate oneself and as a reciprocal sexual experience, unlike the conflict-laden heterosexual encounter. As Moi has noted, this portrayal of lesbianism is rather idealistic, and perhaps rather nostalgic on Beauvoir's part.

In *Le Deuxième Sexe* Beauvoir does not consider the social, historical and political significance of assuming a lesbian identity, as Ann Ferguson has noted.[114] Beauvoir does not examine the difficulties of assuming a lesbian identity in a homophobic and misogynist society. This is surprising because the majority of Beauvoir's text is devoted to the social, historical and political implications of being a (heterosexual) woman. One might conclude therefore that lesbians do not exist in a social, political or historical framework. Furthermore, Beauvoir's refusal to consider the significance of her own sexual relationships with women is regrettable, for elsewhere in *Le Deuxième Sexe* she does draw implicitly on her own experience. As noted previously, the judicial investigation of her sexuality in the early 1940s is likely to have been a factor in Beauvoir's ambivalent stance on lesbianism in the text and in her lifelong denial of her sexual relationships with women.

To summarise, sexuality is described in *Le Deuxième Sexe* as a conflict-laden exchange between an active male and passive female, who are both prisoners of naturalising, reifying biological mythology, or as a reciprocal yet rather narcissistic exchange between women with no historical, social or political significance.

Despite its many inconsistencies, *Le Deuxième Sexe* has been highly influential on both a practical and theoretical level – perhaps, as Denise Warren has argued, because of its understanding of the operation of power in the construction of the female subject. Warren observes:

Finding that its traditional forms fail to explain the male/female asymmetry, she [Beauvoir] turns her attention to the discourse and sets of practices which both constitute and execute gender relations in everyday life, that is, male power in practice. This, combined with her relentless account of "becoming a woman" with its attendant internalization and playing out of Otherness, results in her astute analysis of the micro-politics of the constitution of self as female subject, as Other, in Western culture.[115]

Warren clearly refers here to Foucault's notion of power as operating locally and productively rather than as a monolithic, judicial and repressive force.[116] In *Le Deuxième Sexe*, Beauvoir represents gender relations largely through the everyday transactions between women and men or, as Warren says, the micro-politics of their relationships, which contribute to the production of discourses of sexual difference. Power is not represented as monolithic, repressive or as the unique preserve of men in *Le Deuxième Sexe*, but as a potential for action which, in most cases, can be grasped by either women or men.

In conclusion, in *Le Deuxième Sexe* Beauvoir attempts to demonstrate the 'ambiguïté' of women's situation, to challenge deterministic discourses circumscribing women's subjectivity and to throw women into the world where they might learn how to become subjects on their own terms. The vast majority of *Le Deuxième Sexe* is, for this reason, concerned with women's situation in the world. Beauvoir has often been accused of devaluing feminine activities and experience but, in the late 1940s, there was an abundance of discourses over-valuing traditionally feminine spheres of activity, which she attempted to challenge. The key issue for Beauvoir in *Le Deuxième Sexe* was to articulate how women might achieve agency rather than to confirm discourses of sexual difference. From the 1940s onwards, she made a significant contribution to this theorisation of new forms of subjectivity.

In Beauvoir's memoirs, which will be the focus of examination in Part II, she continues to explore how ethical subjectivity may be assumed – her own life constituting a case study in the elaboration of female subjectivity.

PART II

*Writing the life*

CHAPTER 3

# *Narratives of self-representation*

Simone de Beauvoir's auto/biographical writing will be the focus of the second part of this study. Although she has tended to (re)present herself as a literary writer rather than as a philosopher, in her testimonial auto/biographical writing as in her philosophy, she reflects on the notion of selfhood through the representation of her own life and the lives of others.

In 1985, Kate Millett compared Simone de Beauvoir's auto-biography to *Le Deuxième Sexe*, and argued that Beauvoir had affected women just as deeply by her autobiography, but that its effect was not as well recognised. For Millett, if *Le Deuxième Sexe* had taught women of her generation how to think, Beauvoir's autobiography had taught them how to live.[1] In this chapter, Beauvoir's approach to autobiography will be examined through critical discussion of her relationship to women's autobiographical writing more generally, to the Other in autobiography and her desire to 'tell all' in a narrative production of the temporally-situated self.

In terms of the scope of her autobiography, it is difficult to find many comparable French women autobiographers in the twentieth century.[2] One could cite Colette, who has been described as 'a pioneer in techniques that anticipate the genre of fictional auto-biography'.[3] However, her ahistorical and apolitical textual self-representations in 'impressionist memoir', 'autobiographical fiction' and 'fictional autobiography' seem to have little in common with Beauvoir's testimonial autobiographical project.[4] Clara Malraux and Violette Leduc are potential comparators, although in their autobiographies, as Elaine Marks notes, '[they] create images of victims'. For Marks, Beauvoir's autobiography is essentially a success story.[5]

Writing autobiography can, indeed, be a literal way of 'making a name for oneself'. The 'je qui parle' is bestowed with a name through which he or she can be interpellated and which he or she accepts. This acceptance is manifested by the acts of signing and speaking one's name – acts which are deemed to signal the presence and identity of the subject.[6] As Althusser has argued in his account of interpellation, a subject is interpellated as a potentially active subject and implicated ideologically by the actions of naming and by the recognition of the name as corresponding to oneself as a subject.[7] Yet as Judith Butler has argued, the possibility for the subject's political resistance lies in the inaccurate or unheeded interpellation, for ideological interpellation does not necessarily effect what it names.[8]

In the case of Simone de Beauvoir, desiring to 'make a name for herself', she wrote almost exclusively under her 'own' bourgeois patronym, apart from some articles that she wrote in 1945 under the masculine name 'Daniel Secrétan' and some articles that she wrote for Sartre in 1944 which were published under his name.[9] Unlike Sartre, however, Beauvoir has been attributed with an array of sobriquets, for example, 'La Grande Sartreuse' and the most well-known one, the masculine 'Castor', given to her in the late 1920s by René Maheu. 'La Grande Sartreuse' and other pejorative epithets such as 'La Mère Castor' were assigned to Beauvoir by an often-hostile French press, apparently seeking to diminish her individual intellectual project.

Beauvoir was demonstrably aware of the political importance of using her name in signing petitions, manifestos and prefaces for causes that she supported. Yet this politically subversive use of named identity stands in contrast to Beauvoir's obligation to sign a declaration during the Occupation that she was not Jewish in order to retain her employment.[10] In *Pyrrhus et Cinéas*, as noted in Chapter 1, Beauvoir describes the importance of naming: 'le nom, c'est ma présence totale rassemblée magiquement dans l'objet'.[11] Her literary project, and her autobiography in particular, played a crucial role in this production of 'Simone de Beauvoir' as a well-known name. In 1979, in a film made on her life, she described her early enthusiasm to become a writer:

Pour une femme, c'était la meilleure et peut-être la seule façon que je voyais à l'époque – à moins d'être la reine d'Angleterre – de se faire un nom, d'être quelqu'un.[12]

Yet despite this claim and Beauvoir's celebrity as the author of *Le*

*Deuxième Sexe*, it is problematic to read Beauvoir's autobiography as 'women's autobiography', marked by essentialised gender concerns and rhetorical devices.

In *Women's Autobiography: Essays in Criticism*, Estelle Jelinek argues that women's autobiographies are frequently judged as texts by women rather than as texts in their own right. She notes that most of the 'objective' theories of autobiography are irrelevant to women's lifestories, because they rarely mirror the conventional history of their times. According to Jelinek's somewhat essentialist view, women autobiographers stress the personal aspects of their lives rather than the public sphere and exhibit a self-consciousness and a need to sift through their lives for explanation and understanding. They do not dramatise their lives as success stories, cast their lives in an heroic mould or consider that their lives have any great individual import or connectedness to society. For Jelinek, women's motive in autobiography is rather to convince the reader of their self-worth and to authenticate their self-image. Accordingly, she claims that women use a variety of techniques in autobiography, such as writing elliptically, obliquely or humorously to underplay their feelings or professional lives. If women relate crises in their lives, they distance their crises through understatement. Women's texts are characterised by irregularity and disconnectedness; the life is often related in self-sustaining units, rather than connected chapters. Therefore many more women than men, according to Jelinek, have written diaries, journals and notebooks because these forms mirror women's fragmented lives. Beauvoir was a prolific writer of diaries and letters, as well as four volumes of memoirs. However, few of the features of women's autobiography identified by Jelinek can be found in Beauvoir's autobiography.

In *Life/Lines*, Nancy Miller's 'Writing Fictions: Women's Autobiography in France' considers the autobiographical practice of Beauvoir, George Sand, Daniel Stern and Colette. Miller proposes a 'double reading' or an intertextual reading working in conjunction with a gendered 'overreading', as an approach to women's autobiography which 'would recognise the status of the reader as differentiated subject, a reading subject named by gender and committed in a dialectics of identification to deciphering the inscription of a female subject'.[13] In Miller's view, 'not to perform an expanded reading . . . not to read the fiction with the autobiography is to remain prisoner of a canon that bars women from their own texts.'[14] Although Miller makes many convincing points while deploring women's wrongful exclusion from the canon of auto-biography, she nevertheless appears to uphold this exclusion by arguing that there is a gendered form of autobiographical pro-duction (that women's autobiography is always intertextual) and reception (women readers are privileged decoders of women's autobiography) which may result in women's autobiography be-coming a rather rarefied and marginalised business.

Gender is indeed a key factor in autobiographical production and reception, but it is a factor which is taken up and negotiated differently by every autobiographer. The exclusion until fairly recently of women's autobiography from autobiography studies and the refusal by critics to employ gender as a category of auto-biographical interpretation is regrettable and has impoverished the study of self-representational writing. However, this exclusion and the gender blindness are not satisfactorily remedied by the political strategy of constructing an essentialist tradition of women's auto-biography, for this foregrounds gender at the expense of other possible key factors of autobiographical engagement, such as class, race and sexuality. For many women who write their lifestories – including Beauvoir – sexism may not be the principal or only source of their oppression. As Leigh Gilmore has noted:

Insofar as feminist criticism of autobiography has accepted a psycholo-gizing paradigm, it reproduces the following ideological tenets of individu-alism: men are autonomous individuals with inflexible ego boundaries who write autobiographies that turn on moments of conflict and place the self at the center of the drama. Women, by contrast, have flexible ego boundaries, develop a view of the world characterized by relationships (with priority given to the mother-daughter bond), and therefore represent the self in relation to "others" . . . The extent to which the "women" in "women's autobiography" have been stabilized, have been given a history, have had female identity and been seen as speaking and confirming this identity, obscures the broader ways in which gender is produced through the discourses of self-representation . . . Autobiography is positioned within discourses that construct truth, identity, and power, and these discourses produce a gendered subject.[15]

Gilmore, working within a broadly Foucauldian perspective, suggests that there is not so much 'autobiography' as 'autobiographics', which allow an examination of how the 'I' is multiply coded in a range of discourses, of which gender may be only one.[16] Gilmore focuses on discontinuities in autobiographical identity and focuses on how the autobiographical is represented through technologies of autobiography as historically variable discourses of truth and identity which vary according to every autobiographer. Such an approach avoids reading autobiography according to a logic of the same which tends to elide gender and any other factors which do not 'fit' the established canon of autobiography or the identity category which is privileged, thereby disregarding the autobiographical subject's specific detailed engagement with the dynamics and problematics of self-representation.

In the ensuing discussion of Beauvoir's autobiography, I shall attempt to look similarly at how the 'je' of her autobiographical self-representation is produced through the negotiation of discourses of class, nationality, race, religion, gender and sexuality. It will be argued that in her memoirs Beauvoir largely rejects a confessional approach to autobiography in favour of a testimonial project. She experiments with linear and thematic-linear narrative forms and with different autobiographical forms: autobiography as an authoritative account of an individual who is positioned as the coherent producer of textual meaning; memoirs as an anecdotal representation of self as always already produced in relation to others; and existentialist self-representation, which plays off traditional autobiography and journal form against each other to represent the self as necessary for agency and yet also a contingent construction, formed in relation to others and to the world.

The range of Beauvoir's testimonial autobiographical project (autobiography, memoirs, letters, journals) has indeed constructed her as 'a witness to the twentieth century', and has resulted in her autobiography being cited in many biographies and histories of twentieth-century France.[17] In addition, her autobiography is deemed by many Beauvoir scholars – encouraged perhaps by Beauvoir herself – to be the authoritative source of information on her own fiction and philosophical writing, as if a seamless conflation of woman, life and text were possible.

The range, detail and ostensibly traditional form of Beauvoir's lifestory is striking, particularly in relation to Sartre's slight volume, *Les Mots*, which he described as 'un roman'.[18] By writing *Les Mots* he eschewed writing conventional autobiography and, in later life, he turned to biography and to self-representation in interviews and film.[19] As Mary Warnock has noted, Sartre held that there was little difference between autobiography and biography, and that both were important in order to make and understand history. Warnock argues that, for Sartre, the task of the auto/biographer is to enable us to see how a particular individual is shaped by his or her circumstances, and how he or she then shaped the future by his or her choices and actions.[20]

Given this, Sartre's relative lack of literary interest in himself and his preference for philosophical explorations of subjectivity and biography – rather than the kind of extensive testimonial auto-biographical project undertaken by Beauvoir – is remarkable.[21] Speaking about his notion of literature, Sartre explained in an interview with her:

> Moi, je ne sais pas pourquoi, je n'écrivais pas sur moi. Du moins sur moi comme personnage subjectif, comme ayant une subjectivité, des idées. Ça ne m'est jamais venu à l'idée d'écrire sur moi.[22]

This apparent lack of literary interest in recording his own experience of subjectivity and his decision not to write a sequel to *Les Mots* (which, in any case, cannot really be viewed as a chronological narrative of a life, as Philippe Lejeune has noted,[23] and draws only on material from Sartre's first eleven years), has encouraged some critics to read Beauvoir's extensive autobiography as a compensatory biography of Sartre[24] – despite Beauvoir's claims to the contrary.[25]

In the same series of interviews with Beauvoir, Sartre made some further observations which are of interest here. He said that 'J'ai toujours eu l'idée, à dix-huit ans, vingt ans, d'écrire sur ma vie quand je l'aurais faite, c'est-à-dire, à cinquante ans'.[26] He explained that he began the first version of *Les Mots* (entitled *Jean-sans-terre*) as a result of his 'rapprochement' with the Parti communiste in 1952, in order to represent his life as having 'ce sens politique d'arrivée au communisme'. He then began writing a different, highly stylised literary representation based on his early life in 1961 which became *Les Mots*, as 'une manière de dire adieu' to the apolitical literature he had written during his early writing career.[27]

In another interview with Beauvoir, Sartre described his extensive correspondence as 'en somme l'équivalent d'un témoignage sur ma vie'.[28] She replied, implicitly referring to herself because she was the recipient of the majority of Sartre's letters: 'Oui, mais pour porter ce témoignage il vous fallait un interlocuteur'. Her reminder to Sartre here of the importance of the Other's role is a microcosmic example of the different role attributed to the Other in their respective early philosophical and literary projects. Beauvoir further developed her own notion of the self's relationship to the Other, first theorised in her philosophy of the 1940s, in her project of testimonial autobiography.

### THE OTHER

As Michael Sheringham has observed, autobiography always involves an engagement with alterity in its different forms: 'Desiring the self . . . the autobiographer must first encounter alterity: other texts, other ideas, other people.'[29]

As noted in Part I, the Other plays a crucial role in Beauvoir's philosophical project, because she views subjectivity as assumed and produced always already in terms of our relationships with others. In Beauvoir's memoirs, the Other is ever-present – as lost self, as reader, as all that which is not 'I' and which must be contested or embraced. For Beauvoir as existentialist and feminist, the Other has a philosophical and political existence, and subjectivity is produced in the context of the relationship with the Other.

As temporally-situated reader, the Other enables the production of the autobiographical subject. This (lost) subject is situated in the otherness of history, and is recovered through the collaboration of reader and autobiographer.[30] They are both situated differently in time: the autobiographer is situated in the narrative present and is separated from the past selves which she relates, whereas the reader is situated in a future present, separated from the narrator's present, and the past related. However, this three-fold temporal rupture between the future time of the reader, the present of the narrator and her past autobiographical selves and the alienation which this rupture entails can be overcome by collaboration between the author and the reader.

Beauvoir explains this collaboration in a lecture she gave in Japan in 1966, after she had completed three volumes of her autobiography:

Le récit trahit le mouvement vivant d'une vie. Il y a tout de même une manière de le susciter: une seule. Il faut que le lecteur, qui lui est vivant, qui vit en chair et os dans le temps, me prête son propre temps; au moment où il me lit, il se rappelle tout ce qu'il a lu jusque-là; quand il me voit, à vingt ans, il se rappelle la petite fille que j'ai été, et en même temps il se demande quelle femme je vais devenir. Alors il me prête l'épaisseur de son propre temps et le défaut . . . sera pallié. Mais pour cela, il me faut capter l'intérêt du lecteur, donc il faut que mon livre ait une qualité littéraire. Il faut que par le ton, par le style, par la manière dont je parle, dont je raconte, il faut que je charme, que je séduise, que je retienne la liberté du lecteur; que librement il reste là à m'écouter et à faire de son côté ce travail de création qui lui appartient.[31]

It can be argued, then, that Beauvoir adopts a largely chronological approach to autobiography, and relates the life in much of its contingent detail not with the aim of producing a complete and mimetically true account of her life, but rather to facilitate the recreation of the life in the future time of the reader. Autobiography appears to function for her as an intersubjective locus of (future) self-(re)creation, and as a means of (re)creating a vital agency which the passing of time destroys, because Beauvoir views time as operating by division and diminution, rather than by cumulative progression. The Other as reader-collaborator plays a vital role, then, in the production of past selves in the future time of autobiography.

But what are the characteristics of this self (re)created in auto-biography? In *Tous les hommes sont mortels*, Beauvoir had already demonstrated the futility of immortal life, for existence only assumes significance through being situated, and thus limited by time, space and relationships with others. In her essay, 'l'Existentialisme et la sagesse des nations', Beauvoir explains that for existentialism, 'le moi n'existe pas' and that 'dans la philosophie de la transcendance, c'est uniquement comme point de départ que le sujet existe'.[32] In her memoirs, in *La Vieillesse*, as well as in her philosophical essays, Beauvoir demonstrates that, with the passing of time, the subject is continually and irremediably divided from his or her past. The past is past and does not hold the richness, vitality or urgency of the present. Mary Warnock agrees with Beauvoir's notion of the past as largely irretrievable through memory, and argues that in remembering 'what I cannot do is make it necessary to choose again. In the past I was free; now, looking back on the past, my choices are determined. I can tell the story as it was; but I cannot change the plot at will.'[33] The recreation of past selves in autobiography is a fallacy, for one can never choose twice, and a life without choice and agency is not an option that Beauvoir would endorse. Self-recreation in her autobiography appears to be a form of self-conservation achieved through self-narration, in which the reader assumes the role of curator of Beauvoir's life. Her life is conserved as a potential exemplar for future generations of the female intellectual as witness to history. Yet this leaves Beauvoir open to charges of self-hagiography, recalling perhaps the portraits of the 'immortals' in the Bouville art gallery in Sartre's *La Nausée* (1938), who, inflated with their own sense of legitimacy, look down on the passive spectators of bourgeois history.[34] Yet this history, in addition to being bourgeois, is also patriarchal, and, despite her situation of centrality as a member of the bourgeoisie, Beauvoir subverts its process in assuming a role as female witness.

The reader as Other also facilitates the recovery of lost others for Beauvoir. On several occasions, her memoirs offer the reader micro-biographies of characters in her entourage. Auto/biography and memoirs act as a site of recovery or as an opportunity to rework lost relationships with the Other: friends from whom she is now separated for ideological or personal reasons, such as Nathalie Sorokine and René Maheu (Herbaud in the *Mémoires*) or friends or members of her family who have died, such as Zaza, Jacques, Bourla, her father, Giacometti, Camus, and Merleau-Ponty. In *La Vieillesse*, Beauvoir describes how the death of others entails the death of a part of her life:

Tant qu'ils vivaient, il n'était pas besoin de souvenir pour qu'en eux notre commun passé demeurât vivant. Ils l'ont emporté dans leur tombe; ma mémoire n'en retrouve qu'un simulacre glacé. Dans les "monuments funèbres" qui jalonnent mon histoire, c'est moi qui suis enterrée.[35]

In summary, the Other plays a crucial role in Beauvoir's auto-biography: as she or he through whom subjectivity is assumed from the outset, as lost other self to be recreated in autobiography, as lost Other in the shape of friends or family, and as reader who enables the process of self-recreation in autobiography to take place.

## AUTOBIOGRAPHICAL FORM

Concern for the Other's (negative) judgement is often articulated through anxiety over form in Beauvoir's autobiography. This is not unusual among autobiographers. Montaigne and Rousseau, as well as some of Beauvoir's contemporaries in the twentieth century, such as Violette Leduc, expressed anxiety over autobiographical form in their various declarations of autobiographical intention. Neverthe-less, the linear, chronological and teleological narrative which predominates in Beauvoir's autobiography and memoirs stands in stark contrast to the diverse textual practices of her contemporaries such as Sartre, Leiris, Genet, Leduc, Duras and Sarraute. On first glance, her autobiography might appear ill-at-ease in the twentieth century.

Beauvoir's anxiety over autobiographical form is one indication that her philosophical objectives in autobiography are occasionally at odds with her literary and political objectives. For example, the philosophical objective of representing the temporally-situated self in autobiography, which requires, Beauvoir believes, that she observe a largely chronological, teleological narrative form, poses literary difficulties for her because she recognises that it can seem stylistically tedious and lacking in analysis.[36] What appears interesting philo-sophically – the representation of an individual existence as what Sartre called a 'totalité détotalisée' whose meaning is always deferred[37] – does not necessarily constitute interesting literature. Beauvoir is consequently torn between stylistic concerns as a literary writer, who seeks a position in the predominantly male auto-biographical canon, and her philosophical interest in the notion of selfhood.

Yet despite her somewhat conservative approach to auto-biographical form, Beauvoir's autobiography is more innovative than might initially appear. Her notion of time as operating by division leads her into an interesting diversity of autobiographi-cal narrative forms. This view of time, largely neglected by Beauvoir scholars, offers a fresh perspective on her use of linear historical narrative, diary extracts and thematic-linear narrative in *Tout compte fait* as well as on her experimentation with various forms of autobiographical writing (for example, her representation of autobiography as *Bildungsroman* in *Mémoires d'une jeune fille rangée* and her use of memoir form in the three subsequent volumes).[38] This experimentation demonstrates a continuing commitment to narrating the experience of existence as situated in time, and as experienced differently in time which, as we have seen, is also produced in the future time of the reader.[39] For Beauvoir, the roles of time and memory in the experience of subjectivity and in the autobiographical represen-tation of subjectivity are crucial.

TIME AND MEMORY

Temporality, or how the subject experiences time, is an important theme throughout Beauvoir's writing, and had similarly concerned Bergson, Husserl and Heidegger, with whose work she was well-acquainted. Bergson was an important part of Beauvoir's philosophical education as she noted in her memoirs.[40] According to her account in *La Force de l'âge*, Beauvoir claims to have first become aware of Husserlian phenomenology in the early 1930s, although it is likely that her acquaintance with Husserl's work actually began in the late 1920s.[41] In a celebrated passage, Beauvoir relates how Raymond Aron introduced her and Sartre to Husserl:

> Raymond Aron passait l'année à l'Institut français de Berlin et, tout en préparant une thèse sur l'histoire, il étudiait Husserl. Quand il vint à Paris, il en parla à Sartre. Nous passâmes une soirée au Bec de Gaz, rue Montparnasse; nous commandâmes la spécialité de la maison: des cocktails à l'abricot. Aron désigna son verre: "Tu vois, mon petit camarade, si tu es phénoménologue, tu peux parler de ce cocktail, et c'est de la philosophie!"[42]

Enthusiastic to learn more, Sartre replaced Aron at the French Institute in Berlin and spent 1933–4 studying Husserl's phenomenology. Later in *La Force de l'âge*, Beauvoir explains how she began to study Husserl in her own right:

> Je m'initiai à Husserl. Sartre m'avait exposé tout ce qu'il en savait. Il me mit entre les mains le texte allemand des *Leçons sur la conscience interne du temps* que je déchiffrai sans trop de peine. A chacune de nos rencontres, nous en discutions des passages. La nouveauté, la richesse de la phénoménologie m'enthousiasmaient: il me semblait n'avoir jamais approché de si près la vérité.[43]

Beauvoir rapidly acquired a thorough knowledge of Husserlian phenomenology, including his notions on time-consciousness. Indeed, Sartre observed that her knowledge of Husserl was more thorough than his own at this time.[44]

However, her philosophical notions concerning time were also developed through her reading of Heidegger, whose work she read in the late 1930s.[45] Heidegger's notion of the subject in *Being and Time*, whose existence is always already temporally imbricated and as a 'being-towards-death', who cannot fully experience his or her own death but only the deaths of others, is illustrated more generally across Beauvoir's fictional and auto/biographical writing.[46] In particular, the diversity of auto/biographical forms which she exploited (journal, memoirs, letters, biographical récit) indicates a fascination with the pivotal role time plays in the experience and narrative production of subjectivity.[47]

Moreover, temporality is a significant feature even in her early fiction, as Kate and Edward Fullbrook have also noted.[48] In *L'Invitée*, Beauvoir expresses a view of time and action as co-implicated:

Le temps n'est pas fait d'un tas de petits morceaux séparés dans lesquels on puisse s'enfermer successivement; quand vous croyez vivre tout simplement au présent, bon gré, mal gré, vous engagez l'avenir.[49]

The past, present and future are simultaneously implicated in our projects. We do not accumulate time or progress through time because we do not possess our past. In *Pyrrhus et Cinéas*, Beauvoir expresses this clearly:

Les moments successifs d'une vie ne se conservent pas dans leur dépasse-ment, ils sont séparés; pour l'individu comme pour l'humanité, le temps n'est pas progrès, mais division . . . Il n'est aucun instant d'une vie où s'opère une réconciliation de tous les instants.[50]

Chantal Moubachir, in her discussion of Beauvoir's notion of time, has argued that although she views time as tri-dimensional, each moment is divided from the next. The past is, therefore, irrevocably lost to us. Our lives only assume meaning through our current projects, which characterise our present.[51] Moubachir briefly exam-ines Husserl's influence on Beauvoir's notion of time referring to his 1905 lectures on the *Phenomenology of Internal Time-Consciousness* which, as noted above, Beauvoir had read in the original German in the early 1930s.[52] Moubachir argues that although Beauvoir shares Husserl's view that the present is consciousness as action, she does not agree with his notion of time as a continuous flux, according to which it is always possible to recover what has been experienced, through what Husserl calls 'protention' and 'retention'. Moubachir refers to Husserl's example of listening to a melody, which he uses throughout much of *The Phenomenology of Internal Time-Consciousness*, and is similarly used by Sartre in *La Nausée*.

Husserl says that when we listen to a melody we have a primal impression of the note occuring at a given moment, and also 'retain' an impression of the previous note as having just occurred. We therefore retain an impression of the succession of individual notes. Listening to the melody, we also 'protain' its future course as being within certain limits. For example, even if we do not have prior knowledge of a Schubert string quintet, we do not 'protain' the quintet to break into classical jazz in its second movement for such a development would exceed the horizons of the melody already established. Husserl distinguishes retention (which he also calls primary remembrance) from recollection and protention from anticipation. If, for example, I am attempting to remember an earlier part of the melody, this distracts me from hearing the note occurring now because I am concentrating on an earlier sequence. However, as far as retention is concerned, when I hear the note occurring now, I also retain the notes of the melody I have heard without being distracted from listening to the present note, as Husserl's characterization of retention as 'a comet's tail which is joined to actual perception' indicates.[53] My focus of attention is therefore different in the cases of retention and recollection. Thus, retention and recollection are distinct because in the former, the melody is the object or the very recent object of my perception, whereas in recollection, I am attempting to re-present it to myself from presentifications of earlier perceptions.[54] Yet, both retention and recollection indicate that the past is recoverable in some form.

However, in Beauvoir's writing, consciousness of temporal succession is marked by rupture. We cannot achieve self-coincidence because we are radically separated from ourselves by the three temporal *ekstases* (meaning literally from the Greek 'ek-stasis', a 'standing out from') of past, present and future because the passing of time operates by division rather than progression. Life does not become more meaningful through the accumulation of temporal instances, but through action. The human subject's production of time, manifested corporeally through ageing, diminishes his or her ability to act.[55]

In Chapter 2, it was argued that for Beauvoir, as for Merleau-Ponty, the body is always already anchored in time, space and in relation to others, and constitutes the point at which we assume our subjectivity in the world. For Merleau-Ponty, temporality and corporeality are represented in the *Phénoménologie de la Perception* as deeply imbricated.[56] His theories concerning the 'present body' and the 'habitual body', 'the phantom limb' and bodily disfunctionalism demonstrate how temporality permeates the experience of corporeal selfhood.[57]

In much of Beauvoir's writing, especially in her memoirs and *La*

*Vieillesse,* she similarly represents our relationship to time as inscribed through the body, as a relationship which we experience through the body, in an almost Kafkaesque way.[58] At the end of *La Force des choses* for example, she describes the shock of experiencing time written on her body:

Comment ce qui n'a ni forme ni substance, le temps, peut-il m'écraser d'un poids si lourd que je cesse de respirer? Comment ce qui n'existe pas, l'avenir, peut-il si implacablement se calculer? Mon soixante-douzième anniversaire est aussi proche que le jour si proche de la libération. Pour m'en convaincre, je n'ai qu'à me planter devant la glace. A quarante ans, un jour, j'ai pensé: "Au fond du miroir la vieillesse guette; et c'est fatal, elle m'aura". Elle m'a. Souvent je m'arrête, éberluée, devant cette chose qui me sert de visage . . . Je déteste mon image: au-dessus des yeux, la casquette, les poches en dessous, la face trop pleine, et cet air de tristesse autour de la bouche que donnent les rides. Peut-être les gens qui me croisent voient-ils simplement une quinquagénaire qui n'est ni bien, ni mal, elle a l'âge qu'elle a. Mais moi je vois mon ancienne tête où une vérole s'est mise dont je ne guérirai pas.[59]

Here, the autobiographical subject's experience of time is distinct from other people's perceptions of her, for only she is aware of the physical effects of temporal succession in her memories of her past bodily states. The body acts as sedimented, material evidence of the subject's transtemporal states which can then be interpreted by the Other, for example as a body which is gendered and aged in specific ways, as Beauvoir explores in *Le Deuxième Sexe* and in *La Vieillesse.*

In order to palliate the irrecoverable loss of experience which is etched through the body, Beauvoir's solution is to record her life experiences in narrative which, as we have seen, are then produced in the future time of the reader. For, drawing on her knowledge of Husserl's distinction between retention and recollection described earlier, the reader retains knowledge of Beauvoir's past states as she represents them in autobiography and is able to evoke a present synthesis, whereas Beauvoir herself can only recollect but not achieve that living synthesis of her life apprehended by the reader. There is, then, a necessary collaboration between reader and author to achieve the temporal recreation of lost selves in autobiography, as we have noted earlier. So, although Beauvoir disagrees with Husserl's notion of time as continuous flux as far as the subject's experience of time is concerned, she effectively adapts it within the context of the act of reading, so that the reader imaginatively creates the lost 'self' of autobiography.

In her memoirs and in her 1972 study, *La Vieillesse*, Beauvoir argues that our relationship to time changes as we grow older and she represents the experience of this changing relationship to time in her memoirs and fiction. For example, in *Mémoires d'une jeune fille rangée*, when describing her early adolescence, she represents time as being a bourgeois commodity which she learns to manage carefully – this became a lifelong habit for Beauvoir. In a passage which recalls the temporal disciplining of the subject in Foucault's *Surveiller et punir*,[60] she also represents time as a commodity which the subject both manages and deploys in different ways. Françoise de Beauvoir is presented as the key figure through whom time is mediated:

Ma mère ne gaspillait jamais une seconde; en lisant, elle tricotait; quand elle causait avec mon père ou avec des amis, elle cousait, ravaudait ou brodait; dans les métros et les tramways elle confectionnait des kilomètres de "frivolité" dont elle ornait nos jupons. Le soir elle faisait ses comptes: depuis des années, chacun des centimes qui avaient passé par ses mains avait été marqué sur un grand livre noir. Je pensais que, – non seulement dans ma famille, mais partout – le temps, l'argent étaient si étroitement mesurés qu'il fallait les administrer avec la plus exacte rigueur . . . je demeurais convaincue qu'il faut employer à plein toutes les choses et soi-même.[61]

Moreover, Beauvoir relates how she experienced time differently whenever the teacher entered the classroom at the Cours Désir, and it is significant that in the following quotation, she represents the recording of her remembered existence as important in her perception of her life as purposeful:

A l'instant où Mademoiselle faisait son entrée, le temps devenait sacré. Nos professeurs ne nous racontaient rien de bien palpitant; nous leur récitions nos leçons, elles corrigeaient nos devoirs; mais je ne leur demandais rien de plus que de sanctionner publiquement mon existence. Mes mérites s'inscrivaient sur un registre qui en éternisait la mémoire. Chaque fois, il me fallait sinon me dépasser du moins m'égaler à moi-même: la partie se jouait toujours à neuf; perdre m'eût consternée, la victoire m'exaltait. Mon année était balisée par ces moments étincelants: chaque jour menait quelque part. Je plaignais les grandes personnes dont les semaines étales sont à peine colorées par la fadeur des dimanches. Vivre sans rien attendre me paraissait affreux.[62]

Individual moments assume here a privileged status for the autobiographical subject and, although each performance must begin anew, it is nevertheless measured in terms of past performances and the illusion of progress is created through the accumulation of these privileged moments, which are recorded in narrative. Yet Beauvoir makes clear here that this is a naïve and childishly egocentric conception of time, which she contrasts ironically with the apparently 'purposeless' time of adults.

In *La Vieillesse*, she notes again the subject's changing relationship to time:

Exister, pour la réalité humaine, c'est se temporaliser: au présent nous visons l'avenir par des projets qui dépassent notre passé où nos activités retombent, figées et chargées d'exigences inertes. L'âge modifie notre rapport au temps; au fil des années, notre avenir se raccourcit tandis que notre passé s'alourdit.[63]

Accordingly, Beauvoir explains in the preface to the final volume of her memoirs, *Tout compte fait*, after a certain period of time has elapsed, she is able to take stock of life in so far as she can recollect it, because her situation is no longer liable to be profoundly transformed. This taking stock is a narrative process, which does not restore the past, because as Moubachir notes, she can only fulfil the role of a 'témoin d'un monde aboli'.[64]

In *Pour une morale de l'ambiguïté*, Beauvoir explains that the collective ways in which we experience the past have significant implications for us as individuals. For example, people can act as curators of objects in the same way that they can act as curators of the past. The past can therefore be exploited as a refuge against any change by these curators of the past or 'conservatives'.[65]

Conversely, we cannot deny the past because it is part of us and is needed to forge our future projects:

Le fait d'avoir un passé fait en tout cas partie de la condition d'homme; si le monde derrière nous était nu, nous ne saurions guère apercevoir devant nous autre chose qu'un morne désert. Il faut essayer de reprendre à notre compte, à travers nos projets vivants, cette liberté qui s'est engagée dans le passé et de l'intégrer au monde présent.[66]

Beauvoir describes the past as an appeal to the future, which can only save the past by destroying it; through this perpetual destruction of the past, we assume our existence. Doubt is an inevitable part of action because we cannot predict the future implications of our actions. In time our actions can assume different meanings, which conflict with our original aims. In addition, we may be tempted to use methods which conflict with the ultimate result. Beauvoir asserts that the end only justifies the means if it is completely disclosed from the outset, although it is difficult to see how this is possible if uncertainty is an integral part of action.[67] 'End' has a twin meaning of ultimate target and fulfilment. Beauvoir explains that through festivals and celebrations, we valorise the present moment, as the end or fulfilment of a particular story or historical process. The plural significance of 'end' is demonstrated by the celebration of the Liberation at the end of *La Force de l'âge* – it is the end of the war, the fulfilment of the Resistance struggle and the end to that particular episode of Beauvoir's story, as personal 'histoire' and collective 'histoire' coincide.

For Beauvoir, then, temporality is a crucial feature of the way in which we assume our existence and, in autobiography, it is inextricably linked to the representation of subjectivity in narrative, which must now be examined in more depth.

### TELLING ALL

In her discussion of Beauvoir, Leduc and Clara Malraux, Elaine Marks compares the proliferating detail of their work to the sparseness of their male partners' or friends' autobiographies:

They seem haunted, more than the men, by the possibility of total annihilation and oblivion, they are fearful of dissolution and obsessed with mortality. Thus, they attempt to hold onto every detail; nothing will be forgotten.[68]

Geneviève Idt has succinctly described Sartre's and Beauvoir's divergent attitudes towards remembering the past:

[Sartre's] baroque intuition of change, of the rebirth of ideas and beings in a new form, is opposed in Beauvoir by a classical liking for traces and monuments. One believed in the virtue of forgetting, the other in the virtue of faithfulness, of Kierkegaardian "repetition". For Sartre, the past does not exist, whereas it inhabits, besieges and delights Beauvoir.[69]

Idt refers here to Beauvoir's commentary on *Les Mandarins* in *La Force des choses*, in which she says: 'Un des principaux thèmes qui se dégage de mon récit, c'est celui de la répétition, au sens que Kierkegaard donne à ce mot: pour posséder vraiment un bien, il faut l'avoir perdu et retrouvé'.[70] One might also add that Beauvoir seems to share the view articulated in another observation by Kierkegaard:

It is quite true what philosophy says: that Life must be understood

backwards. But that makes one forget the other saying: that it must be lived
– forwards. The more one ponders this, the more it comes to mean that life
in temporal existence never becomes quite intelligible, precisely because at
no moment can I find complete quiet to take the backward-looking
position.[71]

Beauvoir's proclivity for recording and rewriting episodes of her life
suggests a lifelong commitment to recover and to understand her life
'backwards', hence the desire 'to tell all' runs throughout her
autobiographical project, even though she warns the reader of her
autobiography on several occasions of the inevitability of selectivity.
There appears to be, on the one hand, a desire for self-totalisation in
a Derridean sense;[72] Beauvoir longs to capture the life in the text.
On the other hand, she acknowledges, like many autobiographers,
that it is never possible to record everything because of the
constraints produced by language, knowledge, memory, textual
form, her desire to capture the reader's interest and the need for
discretion concerning other people who appear in her texts.

In an interview with Francis Jeanson in 1965, Beauvoir described
this desire to record her life in autobiography as an effort to recover
lost time:

L'une des idées essentielles de ces trois volumes a été cette espèce de
récupération, qui est en réalité impraticable parce qu'on ne récupère
jamais vraiment le passé: une fois les livres écrits, il vous demeure aussi
étranger qu'auparavant; mais enfin, c'est plus ou moins récupéré, sous la
forme – en tout cas – de langage imprimé dans des livres.

In Sartre's *La Nausée*, Roquentin reasons in his diary that life should
not be confused with narrative because the essentially contingent
quality of life is destroyed by any attempt to capture it in language.
Accordingly, he concludes 'il faut choisir: vivre ou raconter'.[73]
Beauvoir, however, refuses to choose between living and recounting
and instead opts for both.[74] Few events occurred in her life which
did not appear in some written form at some time – a procedure
which caused dismay at times to those in her entourage.

Certain critics have not viewed positively Beauvoir's habit of
recording and relating her experience. In 1958, when *Mémoires d'une
jeune fille rangée* was published, the psychoanalyst, Octave Mannoni
observed in a lecture at the *Collège de philosophie* that, 'Il suffit de lire
ses *Mémoires* pour s'apercevoir comment dès son enfance on peut dire
qu'elle a toujours vécu dans un rapport autobiographique avec elle-
même'.[75]

Mannoni claims not to be interested in the factual content of Beauvoir's autobiography, but rather in what the conceptualisation of her autobiography tells us about how she perceived her life. The tautological notion that Beauvoir lives 'dans un rapport autobiographique avec elle-même' suggests a fragmented, narcissistic self, who observes, records and observes herself recording. The charge of narcissism has been a frequent response to Beauvoir's autobiographical project.[76] It is also a charge levelled at women's autobiography in order to dismiss it. Toril Moi has noted in her survey of the critical reception of Beauvoir's writing:

The very fact of writing a multi-volume autobiography . . . is presented as evidence of her relentless narcissism . . . not only is the fact that she often writes in autobiographical genres used as evidence of her debilitating egocentricity; her discussions of traditional "non-personal" topics, such as politics and philosophy, tend to be disparaged as mere displacements of the personal.[77]

Moreover, as Domna Stanton has noted, the fact that women's writing has been generally devalued on the basis of its autobiographical character suggests that among certain critics there are common political interests in terms of what is received as autobiography.[78]

Yet, Beauvoir's desire to record and to narrate can be viewed as constituting a healthy and productive response to personal and collective events experienced in a social, historical and political framework. John Taylor has noted in his examination of Sartre's use in *La Nausée* of Pierre Janet's work on psychasthenia that the distinction between 'vivre' and 'raconter' derives from Janet's *L'Evolution de la mémoire et de la notion du temps* (1928).[79] According to Taylor, 'for Janet, the reflexive production of a narrative contemporaneous with our acts is the key factor in the creation of 'le sens du réel' essential to mature and healthy existence'.[80] Beauvoir had read Janet's work, and the persistence with which she wrote and rewrote Zaza's story in an attempt to understand this traumatic experience is a powerful example (among many others) of her therapeutic production of narratives in order to organise and to understand her experience.[81] Her vast autobiographical project and the autobiographical character of much of her fiction, when examined in the context of her notion of the self as always already in the world with others, constitutes a continuing commitment to resolve the dichotomy of 'vivre ou raconter' posed in *La Nausée*. For Beauvoir, narrative acts as a bridge between our experience of the world and our understanding of that world, which is shared with the Other.

Beauvoir's repeated recourse to narrative to represent her experience can be characterised as a desire to produce in autobiography what Paul Ricoeur has termed an 'identité narrative'. This concept has been briefly examined in relation to autobiography more generally by Michael Sheringham.[82] An introduction to some of the features of 'identité narrative' is helpful in this discussion of Beauvoir's use of narrative as a testimonial tool to represent her experience as lived with others in a temporal framework.[83]

### NARRATIVE IDENTITIES

Ricoeur introduces the concept of 'identité narrative' at the end of the third volume of *Temps et récit* (1985) and develops it further in *Soi-même comme un autre* (1990). In *Temps et récit*, he argues that the production of narratives makes our experience intelligible to us and to others as it is lived in the three temporal dimensions of past, present and future. Narrative can act as a bridge between an individual's private understanding of the world and the public world in which he or she articulates that understanding. Experience consists of events, which are disruptive because they suddenly occur in a particular configuration of circumstances no matter how we might try to anticipate them. And yet, events are also productive because they ensure a development of some kind. The emplotment of events in narrative is an attempt to resolve the disruptive and productive character of events. Events take place in a temporal sequence, and narrative, in Ricoeur's view, is a response to the problems posed by temporality.

The mediation between narrative and temporality takes place through a three-fold mimetic process which he explains in the first volume of *Temps et récit*. The first stage involves a pre-comprehension of human action and its temporal structures, which is in place prior to narration. The second stage entails the configuration or emplotment of events in a teleological narrative structure. The third stage involves the act of reading as a creative or passive performance of the text's instructions, so that the reader might imaginatively refigure his or her temporal experience against the emplotted experiences represented in the text.

For Ricoeur, as for Beauvoir, narrative plays an important role in the production of identity:

Une vie, c'est l'histoire de cette vie, en quête de narration. Se comprendre soi-même, c'est être capable de raconter sur soi-même des histoires à la fois intelligibles et acceptables, surtout acceptables.[84]

The repetition of 'acceptable' here signals the important role played by the Other as receiver of these stories – a role which Beauvoir acknowledged – and also that the stories that one tells about oneself need to be satisfactorily coherent and ethically acceptable.

Significantly in terms of autobiography's function as a political strategy of resistance, Ricoeur's concept of narrative identity can be understood in terms of narrative agency and can be applied to both individuals and communities. He argues that we are entangled in stories told to us by our culture. Through imaginative variations of these stories, personal and collective narrative identities can be constructed in autobiography, in psychoanalysis, in the law courts and in day-to-day transactions with other people. The production of narrative identities is a continual activity in which previous narratives are perpetually undone by successive ones. Narrative identity is not a panacea, however, because, as Ricoeur argues, its instability makes it as much of a problem as a solution to the question of personal identity. Identity is understood here not as being the *same* individual through time, but as a narrating *subject* through time, who becomes an agent in the act of narration. Narrative identity therefore involves a dynamic production of identity through narrative which, in the context of traditionally marginalised subjects, is an important motive to produce autobiographical selves.

Ricoeur distinguishes here between two uses of 'identity', understood as that which is the same (Latin, 'idem') and as selfhood (Latin, 'ipse'). As far as an individual is concerned, the difference between these two is represented by the opposite poles of self-sameness through time, according to which an individual's character is viewed as determining the same behaviour, opinions and so on, and of 'le maintien de soi', as Ricoeur terms it. In *Soi-même comme un autre*, he describes this 'maintien de soi' in the following way: 'c'est pour la personne la manière telle de se comporter qu'autrui peut *compter* sur elle'.[85] 'Le maintien de soi' is therefore a form of ethical

self-constancy according to which I am there for the Other who is
then able to (choose to) count on me.

Many of Ricoeur's ideas about narrative and more particularly,
narrative identity are productive and illuminating in a consideration
of Beauvoir's project of testimonial autobiography, rooted in the
recognition of an indebtedness to the Other. Initially, however, it is
useful to return to the problematics of Roquentin's view of narrative
in *La Nausée*, as a counterpoint to Beauvoir's use of autobiographical
narrative.

In *La Nausée*, the ability to organise experience into narrative is
represented as a self-deluding activity which masks the fundamental
anguish peculiar to each individual as he or she becomes aware of
the utter contingency and absurdity of existence. For Roquentin, the
central character of *La Nausée*, the link made between 'vivre' and
'raconter' is a false one because the experience of life and the
production of narrative are two quite distinct activities. Life, according to Roquentin is essentially contingent, it has no beginnings and
no ends. He may reflect occasionally on his life, but essentially
experiences it as a continual accumulation of the same. Narrative,
however, transforms 'le quotidien' as it constructs beginnings and
ends to lived experiences and events are related in a teleological
narrative framework. Yet Roquentin sees the narrative representation of experience as a deceitful activity because he does not believe
that 'true stories' exist. Instead, he associates the production of
narratives with 'des professionnels de l'expérience', such as the
smug, bourgeois Dr Rogé, who perpetually explain the present and
future by resorting to an explanatory narrative of a necessary past,
rather than confronting their fear of the novelty of the present.
However, in her memoirs and to some degree in her fiction,
Beauvoir recognises the role of narrative in the dynamic construction of personal identity and offers a more productive view of the
necessary link between narrative and experience than Sartre in *La
Nausée*.

Beauvoir's awareness of the importance of narrative in the
production of identity can be found in her earliest writing. In
*L'Invitée*, in a chapter omitted from the 1943 version of the published
text, Kate and Edward Fullbrook have noted how, as a child,
Françoise sits in the garden pondering over the question of personal
identity as 'une histoire qu'on se raconte' and as a role play, as she
plays at being herself or another person by experimenting with

different narrative identities. This narrative subjectivism re-emerges in *Mémoires d'une jeune fille rangée*, in Simone's identification with George Eliot through the character of Maggie Tulliver in *The Mill on the Floss*. She imagines an ideal other self, who will be moved by her lifestory: 'un jour, une adolescente, une autre moi-même, tremperait de ses larmes un roman où j'aurais raconté ma propre histoire.'[86] In both these examples, identity is represented as a solipsistic narrative process.

Later, in *La Force de l'âge*, Beauvoir unequivocally asserts the power of narrative when she relinquishes any claims to self-knowledge and says that she undertook her autobiographical project because 'on ne peut jamais se connaître mais seulement se raconter'.[87] Self-knowledge is jettisoned here in favour of self-narration through which self-interpretation can be achieved. The essence of Beauvoir's observation here is echoed by Ricoeur in the conclusion to the final volume of *Temps et récit*. He cites Socrates' phrase from the *Apology* that 'the self of self-knowledge is the fruit of an examined life' and explains that an examined life is one purged and clarified by the cathartic effects of historical and fictional narratives conveyed by culture. Ricoeur seems to argue here that the self tries on a set of narratives like a new outfit and, through the cathartic process of 'seeing whether they fit', comes to a temporary resting-place of momentary self-definition or sense of self-coincidence, located within a particular personal and historical context.

Self-narration is a perpetual process for Beauvoir, during which she constructs and re-constructs narrative identities as her relationship to time changes. Perhaps the most obvious example in the memoirs of this re-construction of narrative identity is the thematic reworking of Beauvoir's life in the first part of *Tout compte fait*. This change of autobiographical methodology is often perceived as the result of the failed chronological, teleological approach used in the previous three volumes. Yet there are some valid reasons for a change of narrative methodology at this point. By reworking material related in earlier volumes, Beauvoir appears to recognise that one can construct a number of narrative identities for oneself based broadly on the same material. The shift to a thematic narrative is the result of her recognition of her changing relationship to time as she grows older, which transforms her perception of her temporally-situated existence. As she explains in the prologue to *Tout compte fait*, she has aged and her perspective is now focused on

the past rather than the future. It is now possible at the beginning of
the 1970s to offer a partial 'totalisation' of her life because her
perspective on her life is now unlikely to change radically.

Nevertheless, ethical objections can be raised regarding this
variation of narrative identities within Beauvoir's testimonial framework of autobiography. Is it possible for a testimony to be considered
authoritative if it can be related differently? Does Ricoeur's ethical
'maintien de soi' occur in Beauvoir's testimonial autobiography?
These questions are at the heart of certain negative criticism of her
autobiographical project, which accuses her of mythologising her
past and autobiographical selectivity, as a scientific notion of truth as
correspondence acts as the arbiter of ethics. Reception of Beauvoir's
autobiography has perhaps focused for too long on an inevitably
moving target – namely, did she tell the truth (of correspondence)?
As already noted, perhaps a more productive line of enquiry in an
assessment of the ethics of Beauvoir's autobiography, which does not
'frame' the autobiographer as villain and which acknowledges the
inevitable construction of the text, is to pursue a notion of autobiographical truth as 'coherence' and to examine the positioning of
the Other in autobiography.

For it can be argued that any event – collective or personal – can
always be understood differently and related differently by the
participants involved because of the discrepancy between private
and collective levels of experiencing and understanding the world,
and because perspectives also change over time. But this view, which
seems to accept any testimony as valid, suggests that testimony
might be a narrative performance with no ethical import or
historical and political significance, which appears a dangerously
anti-humanist path to tread. As Ricoeur argues, the difference
between history and fiction must be maintained in order to challenge
moral relativism and revisionist historians, such as Robert Faurisson,
who, in an article published in 1979 in *Le Monde*, said that nothing
real happened in Auschwitz.[88]

Narrative identity understood as an ethical 'maintien de soi' and
self-coherence, manifested through the act of bearing witness, may
constitute a third option. This avoids on one hand, the anti-
humanism and apolitical implications of testimony viewed as a
contingent performance and on the other, a concept of testimony as
a disciplinary activity which produces a hegemonic, univocal truth
of correspondence – aspects of testimony which will be more closely

examined in Chapter 6. Ricoeur argues that 'it is possible to apply to our self-understanding the play of sedimentation and innovation which [. . . is] at work in every tradition'.[89] In the tradition of testimony, the sedimentation of the witness's role may entail producing an account which is received as 'true' because the individual perceives a duty to contribute to a pre-existing, collective understanding of the event (truth as coherence). The individual recognises a specific collective framework as the backdrop to his or her experience, which is in turn recognised by that collectivity. The innovation involved in the act of bearing witness arises in the potential of any testimony to disrupt that collective understanding by producing personal accounts which fall outside current horizons of expectation and experience while simultaneously being recognised by the collectivity. Testimony as a form of narrative identity would involve the play between this sedimentation as a personal obligation to bear witness to an event experienced collectively and the innovation of an individual account to disrupt and refine the collective narrative.

In Beauvoir's negotiation of autobiography, she positions herself within a predominantly masculine-constructed tradition of representing the self as witness to collective history. Yet she disrupts this tradition because she constructs an autobiographical 'ipse' by representing the agential female subject as witness to history. In this way, for a traditionally marginalised subject, writing autobiography can be a means to subvert and rework an earlier trauma of interpellation by the dominant group through the representation of alternative selves.[90] Entangled in discourses of gender, class, and religion, Beauvoir provides a testimony of her own experience within the collective, patriarchal history which would silence her. She exploits narrative to rework her identity of 'une jeune fille rangée' into a witness to the history of the Other, who has been silenced by the apolitical bourgeoisie. From *La Force de l'âge*, the second volume of her memoirs, Beauvoir prioritises the Other and represents identity as assuming meaning only in relation to that Other as always already part of her 'situation'. This attention to the Other is manifested in several ways: first, on a general level, in her notion of the literary text as the privileged locus of intersubjectivity. Then, in specific ways in her memoirs, for example, in her narrative positioning of a series of privileged interlocutors such as Zaza, Sartre and Sylvie Le Bon de Beauvoir; in the individual case histories of friends and acquaintances to be found throughout her memoirs and in her notion of autobiography as a testimonial project, in which she bears witness to the twentieth century.

Ricoeur's notion of history as a 'connaissance par trace' because historical events leave behind traces, and as a form of indebtness to the Other, outlined in *Temps et récit*, is especially relevant to Beauvoir's autobiographical practice. Her preoccupation with documenting the evidence of her past, as already noted, can be interpreted as a gesture of anxiety; yet it can also be viewed as a recognition of an indebtedness to the Otherness of history, as an attempt to make history live on. Beauvoir makes direct reference to her sense of personal and collective debt on numerous occasions. A frequently-cited example of personal debt is the final line of *Mémoires d'une jeune fille rangée* where she says that the death of her friend Zaza was the price for her own freedom. Zaza's death may be interpreted, as we will see in Chapter 5, as a convenient 'deus ex machina' device which allows Beauvoir to assume her adult life with Sartre, and as a final, crushing example of her indictment of the bourgeoisie. Yet this monumental, tragic death serves to shape Beauvoir's subsequent engagement with autobiography and history as an indebtedness to the Other and, following Ricoeur, as a recognition of the past's right to 'have been' rather than as a silent absence. Therefore, in response to the question raised earlier, Ricoeur's notion of narrative identity as a form of ethical self-constancy for and with the Other would seem to be exemplified in Beauvoir's testimonial autobiography.

In this chapter it has been argued that, for Beauvoir, autobiographical writing is a collaborative activity in which she attempts to construct a temporally-situated narrative identity by recreating her life experienced in history, with and for others. In the more detailed reading of her memoirs which follows, it will be argued that as a woman writer shaped by discourses of gender, sexuality, nationality and class, Beauvoir uses autobiographical narrative in order to represent herself as both discursively constituted and as a constituting autobiographical subject. Her engagement with truth-telling, intention, memory and time, autobiographical forms, and self-knowledge will be considered next as features of her explicit negotiation of autobiography with the reader.

CHAPTER 4

# *Negotiating autobiography*

Beauvoir declares her autobiographical intentions frequently: in her memoirs (in paratextual statements à la Rousseau), in interviews and notably in a lecture given in Japan in 1966.[1] These statements have frequently been received as authorial directives by critics who perhaps underestimate the philosophical and political dimensions of Beauvoir's autobiography.[2] Given the importance of the Other in her notion of subjectivity and the Other's role in the production of subjectivity in auto/biography and memoirs, these statements are unremarkable. They form part of Beauvoir's negotiation of auto/biography with the reader and reflect her view that selfhood and auto/biography are intersubjectively produced. These explicit negotiations with the reader will be considered in this chapter. They take place in the prologues, mid-textual reflections on the autobiographical task and conclusions to the texts. It will be argued that she exploits these paratextual spaces to negotiate with a reader-collaborator the production of the life within a testimonial framework of autobiography.

## MÉMOIRES D'UNE JEUNE FILLE RANGÉE

It is extraordinary, perhaps, that Beauvoir does not explicitly negotiate with the reader from the outset in the *Mémoires*, but rather in *La Force de l'âge*. This may be because she initially had no intention of writing a sequel to the *Mémoires*, as is evident from a letter she wrote to Nelson Algren on 2 January 1959, in which she told him that she had enjoyed writing the story of her childhood, that it had sold well, but that she did not know what to write next, especially in the current political situation, namely that of the Algerian War.[3] It may also have been difficult for Beauvoir to know *how* she could relate the difficult events of her life after 1929 in an autobiographical

87

sequel. Her innovative 'pacte' with Sartre, the triangular relationship with Olga, her early writing difficulties, her various male and female lovers and her political inactivity during the 1930s constituted interesting autobiographical material, but of a kind that was likely to provoke further scandal similar to that which she had experienced after the publication of *Le Deuxième Sexe*.[4]

Philippe Lejeune has criticised the mimetic use of language and the lack of 'pacte' (as he terms it) in the *Mémoires*:

Simone de Beauvoir, loin d'afficher la subjectivité liée au récit autobiographique, a l'air de raconter les choses "telles qu'elle furent": il n'y a aucun pacte autobiographique au début du livre et les intentions avouées du narrateur se comptent sur les doigts de la main.[5]

Leah Hewitt takes up Lejeune's terminology and says that a pre-autobiographical pact exists in the *Mémoires*,[6] which is evident in the character Simone's identification with Maggie Tulliver in George Eliot's *The Mill on the Floss*:

A travers son héroïne, je m'identifiai à l'auteur: un jour une adolescente, une autre moi-même, tremperait de ses larmes un roman où j'aurais raconté ma propre histoire.[7]

This seems rather cursory compared to Beauvoir's later statements of autobiographical intention and appears to signal that at this stage in her autobiographical project she would like her text to be read by a benign Other like herself who would be moved by her story.

Conversely, Marylea Macdonald has argued that there is no pact in the *Mémoires* and that this is the result of Beauvoir's anxiety over its reception and an indication of uncertainty over the text's status.[8] This anxiety would explain Beauvoir's veiled directive to the reader to be moved by her story, and the existence of various control mechanisms in the text, which will be examined in Chapter 5. As Macdonald notes, the absence of pact in the *Mémoires* is by no means unusual in twentieth-century French autobiography: 'l'absence de pacte préfigure les autobiographies contemporaines qui ont apporté des modifications radicales à la forme du genre.'[9] Macdonald notes in a later article that Lejeune's criticism of Beauvoir on this occasion is symptomatic of his largely negative appraisal of her auto-biography. She argues that Lejeune avoids examining Beauvoir's autobiography in any depth and stigmatises her work as an auto-biographical failure to the benefit of Sartre's *Les Mots*, particularly with respect to her chronological methodology.[10]

In short, the lack of an explicit declaration of autobiographical intention in the *Mémoires* leaves Beauvoir free to gauge the text's reception because writing autobiography was a new departure for her. She appears to have considered the *Mémoires* as a single volume at this stage. The narrator-reader relation functions solipsistically at this point for the reader is envisaged as a benign other self, who will be moved by Beauvoir's story.

## LA FORCE DE L'ÂGE

In *La Force de l'âge* and the remaining volumes of her autobiography, Beauvoir anticipates and responds to the reader's expectations that she might write within a confessional framework of autobiography. In the 'Prologue' to *La Force de l'âge*, she alerts the reader to the impossibility of her undertaking: 'Je me suis lancée dans une imprudente aventure quand j'ai commencé à parler de moi: on commence, on n'en finit pas'.[11] The desire to record and relate her past life to herself is ever-present, although in this volume she begins to address the reader directly, having become acquainted with her autobiographical readership since the publication of the *Mémoires*. On several occasions, Beauvoir expresses the desire to save her past selves in autobiography, as if the self is her literary capital.

Discovering the meaning of her existence is posited as a motivating factor for continuing her autobiography, although this inevitably involves other people. Like Rousseau, Beauvoir demonstrates her awareness that the production of her autobiography impinges on others' lives. And, following Montaigne's example of offering an account of himself in the form of an individual case study from which universal precepts might be drawn, Beauvoir writes herself into the male autobiographical canon.

From *La Force de l'âge* onwards, autobiography becomes a privileged locus of intersubjectivity for Beauvoir: a chance to communicate directly with her readers, albeit on her terms. Accordingly, she distinguishes her desire to record and to tell all from the need for autobiographical selectivity. As Geneviève Idt has observed: 'Beauvoir never swore to tell everything . . . she has always reserved the right to omit things and she does.'[12] To this effect, Beauvoir warns readers who expect a complete confession that 'Je laisserai résolument dans l'ombre beaucoup de choses'. Yet her autobiographical project is one of 'témoignage', in which 'toute vérité peut intéresser et servir'.[13] As for Rousseau, how to tell the truth is no simple matter for Beauvoir, for she distinguishes between omissions (which she allows), lies (of which she is not guilty) and minor mistakes, caused perhaps by memory lapses (which she has probably made).[14] These aspects of her negotiation of truth-telling, however, do not affect 'la vérité de l'ensemble'.

Later, in *La Force de l'âge*, Beauvoir reflects on the unreality of her early life with Sartre, and her naïve belief that her life could be 'une belle histoire qui devenait vraie au fur et à mesure que je me la racontais', which neglected the existence of the Other and the constraints of her 'situation'.[15] She questions the value of what she has related in the first part of *La Force de l'âge*, effectively distinguishing between one's relationship to what is true or real and the act of relating that relationship to the truth. Beauvoir assumes a vantage point in autobiography in relation to her past life and, by implication, asserts that her current position is one of good faith.

In her negotiation of truth-telling here, Beauvoir begins to anticipate criticisms from a reader who is not the benign other self whom she had imagined would read her *Mémoires*. She begins a polemic with critics and readers which will be continued throughout her autobiography. She responds to two critical camps here: those who claim that her portrait of subjectivity in her autobiography conflicts with her arguments in *Le Deuxième Sexe*, and those who perform reductive psychoanalytic readings on her autobiography. As far as her representation of her femininity in autobiography is concerned, she asserts 'mon effort a été au contraire de définir dans sa particularité la condition féminine qui est mienne', which suggests her autobiography constitutes her own 'cas particulier' of the generalised arguments concerning the construction and experience of femininity advanced in *Le Deuxième Sexe*. As far as psychoanalysis is concerned, Beauvoir's objections to its methodological reductiveness have not changed substantially since writing *Le Deuxième Sexe*. However, her comments at the end of this mid-textual commentary in *La Force de l'âge* might sound like a plea for the 'talking cure' of psychoanalysis, although they refer to Sartre's notion of the transcendental ego, developed in the mid-1930s:[16]

Je crois encore aujourd'hui à la théorie de "l'Ego transcendental"; le moi n'est qu'un objet probable et celui qui dit *je* n'en saisit que des profils; autrui peut en avoir une vision plus nette ou plus juste. Encore une fois, cet exposé ne se présente aucunement comme une explication. Et même, si je l'ai entrepris, c'est en grande partie parce que je sais qu'on ne peut jamais se connaître mais seulement se raconter.[17]

Beauvoir here relinquishes a claim to self-knowledge, and again frustrates any expectations that she might observe a confessional format in her autobiography. Instead she dismisses self-knowledge as impossible, because according to an existentialist notion of selfhood, the self cannot be an object of knowledge for itself.[18] Again she emphasises the role of narrative in the production of identity, asserting that it is only possible to relate one's experience of selfhood in collaboration with the reader.

However, this does not give the reader licence to impose any number of facile interpretations, for at the end of *La Force de l'âge*, Beauvoir alludes to the complexity of her autobiographical project and reiterates that it is impossible to tell all:

La sincérité littéraire n'est pas ce qu'on imagine d'ordinaire: il ne s'agit pas de transcrire les émotions, les pensées, qui instant par instant vous traversent, mais d'indiquer les horizons que nous ne touchons pas, que nous apercevons à peine, et qui pourtant sont là; c'est pourquoi, pour comprendre d'après son oeuvre la personnalité vivante de son auteur, il faut se donner beaucoup de peine. Quant à lui, la tâche dans laquelle il s'engage est infinie, car chacun de ses livres en dit trop et trop peu. Qu'il se répète et se corrige pendant des dizaines d'années, il ne réussira jamais à capter sur le papier, non plus que dans sa chair et son coeur, la réalité innombrable qui l'investit.[19]

This appears to be an acknowledgement of the existence of the unconscious. It is congruous with Beauvoir's notion of subjectivity as constituted and constituting, outlined in Part I: we are both agents and yet discursive productions, and how we have been shaped by discourses (understood in the Foucauldian sense, as historically contingent ways of producing forms of knowledge, truth and identity) is often beyond our ability to apprehend. Nevertheless, aspects of this experience may be communicated in autobiography if the reader is sufficiently attentive to the dislocations and silences of the autobiographical discourse. In the main text of *La Force de l'âge*, in one of several observations in her autobiography on the function of silence, Beauvoir observes that speech and silence are not mutually exclusive: 'La parole ne représente parfois qu'une manière, plus adroite que le silence, de se taire'.[20] The process of writing autobiography can thus be viewed as a negotiation of what it is possible to say at any given time.

In the 'Prologue' to this text, Beauvoir discusses a number of reader responses to her autobiography so far: that she owes her readers an end to her story, that she should wait to write until she has a more established reputation or until she can tell all because 'des lacunes, des silences, ça dénature la vérité', and that her fiction is more self-revelatory. She responds with litotes, assuming the role of arbiter of truth: 'rien de tout cela n'est faux.' She explains that time changes her relationship to her story and that she has no choice but to continue if she is to capture the vital moment of self-interrogation before old age sets in. The body of the text is represented as co-extensive with her body: 'j'ai voulu que dans ce récit mon sang circule; j'ai voulu m'y jeter, vive encore, et m'y mettre en question.' Recalling Beauvoir's pious Catholic upbringing, the co-extensive relationship of body and text functions to constitute a form of corporal endurance through which confession is produced. Beauvoir claims to have no choice, which may be considered a surprising admission for an existentialist philosopher. However, as we have seen in Chapters 1 and 2, Beauvoir's notion of subjectivity is that choices are made 'en situation', and here her choice is made according to temporal and physical constraints produced by the ageing process.

There are several instances in the 'Prologue' of Beauvoir asserting her autobiographical authority over her 'own' story: only she is able to 'dissiper des malentendus' by relating her life 'en vérité'. Again, she does not appear to employ a notion of truth as correspondence, but rather a truth of coherence, which functions as a detailed testimony of experience, produced by an authoritative eye-witness. Presence takes priority over the factual accuracy of a complete confession, which is never possible.

Beauvoir exhibits anxiety here over literary form, and by implication, condemns the reader in advance as preoccupied with bourgeois 'convenances', if he or she criticises her autobiography on aesthetic grounds. She rejects the label 'oeuvre d'art' for the autobiographies of Rousseau and Montaigne, as much as for her own, and thereby positions herself squarely in the autobiographical canon once more. Like Rousseau, Beauvoir relates her life in great detail and stylistic considerations are subordinated to capturing the experiential truth of the life. As Heath notes, Beauvoir's apparent disregard for aesthetic concerns in her autobiography echoes Montaigne's claim to artlessness; compare for example, her statement: 'Non, pas une oeuvre d'art, mais ma vie dans ses élans, ses détresses, ses soubresauts, ma vie qui essaie de se dire et non de servir de prétexte à des élégances' with Montaigne's address to the reader: 'Je veus qu'on m'y voie en ma façon simple, naturelle et ordinaire, sans contantion et artifice: car c'est moy que je peins'.[21]

A further reference to psychoanalysis occurs in the 'Prologue' to *La Force des choses*, when Beauvoir acknowledges that a psychoanalytic reading of her life might upset or embarrass her. She asserts her authority to describe herself within her own frame of reference. She concludes that the truth of her account is in the totality of her story, rather than in isolated incidents, and reassures the reader: 'je répète que jamais je n'ai délibérément triché.'

What does 'tricher' mean here in the context of Beauvoir's project of testimonial autobiography, which cannot produce a disciplined, objective truth of correspondence and cannot tell all? Beauvoir's autobiographical authority derives from the fact of being there and bearing witness to and for others. Josyane Savigneau has argued that one of the strengths of *La Force de l'âge* is 'l'acharnement à se regarder avec clarté' on Beauvoir's part.[22] It can be argued that this is a feature of her autobiographical project more generally, and that despite the fact that certain aspects of her life (for example, her experiences of sexuality and the death of her father) are passed over in silence, Beauvoir often signals the gaps and dislocations in her narrative to the reader.

Halfway through *La Force des choses*, Beauvoir reflects again on her autobiographical method. Employing a cartographic metaphor, 'le territoire n'est pas la carte', she says that a certain 'mise au point' is necessary. It is not enough for Beauvoir to travel and colonise the territory of her past selves, she must also be able to navigate her way within the male tradition of autobiography in which she has positioned herself.

She notes here that a common fault in autobiographies is that what goes without saying (for Beauvoir, her work as a writer) is literally left unsaid, and so the fundamental part of the life is omitted. As noted earlier, her decision to employ a chronological method of narration is, in part, philosophically motivated, for it enables the temporally situated reader to recreate the lost auto-biographical self in the future. However, the disadvantages of such a method are that meaning appears always deferred, the narrative can be laborious reading and the detail of the life represented can appear uninteresting and insubstantial.

Philippe Lejeune, in his reading of *Les Mots*, describes Beauvoir's chronological method again as a naïve failure, because it renders the past as a series of separate moments, disguised as a dialectical progression.[23] This demonstrates, as far as Lejeune is concerned, Beauvoir's inability to understand Sartre's notion of temporality, namely that 'le passé en soi' does not exist, and that the past only assumes significance in the light of my present project.[24] In Lejeune's view, '[Beauvoir] devrait plutôt pratiquer franchement le journal intime, au lieu d'essayer de le déguiser en autobiographie'.[25] In response to Lejeune's (gendered) criticisms, Leah Hewitt has argued that Beauvoir's chronological method is successful precisely because:

> it reveals its own impossible underpinnings and responds to the structure of the broken promise. Given that chronology is conventional and arbitrary, it is particularly apt for portraying the breakdown in a necessity or absolute through the writing and the life. Although de Beauvoir is not intending such an outcome, and seems to ignore it by the end of her autobiography, the collapse of the chronological structure of the first three books successfully registers the broken promise. The "failed" structure enacts both her continuing belief that a totality can be revealed and its textual impossibility through time.[26]

In the sense that the chronological method conveys the progression and purpose of the life represented and its subsequent decline through ageing, Beauvoir's method appears to work. For as Lejeune points out earlier in his discussion:

> C'est la chronologie qui règle tous nos rapports avec autrui, de la vie sentimentale aux accomplissements sociaux, et qui finit par prétendre régler tous nos rapports avec nous-mêmes. Nous ne sommes constitués comme sujet que par ce rapport à autrui, et il est naturel que la chronologie, base de notre histoire, tienne une place capitale dans le récit de vie.[27]

Beauvoir acknowledges that the past is a narrative construction of her own making, and seeks to recreate the process of that past in so far as it has culminated in the existence of the celebrated writer of the autobiographical present. What is appropriate methodologically in a brief aperçu of a future writer's life in Sartre's *Les Mots* is evidently not appropriate in Beauvoir's multi-volume project of testimonial autobiography, in which she seeks to bear witness to her own experiences, as a temporally situated subject.

At the end of this 'Intermède' to *La Force des choses*, Beauvoir explains the difficulties of autobiographical narration and the impossibility of rendering her experience as a constituted and constituting autobiographical subject:

Plus je vais, plus le monde entre dans ma vie jusqu'à la faire éclater. Pour la raconter, il me faudrait douze portées; et une pédale pour tenir les sentiments – mélancolie, joie, dégoût – qui en ont coloré des périodes entières, à travers les intermittences du coeur. Dans chaque moment se reflètent mon passé, mon corps, mes relations à autrui, mes entreprises, la société, toute la terre; liées entre elles, et indépendantes, ces réalités parfois se renforcent et se harmonisent, parfois interfèrent, se contrarient ou se neutralisent. Si la totalité ne demeure pas toujours présente, je ne dis rien d'exact. Même si je surmonte cette difficulté, j'achoppe à d'autres: une vie, c'est un drôle d'objet, d'instant en instant translucide et tout entier opaque, que je fabrique moi-même et qui m'est imposé, dont le monde me fournit la substance et qu'il me vole, pulvérisé par les événements, dispersé, brisé, hachuré et qui pourtant garde son unité.[28]

She obliquely alerts the reader and warns herself not to be duped by the allure of transparency and authority: 'les paroles souvent ne sont que du silence et le silence a ses voix'.[29] For a writer such as Beauvoir whose writing project is marked by an apparent confidence in language and a powerful desire to communicate, this may appear a surprising observation.

Such remarks suggest a slight 'rapprochement' on her part with the new developments in the French novel, which had been taking place from the 1950s.[30] The Nouveau Roman was in part a reaction against Sartre's notion of 'littérature engagée', which communicates a realist representation of the world and uses language as an instrument for social change.[31] Although Beauvoir uses language instrumentally to offer a realist representation of events in her project of testimonial autobiography, she acknowledges that she is offering an account of 'un cas particulier' and that 'reality' is multiple and beyond her knowledge and communicative ability.[32] As well as reflecting in paratextual statements on the limitations of language's ability to communicate, in the main text of her auto-biography Beauvoir signals her dissatisfaction with language as a mimetic instrument to convey a realist representation of the world.

She concludes this 'Intermède' to the first volume of *La Force des choses*, by defending her use of a chronological method:

Le fond, tragique ou serein sur lequel mes expériences s'enlèvent leur donne leur vrai sens et en constitue l'unité; j'ai évité de les lier par des transitions qui seraient univoques, donc artificielles. Alors puisque la totalisation me paraît si nécessaire, pourquoi me suis-je asservie à l'ordre chronologique au lieu de choisir une autre construction? J'y ai réfléchi, j'ai hésité. Mais ce qui compte avant tout dans la vie, c'est que le temps coule; je vieillis, le monde change, mon rapport avec lui varie; montrer les transformations, les mûrissements, les irréversibles dégradations des autres et de moi-même, rien ne m'importe davantage. Cela m'oblige à suivre docilement le fil des années.[33]

Once more, communicating the temporal situation of subjectivity assumes pre-eminent importance for Beauvoir.[34] The meaning of one's life is always deferred, unless, like Beauvoir, one attempts a partial totalisation by writing a chronological autobiographical narrative, which, in its linear form, attempts to mime the projective movement of the lost autobiographical subject.

In the epilogue to *La Force des choses*, Beauvoir begins by explaining her working relationship with Sartre, in a further bid, à la Rousseau, to use the autobiographical space to correct misconceptions about her life – here, that Sartre writes her books. By addressing this criticism at this point, Beauvoir asserts her authority over her entire work and manifests her awareness of her situation as a woman writer in a traditionally patriarchal society. Nevertheless, Sartre is represented once more as the philosophical and political initiator: 'Reste que philosophiquement, politiquement, les initiatives sont venues de lui.'[35] Proclaiming intellectual honesty and responding to criticisms from those who find discrepancies between her account of female subjectivity in *Le Deuxième Sexe* and her life represented in autobiography, Beauvoir says:

Sartre est idéologiquement créateur, moi pas . . . C'est en refusant de reconnaître ces supériorités que j'aurais trahi ma liberté; je me serais butée dans l'attitude de challenge et de mauvaise foi qu'engendre la lutte des sexes et qui est le contraire de l'honnêteté intellectuelle. Mon indépendance, je l'ai sauvegardée car jamais je ne me suis déchargée sur Sartre de mes responsabilités: je n'ai adhéré à aucune idée, aucune résolution sans l'avoir critiquée et reprise à mon compte.[36]

Despite Beauvoir's protestations of her lack of philosophical initiative, this last statement encourages readers to re-appraise her work in order to ascertain how she develops Sartrian philosophy.

In the epilogue to *La Force des choses* Beauvoir discusses the process of celebrity and her image as a woman writer. She clearly does not underestimate here (if ever) her role in shaping public perception of her work. Her memoirs belong in this respect to what Philippe Lejeune has identified as 'une tradition contestataire' of auto-biographical writing, which he associates with Rousseau, Gide, Leiris and Guibert, in which 'leur souci commun est de rompre le mur du silence, de faire éclater les mensonges'.[37]

Beauvoir explicitly refers to her changed relationship to her middle-class public:

Depuis les *Mémoires d'une jeune fille rangée*, surtout depuis *La Force de l'âge*, mon rapport au public est devenu très ambigu parce que la guerre d'Algérie a porté au rouge l'horreur que m'inspire ma classe. Il ne faut pas espérer, si on lui déplaît, toucher un public populaire: on n'est imprimé dans une collection bon marché que si l'édition ordinaire s'est bien vendue. C'est donc, bon gré, mal gré, aux bourgeois qu'on s'adresse.[38]

The alienation which Beauvoir claims to have experienced since the late 1950s is represented as motivated by her political stance during the war, supporting Algerian independence.[39] However, since the publication of *Le Deuxième Sexe*, Beauvoir was also receiving regular letters from women readers who viewed her work positively.[40] But this positive reception does not change her analysis of her situation as a woman writer, for she notes: 'en France si vous écrivez, être une femme c'est donner des verges pour vous battre.'

The female reader of her autobiography is, indeed, not the benign 'dédoublement' whom she imagines in the *Mémoires* ('un jour une adolescente, une autre moi-même, tremperait de ses larmes un roman où j'aurais raconté ma propre histoire'[41]). Beauvoir observes here how too many female readers of the *Mémoires* identified with the bourgeois milieu which she evoked, without being interested in her efforts to liberate herself from the bourgeoisie.[42] As Leah Hewitt notes, such readers 'have taken the work to be an authentic, straightforward representation of reality rather than a literary reworking of the life material'.[43] This is likely to have been partly the result of the lack of explicit statement of autobiographical intention in the *Mémoires* discussed above.

Two reasons are given here for the changed relationship between Beauvoir and the not-so-benevolent reader as Other: the conservative bourgeoisie's stance during the Algerian war and the misogyny of French society. Beauvoir's dilemma is to have always wanted to escape her middle-class background, and yet to have written books representing middle-class experience with which predominantly only the bourgeoisie would identify. Within the confessional framework of autobiography, Beauvoir finds herself, therefore, in the paradoxical position of desiring to be understood and perhaps even absolved by the class which she despises.

At the end of *La Force des choses* Beauvoir represents herself as alienated from her readers, yet still needing to write. In terms of the recovery of her lost past facilitated by the reader of autobiography, this alienation is significant, for it logically implies that Beauvoir's past is definitively lost to her.

In a strikingly Catholic passage, Beauvoir reflects on the transcendental power of the Word:

Il y a des jours si beaux qu'on a envie de briller comme le soleil, c'est-à-dire d'éclabousser la terre avec des mots; il y a des heures si noires qu'il ne reste plus d'autre espoir que ce cri qu'on voudrait pousser. D'où vient, à cinquante-cinq ans, comme à vingt ans, cet extraordinaire pouvoir du Verbe? . . . Sans doute les mots, universels, éternels, présence de tous à chacun, sont-ils le seul transcendant que je reconnaisse et qui m'émeuve; ils vibrent dans ma bouche et par eux je communie avec l'humanité.[44]

This vision of writing recalls similar observations made by Beauvoir during her life, in which she likens her literary vocation to religious belief, such as her observation to Madeleine Chapsal that 'écrire, à mes yeux, c'était une mission, c'était un salut, ça remplaçait Dieu'.[45] Beauvoir ends this passage with another powerful religious image: 'Peut-être est-ce aujourd'hui mon plus profond désir qu'on répète en silence certains mots que j'aurai liés entre eux.'[46] She seems to desire for her texts the status of the Holy Writ, which the reader would repeat silently as if in prayer.

At the end of *La Force des choses*, Beauvoir describes her alienation from the reader, she no longer knows for whom or why she writes, she has no desire to travel any longer, she is keenly aware of her age and feels alienated from her past.[47] In sum, her life appears suddenly over. She reflects again on her relationship to her life and the inadequacies of her chronological method:

Le stock de mes souvenirs, même s'il s'enrichit un peu, demeurera. J'ai écrit certains livres, pas d'autres. Quelque chose, à ce propos, me déconcerte. J'ai vécu tendue vers l'avenir et maintenant, je me récapitule, au passé: on dirait que le présent a été escamoté. J'ai pensé pendant des années que mon oeuvre était devant moi, et voilà qu'elle est derrière: à aucun moment elle n'a eu lieu . . . J'apprenais pour un jour à me servir de ma science; j'ai énormément oublié et, de ce qui surnage, je ne vois rien à faire. Me remémorant mon histoire, je me trouve toujours en deçà ou au-delà d'une chose qui ne s'est jamais accomplie. Seuls mes sentiments ont été éprouvés comme une plénitude.[48]

This sense of emptiness and the inability to remember or convey her past is represented here as the result both of the chronological method used and of Beauvoir's relationship to her life. Like Rousseau in the *Confessions*, in this instance she falls back on the primacy of affective truth when factual truth proves elusive.[49] In an interview with Francis Jeanson, she explains that 'Je croyais, quand j'étais jeune, que j'*avais* une vie devant moi; mais une vie, n'*est* jamais ni devant ni derrière, ce n'est pas quelque chose *qu'on a*, c'est quelque chose *qui passe*'.[50]

It is in this context that the chronological methodology of the first three volumes of Beauvoir's autobiography and memoirs can be understood, as an attempt to render this temporal progression. The ontological disappointment involved (her belief that she exercised control over a life which she possessed) is articulated by the final, controversial phrase of the volume: 'tournant un regard incrédule vers cette crédule adolescente, je mesure à quel point j'ai été flouée.'

## TOUT COMPTE FAIT

In the final volume of her memoirs, Beauvoir's reflections on her methodology are built into the main narrative, as well as appearing in a brief prologue. While the narrative respects a certain chronology, it is largely thematic and more analytical in character. It is ambiguously titled: has everything already been told, have scores been settled *before* the reader opens the text or *after* the text has been read? Such ambiguity signals the impossibility of the closure which Beauvoir seems to desire in her autobiographical project and to which she refers in the prologue to *La Force de l'âge* ('je me suis lancée dans une imprudente aventure quand j'ai commencé à parler de moi: on commence, on n'en finit pas'[51]).

In the prologue of *Tout compte fait*, Beauvoir explains her decision to change her narrative methodology from a chronological to a thematic presentation, saying that as she approaches the end of her life, it is now possible to consider it as a whole and draw certain conclusions. In existentialist terms, Beauvoir is claiming that the change of autobiographical method will enable a partial *totalisation* or analysis of the significance of the sum of her life, as the majority of her life (her past as 'en-soi') is behind her.

The tensions present in *La Force des choses* regarding her auto-biographical method resurface here. Beauvoir appears to be suffering from a radical lack of self-coincidence, in the sense that Sartre explains in his account of the structure of transcendental consciousness in the second and third sections of *L'Etre et le néant*. He explains how the 'pour-soi' is separated from itself by three ekstases: temporality, reflection and 'être-pour-autrui'. In this crisis of autobiographical method which Beauvoir tries to resolve by adopting a thematic approach, all three ekstases are operative in her failure to achieve autobiographical self-coincidence.

Firstly, she comments on the lack of temporal self-coincidence. Her account relates a series of past selves which she no longer is. Her chronological récit represents time falsely as 'un chapelet d'instants figés', whereas 'en chaque passé, présent et avenir étaient indissolublement liés'.[52] The rosary image here recalls the earlier Catholic image of the autobiographical text as Holy Writ which the reader mouths silently.

Secondly, Beauvoir comments on the inadequacy of the reflective process: she can recall the past, but can never render it within its three dimensions of past, present and future. Every episode she relates is temporally interrelated, but she cannot communicate this interrelation. She is reduced to recounting a form of perpetual present which fails to convey the lived experience.

Thirdly, Beauvoir's concern for her reception (that is, her 'être-pour-autrui') is evident in the decision to change her autobiographical method and in her motivation for finishing her memoirs. She relates readers' reproaches that in *La Vieillesse* she had not spoken much about her personal experience of ageing (as in *Le Deuxième Sexe* she had not spoken explicitly of her own experience of gendered subjectivity). This need to supply a personal testimony of her experiences for herself and for others is clearly a reason to continue with her autobiographical project.

The decision to adopt a thematic approach can be explained in other ways. It may be considered as a strategy to avoid confronting ageing and the passage of time at the end of her life. It might also be viewed as an attempt to psychoanalyse herself, because she takes aspects of her life, such as her childhood, dreams, writing, reading, friendships and travelling, which have already featured in the first three volumes, and reworks them thematically. Her discussion of these topics is more analytical in *Tout compte fait*, and, in her attempt at self-psychoanalysis, Beauvoir occupies the roles of both analyst and analysand. This is clearly impossible from both a psychoanalytic and an existential viewpoint because the self cannot be an object for itself. But perhaps as far as Beauvoir is concerned, it represents a much less daunting way of entering psychoanalysis.[53]

Writing about herself within a chronological framework seems to defer any significance her life might have, and leaves Beauvoir stranded like Coleridge's *Ancient Mariner*, needing to tell and re-tell her tale, but with no guarantee of any final catharsis. In an interview with Francis Jeanson, she comments, expressing her desire for catharsis and autobiographical closure: 'J'avais cru qu'au bout de ces trois volumes je serais complètement délivrée de moi: il se trouve que je ne le suis pas encore. Mais j'espère bien que si j'en fais encore un, alors là, cette fois, je pourrais parler d'autre chose.'[54]

The shift in methodology in *Tout compte fait* is also significant in terms of Beauvoir's relationship with the reader. As noted earlier, by the end of *La Force des choses*, she feels alienated from her readership, whom she categorises as mainly middle-class. She feels similarly estranged from the feminine readership which she had gained with the publication of *Le Deuxième Sexe*, her volumes of autobiography and with the publication of extracts from *La Femme rompue* which appeared in *Elle*. Adopting a thematic rather than a chronological approach, Beauvoir assumes greater narrative control to decide which are the themes which interest her and can incorporate her interpretation of the events related. In a chronological narrative, it is more difficult for Beauvoir to analyse her experiences and to omit segments of her life because overt analysis and omission disrupt the temporal sequence. As noted earlier, she needs to respect the chronological process because she seeks to communicate the experience of her temporally-situated existence to the reader. *Tout compte fait*, as a largely thematic narrative, is less vulnerable, then, to the reader's analysis and negative judgement.

## REFLECTIONS ON AUTOBIOGRAPHY

To conclude, it is worth looking briefly at some of Beauvoir's general statements on autobiography. Her observations on autobiography in the 1966 lecture, 'Mon expérience d'écrivain' will first be considered,[55] and then, some remarks she made in an interview in 1982 about her autobiography and writing more generally.[56]

In her 1966 lecture, Beauvoir explains that she began writing autobiography as a result of her dissatisfaction with the limitations of the novel form because autobiography is able to exploit the existential contingency and facticity which are eliminated in a novel. Through the singularity of her life, Beauvoir can communicate a portrait of her milieu and her era: 'pour que l'autobiographie ait un intérêt, il faut avoir eu des expériences qui concernent un grand nombre de gens.'

By advocating the universalistic quality of autobiography, Beauvoir thereby participates in the deployment of power by the constructed Western autobiographical tradition which 'rests upon the commonsense identification of one individual with another'.[57] In her lecture, Beauvoir refutes charges of narcissism by emphasising this universal dimension of her memoirs:

Le "je" dont je me sers est très souvent en vérité un "nous" ou un "on", qui fait allusion à l'ensemble de mon siècle plutôt qu'à moi-même . . . Par conséquent en écrivant "je . . ." j'ai l'intention de porter le témoignage sur mon époque et sur d'autres gens qui ont vécu avec moi des événements que j'ai vécus. D'autre part ce "je", lorsque je le prononce, c'est aussi le "je" d'une femme. Dans cette époque de transition pour les femmes . . . je pense qu'il est intéressant de voir une vie de femme; le "je" que j'utilise est un "je" qui a une portée générale, il concerne un grand nombre de femmes. Enfin dans la mesure où, comme tout le monde j'ai eu une vie singulière . . . mon "je" recouvre les problèmes de la condition humaine en général.[58]

It might be argued that Beauvoir refutes the charge of personal narcissism by expressing a cultural narcissism and universalism which assumes that a bourgeois, privileged Frenchwoman can speak for her century. However, this would be to attribute a cultural and political myopia to Beauvoir which is easily disproved by her political positions and activities as a committed intellectual. The statement appears to signal instead Beauvoir's notion of her autobiography and memoirs as a testimonial project, which relies on a transcendental, universalistic notion of the subject, manifested as the female witness who is always already situated in relation to others. Aware of her privileged status and her ability to use that status by acting as witness to and for others, Beauvoir assumes and exploits a mainstream position in the French autobiographical canon.

In the 1966 lecture Beauvoir also reflects on her autobiographical method. She comments on her use of a chronological method and her documentary approach to recreating her life, which is a further indicator of her testimonial approach to autobiography. Describing her alienation from her past, she cites Chateaubriand's phrase 'le désert du passé'. This image recalls a phrase of Violette Leduc's, 'je suis un désert qui monologue',[59] written to Beauvoir, by a writer who observed on the first page of her explicitly autobiographical text, *La Bâtarde*, that 'le passé ne nourrit pas'.[60] However, whereas Leduc's past is a tragic one from which she finds it difficult to distance herself, for Beauvoir, communicating her past is a philosophical, political and literary challenge.

Describing the past is the task of a historian: 'il s'agit en vérité de construire une histoire du passé, grâce à un travail de logique et de documentation.'[61] Beauvoir used newspaper accounts, letters, diaries, her own memory and the memories of her friends and family in documenting her past. In her lecture, unlike her memoirs, she emphasises that she is a historian. However, the epistemological problems associated with this historical approach to the past are highlighted by Beauvoir's comments in *La Vieillesse*, indicating the necessary fictionalising involved in writing about the past. Incidents are omitted because her memory is unreliable: 'il m'est arrivé, quand j'écrivais mes *Mémoires*, de revoir avec vivacité des scènes que, faute de coordonnées, il m'a été impossible d'intégrer à mon récit et que j'ai renoncé à raconter.'[62] Alternatively, incidents are condensed and creatively reworked in the process of memory which can collapse the temporal framework of the 'lived experience' of the past:[63]

Souvent j'amalgame en un seul souvenir des données appartenant à différentes époques: à travers toute mon enfance, les visages de Louise, de mon père, de mon grand-père sont immuables. Même quand je me rappelle une scène singulière, elle est construite à partir de schèmes généraux. Agée de 12 ans, Zaza dans la salle d'étude des cours me remercie d'un sac dont je lui fais cadeau: elle a la silhouette et les traits de ses 20 ans.[64]

In *La Vieillesse*, Beauvoir gives several examples from personal experience that her memory, as a factual record of the past, is unreliable,[65] and asserts 'la vie, c'est seulement la mémoire que nous en avons, et la mémoire n'est rien'.[66]

In the interviews with Deirdre Bair in 1982, four years before her death, Beauvoir commented further on her autobiography. First she claimed that the only selectivity she practised in her autobiography was the result of consideration towards other people, effectively reiterating her statement in the prologue to *La Force de l'âge*. However, the two obvious exceptions which were not subject to Beauvoir's discretion are Nelson Algren and Bianca Lamblin, both of whom had expressed their wish not to appear in her writing.[67]

She also rejected any comparison between her autobiographical project and Colette's autobiographical writings, on the grounds that Colette did not try, as Beauvoir had done, 'to capture her existence as a whole'. According to Beauvoir, her own memoirs were 'so total and complete, at least in the sense that they recount my entire life'.[68]

Colette is one of the most frequently cited women writers in *Le Deuxième Sexe*, yet evidently does not constitute a model for writing autobiography as far as Beauvoir is concerned.[69] She explains in the interview with Bair that:

When I wrote my *Memoirs*, it was much less fashionable to write an autobiography than it is now. I know, of course, that we French have a long tradition of autobiography and memoir, but when I started, I could think of nobody as a model. I just wanted to tell my own story, and so I started to write, not really thinking that I would follow my life up to the present.[70]

This is a surprising assertion on Beauvoir's part because, apart from her extensive personal readings of autobiography, she refers to several women autobiographers and journal writers in *Le Deuxième Sexe*, such as Colette, Marie Bashkirtsev, Sophie Tolstoy, Virginia Woolf, among others. Beauvoir's claim that models were lacking appears to refer to what she sees as women's failure to attain the universal in their autobiographies:

Il y a par exemple des autobiographies féminines qui sont sincères et attachantes: mais aucune ne peut se comparer aux *Confessions*, aux *Souvenirs d'égotisme*. Nous sommes encore trop préoccupées d'y voir clair pour chercher à percer par-delà cette clarté d'autres ténèbres.[71]

She makes a further significant observation in 1982 regarding her notion of autobiography, namely: 'the autobiographer has to be like a policeman writing his report: accuracy is paramount.'[72] Her juridical analogy suggests again a desire on Beauvoir's part for an unambiguous relationship with her reader. It also implies that her life may have some potentially culpable dimension, that it might be subject to cross-examination at some point. The policeman image suggests that the autobiographer is a male figure of authority, who is uniquely empowered to establish a single accurate version of events. Beauvoir's emphasis on accuracy – when she has repeated throughout her autobiography that self-knowledge is impossible and that language cannot convey the multiple realities of lived experience – indicates a rather naïve view of discourse as unproblematically referential. At the end of her life, then, she reverts to advocating that words are a faithful instrument in the representation of 'reality' and that it is possible to communicate a 'universal' meaning.

In this chapter, Beauvoir's explicit negotiation of the writing of autobiography and memoirs in paratextual and extratextual reflections on the task in hand has been analysed. It is now appropriate to consider her autobiography and memoirs in more detail, and in the following chapter *Mémoires d'une jeune fille rangée* will be examined.

# CHAPTER 5

# *Writing the self:* 'Memoires d'une jeune fille rangée'

This chapter offers a reading of the *Mémoires* as an ironic text which seeks to communicate to a benevolent reader, as other self,[1] how Beauvoir sought to subvert the discourses of class, religion, gender and sexuality to which she was subjected, simultaneously writing herself out of the contemporary political context of the Algerian War. It will be argued that Simone's erotic attachment to Zaza represented in the *Mémoires* enables her to envisage an alternative to the monolithic bourgeois truth which seeks to discipline Simone into 'une jeune fille rangée'.

In the *Mémoires*, Beauvoir constructs a self in opposition to hegemonic discourses of social class, religion, gender and sexuality. In the subsequent volumes of her autobiography, she represents the self as shaped by relationships with others and situated at the interstices of personal and collective history. In this and the following chapter, a shift will be charted from the disciplined self of the *Mémoires* to the multiple, discontinuous subject represented in the subsequent volumes of memoirs, who increasingly relinquishes the space of personal 'histoire' to achieve autobiographical agency as witness to history.

## COMING TO AUTOBIOGRAPHY

Beauvoir's intention to write her autobiography can be traced back to the immediate post-war period. She began taking notes for a projected autobiography in 1946. In *La Force des choses*, she relates how, sitting in Les Deux Magots at a loss for something to write, she asked Giacometti's advice. He suggested that she write 'n'importe quoi' – possibly the best advice to a writer as 'réfléchi' as Beauvoir, although probably received as the least helpful. She wanted to write about herself and this autobiographical impulse developed into a theoretical enquiry into gender, in which Beauvoir became so interested that she abandoned her plans for 'une confession person-nelle' and began to research what became *Le Deuxième Sexe*.[2]

The experience of living through the Second World War seems to have had a two-fold effect on Beauvoir. Firstly, it enabled her to discover her own historicity and her ethical relationship to others (which is evident in her fiction of this period, notably *Le Sang des autres*). Secondly, it encouraged her to analyse her own experience of selfhood, manifested at this time in her desire to write auto-biography, although she did not begin to write it until the mid-1950s.

Writing autobiography is often considered to be a literary rite of passage, and many writers of Beauvoir's acquaintance wrote their autobiographies between the late 1930s and the late 1950s.[3] Among her contemporaries' autobiographies, Beauvoir read and re-read Leiris's *L'Age d'homme* (1939), especially after she began to write the *Mémoires* in 1956.[4] In *La Force des choses*, she writes 'j'aimais *L'Age d'homme* de Leiris; j'avais du goût pour les essais-martyrs où on s'explique sans prétexte'.[5] Leiris's text cannot be considered a model, however, because his textual practice is quite different from Beauvoir's. Her liking for Leiris's and Leduc's autobiographies as well as Colette's writing was probably motivated by their open treatment of sexuality – a theme which, for Beauvoir, represented a stumbling-block in her own memoirs.

The attraction of autobiography for Beauvoir and Leiris is evident from the scope of their autobiographical projects. It is worth comparing briefly their autobiographical practice because it sheds some light on Beauvoir's approach to writing autobiography, notably her relative silence on the issue of her sexuality. An important difference between the two writers' approach to auto-biography is that Leiris's methodology is heavily influenced by his early interest in surrealism and his experience of psychoanalysis. In contrast to Leiris and consistent with her ambivalence towards psychoanalysis, Beauvoir relies on the universalising presence and integrity of the autobiographical 'je' and predominantly uses a chronological and teleological narrative form. Philippe Lejeune argues that *L'Age d'homme* is 'une sorte de kaléidoscope dans lequel il [Leiris] essaie de voir se composer sa véritable identité.'[6] Autobiography is, inevitably, always concerned with the construc-tion of a textual self; however, in *L'Age d'homme*, Leiris foregrounds the textuality of the self, eschewing traditional autobiographical form and representing his life in fragments, as a collage of textual identity.

When he began writing his autobiography, Leiris's notion of literature was also different from that espoused by Beauvoir. It is outlined in 'De la littérature considérée comme une tauromachie', which was attached as a preface to *L'Age d'homme* in 1946. Leiris embraces literature (and particularly confessional autobiography) for its cathartic function. He is specifically drawn to confession as a dangerous activity, as a stylised ritual poised on the edge of (social) death, as the bullfighting analogy suggests:

Mettre à nu certaines obsessions d'ordre sentimental ou sexuel, confesser publiquement certaines des déficiences ou des lâchetés qui lui font le plus honte, tel fut pour l'auteur le moyen – grossier sans doute, mais qu'il livre à d'autres en espérant le voir amender – d'introduire ne fût-ce que l'ombre d'une corne de taureau dans une oeuvre littéraire.[7]

Leiris wants to confess that which is most dangerous – for example his erotic life – as truthfully as possible. The abandonment of control constitutes a privileged source of creativity for Leiris, whereas retaining control over narrative form and content is important for Beauvoir, as a woman writer seeking to write herself and her experience into the twentieth-century autobiographical canon.

The representation of sexuality is a key area for comparison of Leiris's and Beauvoir's autobiographical practices. Like auto-biographical accounts of sexuality offered by other male writers of roughly the same period, such as Gide in *Si le grain ne meurt* (1926), or women writers such as Colette and Leduc, Leiris's account of his sexuality stands in stark contrast to Beauvoir's relative silence on the issue. A frank account of her sexuality was difficult for her, for several reasons: first, although Beauvoir seems to have partially shaken off her strict Catholic upbringing as far as her own behaviour was concerned, it is important to remember that homosexuality was and continues to be condemned by the Catholic church and, even in the more sexually-liberated France of the 1990s, there is no independent lesbian political movement to fight for lesbian equality and visibility.[8] Given the institutionalised and personal pressure to ignore her own lesbian experiences back in the 1950s, it is understandable that Beauvoir dismissed this area of her life. Second, as Barbara Klaw has argued, Beauvoir's two early attempts at writing about sexuality in *L'Invitée* and *Quand prime le spirituel* were rejected by publishers.[9] Klaw argues that Beauvoir deliberately toned down the representation of sexuality in her early writing in order to ensure publication.[10] Third, there is the 'disciplinary effect' of the judicial investigation into Beauvoir's sexuality between 1941–43, noted in Chapter 2. Finally, the furore unleashed in 1949 over *Le Deuxième Sexe* was partly the result of the text's representation of women's sexuality.[11] By 1954, Beauvoir was very well-known and was building up a female readership, following the publication of *Le Deuxième Sexe*. These women may have wanted to read about her experience of sexuality, and she gave a disguised account of her sexually-charged relationship with Nelson Algren in *Les Mandarins*, in the depiction of the relationship between Anne and Lewis.[12] Representing and thereby 'owning' her lesbian and heterosexual erotic experiences in autobiography was a different matter, however, for it implicated other men and women, who may not have wanted their private lives to appear in print. All these factors add up to a powerful force of internalised and external censorship.

After another false start in 1954 Beauvoir returned definitively to autobiography in 1956, having won the Prix Goncourt and with most of her fiction and *Le Deuxième Sexe* behind her. During this time, she had been reading and discussing autobiography with Sartre (who had written a first draft of *Les Mots* between 1953–54) and the *Temps modernes* team. She had also used autobiographical material in her fiction for many years: for example, writing a version of Zaza's tragedy and of her own early life in *Quand prime le spirituel*, written between 1935–37, and another version of part of her childhood in the omitted chapters of *L'Invitée*.

Embarking on her autobiography in the mid-1950s, Beauvoir found herself writing again during a period of war. Just as the majority of her first three novels had been written through the Second World War, most of the first three volumes of her memoirs were written during the Algerian War. As the Second World War had enabled Beauvoir to discover her historicity, the Algerian War constituted the backdrop to the narration of her experience of selfhood.

## THE ALGERIAN WAR AS AUTOBIOGRAPHICAL CONTEXT/COUNTERTEXT

Leah Hewitt, in her discussion of the *Mémoires*, has noted Beauvoir's sense of isolation in 1956 as a result of her opposition to the Algerian

War.[13] In *La Force des choses*, Beauvoir makes a direct comparison between her situation in 1940 and her situation in the early years of the Algerian War:

Je me sentais aussi dépossédée qu'aux premiers temps de l'occupation. C'était même pire parce que, ces gens que je ne supportais plus de coudoyer, je me trouvais, bon gré, mal gré, leur complice. C'est ça que je leur pardonnais le moins. Ou alors il aurait fallu me donner dès l'enfance la formation d'un S.S., d'un para, au lieu de me doter d'une conscience chrétienne, démocratique, humaniste: une conscience. J'avais besoin de mon estime pour vivre et je me voyais avec les yeux des femmes vingt fois violées, des hommes aux os brisés, des enfants fous: une Française.[14]

Julien Murphy argues that the look of the (colonised) Other is represented here as provoking a moral response on Beauvoir's part,[15] in contrast to Sartre's representation of the objectifying, appropriating look in *L'Etre et le néant*.[16]

Beauvoir's anger and shame at the time of writing the *Mémoires* came from her sense of being assimilated into the mass of the French bourgeois public, who were either indifferent to or supported the atrocities perpetrated by the French military, whom she equates here with the Nazis. Her own political inaction and privileged lifestyle (for example, going ski-ing with Lanzmann and meeting the bourgeoisie whom she claimed she had hoped to leave behind in Paris) suggests, however, a degree of 'mauvaise foi' on Beauvoir's part. Her intention to show in the *Mémoires* how she had escaped the role of bourgeois 'dutiful daughter' was rendered more urgent by the contemporary political situation and by her own guilt.

Beauvoir's sense of moral guilt and isolation were compounded by the fact that, despite her opposition to the war, she was not initially as involved as Sartre in direct political action to oppose it.[17] She had lived through the Spanish Civil War and the Second World War without being involved in direct political action. Beauvoir did, however, actively oppose the Algerian War and it is necessary to consider why she chose to act at that point to assess her situation while she was writing her autobiography.

Since the Second World War, Beauvoir had become increasingly aware of the politics of gender, race, sexuality and religion. In *La Force des choses*, she represents herself as having assumed an anti-colonialist position before the outbreak of the Algerian War; she records her delight at the French defeat at Dien Bien Phu, which brought an end to the Indo-China War (1946–54).[18] During the

Algerian War, Beauvoir read articles on different aspects of the war submitted to *Les Temps modernes* for publication. She also knew Francis Jeanson well. He was closely involved with *Les Temps modernes*, had considerable knowledge of the Algerian situation, and had worked with the FLN (Front de Libération Nationale) since the beginning of the war.[19] Beauvoir signed petitions, notably the 'Manifeste des 121' of 1960, which opposed compulsory military service in Algeria. She was involved in meetings and gave speeches supporting an independent Algeria. She defended a former Rouen student, Jacqueline Guerroudj, who was a teacher in Algeria and involved with the ALN (Armée de Libération Nationale), and helped save her from capital punishment.[20] She also defended Djamila Boupacha who, accused of planting a bomb in Algiers, had been raped and tortured by French soldiers. With Beauvoir's participation in her campaign, Boupacha was freed in 1962.[21]

Julien Murphy argues that Beauvoir became politically active during the Algerian War because she felt implicated in the war as a Frenchwoman, who was bound to the colonisers through her sense of national identity.[22] The war is represented in *La Force des choses* as an assault on Beauvoir's *image of herself* as a non-oppressor. She portrays herself, as a Frenchwoman in the 1950s, as an accomplice to the worst atrocities of war. To rid herself of this feeling of guilt, to recapture a sense of herself as a non-oppressor, and to defend the oppressed Other, she became politically active and simultaneously began to write her autobiography.

Another reason for her active political commitment is that she had discovered an alternative to the masculine world of politics from which she felt excluded. This alternative involved the exploitation of her public profile to support (mainly female) others, as a form of political commitment which engaged Beauvoir's own experience as a left-wing female intellectual. Carol Ascher has observed that the collaboration with Gisèle Halimi, on behalf of Boupacha, was 'one of her first political activities with another woman', and that Beauvoir had discovered 'a new "we"'.[23] This political solidarity with women was a logical extension to writing *Le Deuxième Sexe*, and anticipated her later involvement in post-1968 feminist politics. In the context of Beauvoir's adolescence, this new political solidarity with women might also be interpreted as a means to recover the female symbiotic relationship which she had experienced with Zaza and as a way of expiating for her death.

In writing the *Mémoires* during the Algerian War, Beauvoir constructs an individuated textual identity to be distinguished from the conservative bourgeois masses of her childhood and of the mid-1950s. Beauvoir conceptualised the intellectual as a contestatory figure, both in relation to society and in relation to him or herself. Moreover, in *Plaidoyer pour les intellectuels*, Sartre specifically notes that the intellectual has a duty to fight against his or her class and the bourgeois ideology which he or she has internalised.[24] Both Beauvoir and Sartre have spoken of the importance of crisis points for the production of literature, and the Algerian War can be viewed as a key crisis point in Beauvoir's life during which she seeks to extricate herself from her apolitical bourgeois past through political engagement and writing autobiography.[25]

## AUTOBIOGRAPHICAL DEVICES[26]

The order, self-restraint and literary quality of the *Mémoires* bear witness to an autobiography long in preparation. Beauvoir explained to Francis Jeanson that this first volume was 'le plus réussi du point de vue de la construction: une jeunesse, ça a l'air d'aller quelque part'.[27] The purposefulness of youth is presented as unquestionably mirrored in the text's construction, as textual content doubles as textual form.[28]

At a stylistic level, Beauvoir uses various control mechanisms within a chronological and teleological narrative. Elaine Marks has noted that the text is organised into four parts, which correspond to increasingly shorter periods of time as Simone grows older.[29] The protagonist's relationship to time is represented as changing in the course of the *Mémoires*: as she gets older, her time is less subject to bourgeois control and she experiences time as passing more slowly as she assumes increasing control of her life. Part I covers the years from 1908 until 1919; Part II 1919–25; Part III, the longest section, covers 1925–28 and the final part relates 1928–29. The length of this final part is significant.[30] The death of Zaza and the meeting with Sartre, important autobiographical events, are recounted in considerable detail. Other key events open each of the four sections of the *Mémoires*. Part I opens with Simone's birth; Part II with the move to 71, rue de Rennes and the decline in the family fortunes; Part III with the beginning of Simone's independent student life; and Part IV, with the 1928 'rentrée' and her final year of study for the 'agrégation', which was the path to earning her own income.

Francis Jeanson has analysed the summarising technique of the *Mémoires*, which he calls 'un processus téléscopique':

Nous nous trouvons en présence d'une espèce de phénomène "à tiroirs", d'un mouvement de totalisation dont chaque moment se donne pour absolument décisif, aux dépens de ceux qui l'ont précédé: un peu comme si nous assistions à la reconstitution magique d'une poupée-gigogne à partir de son plus petit élément, chacun des éléments successifs disparaissant à son tour sous un élément qui l'englobe.[31]

Jeanson argues that this technique is the result of the narrator's juxtaposition of the representation of incidents in her life with the later meaning she came to attribute to them. For Jeanson this is evidence of Beauvoir's 'remarquable lucidité' in relation to her own life.[32]

As far as other stylistic considerations are concerned in the *Mémoires*, Beauvoir uses irony extensively. This is often conveyed, as Michael Sheringham has noted, in lapidary formulae, such as 'j'avais une petite soeur: ce poupon ne m'avait pas' and 'enfin le Mal s'était incarné'; these formulae are used to emphasise or to summarise events related.[33]

Irony achieves a wide range of effects in this text. By using irony, particularly at the expense of the bourgeoisie, Beauvoir situates herself in a predominantly male literary tradition, exemplified by writers such as Flaubert and Stendhal. In *Les Mots*, Sartre similarly uses the device at the expense of both himself and the bourgeoisie. Irony can be viewed as a rhetorical strategy used by the bourgeois writer to distance him or herself from his or her class. For Beauvoir, this need to separate herself from her class was particularly important because in the *Mémoires*, she implicates the bourgeoisie in Zaza's death, and in *La Force des choses* she represents them as accomplices in the atrocities committed during the Algerian War.

Autobiography's inherent 'dédoublement' of the past self represented and the self who narrates makes it potentially the ironical literary form par excellence. In his discussion of irony in Flaubert's writing, Jonathan Culler notes that 'irony is the desire of the subject never to let itself be defined as object by others but always to undertake a protective self-transcendence, which, however, exposes more than it protects'.[34] Beauvoir's use of irony to avoid being contained by the bourgeoisie may be motivated by her fear of being judged guilty of colluding in Zaza's death and of political inaction during the Spanish Civil War, the Second World War and at the beginning of the Algerian War. Writing ironically, it can be argued, serves as a means of staving off personal and political guilt which Beauvoir experiences as a surviving witness. It also allows her to maintain a distance from the pain of remembering these events for, as Freud argues in *Jokes and their Relation to the Unconscious*, '[irony] brings the person who uses it the advantage of enabling him readily to evade the difficulties of direct expression'.[35]

Culler says that the perception of irony depends on four factors: our models of human behaviour which provoke judgements of what the text presents; our expectations about the world of the text which suggest possible interpretations and act as criteria within the text; potential incongruities of assertions made in the text which we recuperate as irony; and lastly, a sense of the habitual procedures of the text which allow an ironic reading and which reassures us that we are only participating in the ironic play of the text.[36]

By using irony in the *Mémoires*, Beauvoir constructs a potentially dualistic rhetorical relationship with the reader, rooted either in an alienation between narrator and reader or in a relationship of reciprocal intersubjectivity when the reader shares the world view implicit in the narrator's use of irony. Conflictual and reciprocal self-Other relations are thus played out at a rhetorical level in Beauvoir's relationship with the reader. Irony, nevertheless, provokes an initial anxiety on the part of the reader who, within the ironical process, as Culler explains, is thrown back into the problems of his or her own subjectivity, wondering whether his or her interpretation is 'right' and wondering what made him or her decide on a particular meaning in the first place.[37] As an alienating device, irony prevents autobiography from functioning as a locus of intersubjectivity. Writing autobiography then becomes a solipsistic narrative activity for Beauvoir, who controls the 'right' meaning and effectively relates herself to herself. As far as the reader is concerned, Culler argues that, at worst, irony provides an excellent means of recuperation, whereby the reader allows the text to say whatever he or she wishes to read. Beauvoir discovered this, to her dismay, when the *Mémoires* was well-received by bourgeois readers, who 'misunderstood' her intentions.[38] At best, the ironical text exploits the play of potential meanings and may offer the hard-working reader an answer to the questions he or she asks of the text – in Beauvoir's case, this would explain the greater critical interest in the *Mémoires* than any other volume of her autobiography and its largely positive reception in 1958. While Beauvoir denied that she intended to give a moral lesson in the *Mémoires*,[39] she nevertheless acknowledged that 'toute vérité peut intéresser et servir'.[40] This remark suggests that she recognised that her text might have a didactic purpose – to encourage her readers to abandon bourgeois values.

If, as Robert Cottrell has noted, 'irony informs nearly every page of *Mémoires d'une jeune fille rangée*', how do we know irony is at work?[41] The title may alert us to the possibility of irony, because the name 'Simone de Beauvoir', hardly a model of middle-class respectability, is juxtaposed on the text's cover with the epithet 'jeune fille rangée'. At this point, however, it is not certain that Beauvoir intends irony because, according to Culler's criteria, the habitual operations of the text are not yet evident.

There is a further irony in the use of the term 'mémoires'. Elaine Marks has argued that in using this term, Beauvoir 'deliberately implies that her major preoccupation is neither her inner life nor her mental processes, but the development of her total life in relation to a specific historical context'.[42] Describing her first autobiographical volume as 'mémoires' is ironic because writing 'mémoires' has traditionally been constructed as a bourgeois prerogative, and in the *Mémoires*, Beauvoir constructs a textual self in opposition to the conventional identities on offer to her.[43] Distinguishing between 'autobiography' and 'memoirs', Lee Quinby has argued that:

Whereas autobiography promotes an "I" that shares with confessional discourse an assumed interiority and an ethical mandate to examine that interiority, memoirs promote an "I" that is explicitly constituted in the reports of the utterances and proceedings of others . . . Unlike the subjectivity of autobiography, which is presumed to be unitary and continuous over time, memoirs . . . construct a subjectivity that is multiple and discontinuous. The ways that an "I" is inscribed in the discourse of memoirs therefore operate in resistance to the modern era's dominant construction of individualised selfhood, which follows the dictum to, above all else, know thy interior self. In relation to autobiography, then, memoirs function as countermemory.[44]

The self of the *Mémoires* is constructed in resistance to the bourgeois individualism and the self-analysis of autobiography, which suggests that the text functions as memoirs, and, according to Quinby, against memory and self-knowledge. In the *Mémoires*, Beauvoir appears not to seek to remember or to recapture her past, but rather to record the event of her escape from the bourgeoisie and to indict her class.

From the first page of the *Mémoires*, the narrator uses irony. She inverts the powerlessness of Simone's childhood state, so that she appears to be a monster of egotism. Robert Cottrell condemns the conflation of bourgeois privilege and childhood egocentricity in the *Mémoires* as part of the ideological agenda of the adult narrator.[45] However, his criticism assumes (erroneously in my view) that a non-ideological position is possible for the subject and that such a position would be more desirable in this instance. Beauvoir does indeed assume an ideological position in her indictment of the bourgeoisie through the use of irony. Her purpose is to extricate herself from their hegemonic discourses, both at the time of writing in the mid-1950s and in relation to her earlier self. For Kierkegaard has argued that irony can act as a liberating, metaphysical device:

When an ironist exhibits himself as other than he actually is, it might seem that his purpose were to induce others to believe this. His actual purpose, however, is merely to feel free, and this he is through irony.[46]

To summarise, irony is established early in the text as the principal rhetorical strategy. The combination of irony and Beauvoir's lack of explicit comment on her autobiographical methodology result in a relationship with the reader (the 'real' reader rather than her benevolent, imaginary one) which, for those who do not understand the irony, is potentially fraught with narrative control and anxiety. For those who do understand the irony of the *Mémoires*, they achieve a solidarity with Beauvoir in opposition to French bourgeois ideology which is contested and indicted. The confessional relationship of traditional autobiography is also subverted, as Beauvoir plays with the reader's expectations of how and what she is to communicate in her autobiographical account. The use of these various rhetorical mechanisms of control and solidarity is nevertheless interesting in a text which purports to denounce the bourgeois control to which its protagonist was subjected, for as Leah Hewitt notes in her discussion of irony in the *Mémoires*:

One senses that the adult narrator continues to be involved in the double movement of attachment to, and separation from, her past, that is characteristic of the way the child internalises *her* milieu.[47]

### SUBJECT TO BOURGEOIS CONTROL

Beauvoir opens the *Mémoires* with the conventional autobiographical phrase 'Je suis née', and the linguistic representation of two photographs: the first, a photo of the extended Beauvoir family admiring Simone as a baby, and the second, of her mother with her sister, Hélène, in her arms and Simone nearby, dressed up as Little Red Riding Hood. The two photographs respectively represent Simone within a bourgeois patriarchal milieu and within a maternal universe, against which she will rebel during the course of the text.

Susan Sontag has observed that 'photographs furnish evidence . . . A photograph passes for incontrovertible proof that a given thing happened. The picture may distort; but there is always a presumption that something exists, or did exist'.[48] Beauvoir's inclusion of photographs of her bourgeois past serve to prove her past subjection to the class she despises. Sontag argues that photographs are a rite of family life: 'each family constructs a portrait-chronicle of itself – a portable kit of images that bears witness to its connectedness.'[49] Photographs can be taken to freeze time, to preserve the status quo and to perpetuate institutions under threat:

Photography becomes a rite of family life just when, in the industrializing countries of Europe and America, the very institution of the family starts undergoing radical surgery.[50]

As ideological tools which reify the contingent states of the objectified subject, photographs falsely promise knowledge to their spectators. But, as Sontag notes, this is only a semblance of knowledge:

The limit of photographic knowledge of the world is that, while it can goad conscience, it can, finally, never be ethical or political knowledge. The knowledge gained through still photographs will always be some kind of sentimentalism, whether cynical or humanist. It will be a knowledge at bargain prices – a semblance of knowledge, a semblance of wisdom; as the act of taking pictures is a semblance of appropriation, a semblance of rape. The very muteness of what is, hypothetically, comprehensible in photographs is what constitutes their attraction and provocativeness. The omnipresence of photographs has an incalculable effect on our ethical sensibility. By furnishing this already overcrowded world with a duplicate one of images, photography makes us feel that the world is more available that it really is.[51]

Like Roland Barthes, in his analysis of bourgeois iconography in *Mythologies*, Beauvoir uses photographs at the beginning of the

*Mémoires* to expose the deception involved in bourgeois myth which works by naturalising and promoting its institutions, such as the family, as the unique object and provider of knowledge. Yet, as Sontag argues, such bourgeois photographs offer only a surface knowledge, namely myth. Exposing their ideological function, Beauvoir subverts their power by counterposing her own ironical commentary and inscribing her subversive self – in Trojan horse style – into framed bourgeois space. In the *Mémoires*, photographs are *represented* as symbols of static time and of the status quo, from which Beauvoir will escape, by becoming an intellectual and writer.[52] Unlike Barthes, who opens *Roland Barthes par Roland Barthes* (1975) with copies of photographs, Beauvoir assumes subversive, linguistic control immediately over these images of her bourgeois past by describing them ironically, rather than including copies in her autobiography to 'speak for themselves'. She establishes 'le Verbe' as the path to construct a self in opposition to the bourgeoisie and to escape the reified, gendered self of the photographs.

For Beauvoir these images represent a dead past, which she will try to recreate in autobiography. In *La Vieillesse*, she explains that neither mental images of the past nor photographs can recapture past events:

Les images dont nous disposons sont bien loin d'avoir la richesse de leur objet. L'image, c'est la visée d'un objet absent à travers un analogon organique et affectif . . . L'image n'obéit pas forcément au principe de l'identité; elle livre l'objet dans sa généralité; elle se donne dans un temps et un espace irréels. Elle ne saurait donc ressusciter pour nous le monde réel d'où elle émane et c'est pourquoi si souvent des images surgissent qu'on ne sait pas où situer.[53]

Looking at a photograph of herself in 1929, she does not recognise herself or the surroundings:

Une autre [photographie] des Champs-Elysées en 1929; j'ai porté un de ces chapeaux cloches . . . il ne me semble pas que ce décor ait jamais appartenu à ma vie. Au fur et à mesure que les années passent, le moment présent nous semble toujours naturel; nous avons la vague impression, puisqu'il nous semblait naturel aussi, que le passé était pareil: en fait les images que nous en retrouvons datent. De cette manière-là encore, notre vie nous échappe: elle était nouveauté, fraîcheur; cette fraîcheur même s'est périmée.[54]

Mental images of the past and photographs appear to act, then, as a trigger only to create another version of the past rather than to capture an earlier past.[55]

In the *Mémoires*, the bourgeois world that Simone inhabits is characterised by constraints against which she tries to rebel: 'partout je rencontrais des contraintes, nulle part la nécessité'.[56] As in *Pour une morale de l'ambiguïté*, the child's world is given and absolute, yet also metaphysically privileged because he or she escapes the anguish of freedom as a result of the existential unimportance of his or her actions. Simone achieves 'menues victoires' in the *Mémoires* by aggression or acts of rebellion, such as turning her back to the camera in family photographs, rejecting her place in bourgeois iconography. At this stage, however, there is no question of any ideological rebellion against the bourgeois family. The adult narrator reflects:

Jamais je ne mis sérieusement en question l'autorité. Les conduites des adultes ne me semblaient suspectes que dans la mesure où elles reflétaient l'équivoque de ma condition enfantine: c'est contre celle-ci qu'en fait je m'insurgeais. Mais j'acceptais sans la moindre réticence les dogmes et les valeurs qui m'étaient proposés.[57]

In several passages reminiscent of Lacan's account of ego formation in the Mirror Stage, according to which the infant first (mis)recognises its individuated being in an external mirror image, the narrator conveys the gradual internalisation of a self-image which is imposed on her by the surrounding adults, particularly her mother and Louise, the maid.[58] The child, within this predominantly female universe is 'la proie de leurs consciences', according to which her mother and Louise 'jouaient parfois le rôle d'un aimable miroir'.[59]

In this privileged state of childhood, the 'décalage' between bourgeois appearance and reality is nevertheless quickly perceived and accommodated by Simone. Learning, for example, that her parents' relationship is not the marital idyll that she had supposed constitutes a lesson in the repression of feelings and submission to parental authority. The adult narrator notes 'cette aptitude à passer sous silence des événements que pourtant je ressentais assez vivement pour ne jamais les oublier, est un des traits qui me frappent le plus quand je remémore mes premières années'.[60] Beauvoir signals obliquely to her reader here that some of the most deeply experienced events of her life might have been excised from her autobiographical narrative.

The narrator emphasises her early induction to bourgeois language, which is portrayed as at odds with her experience. Simone is represented as languishing uncritically in the bourgeois myths and clichés perpetuated by adults:

Entre le mot et son objet je ne concevais donc nulle distance où l'erreur pût se glisser; ainsi s'explique que je me sois soumise au Verbe sans critique, sans examen, et lors même que les circonstances m'invitaient à en douter.[61]

Her world is presented as sharply divided by gender differences: the women of the family are religious whereas the men are not; her father represents intellectual concerns and creativity (such as his interest in the theatre) whereas her mother incarnates duty and spirituality.

Religion is a dominant influence in Simone's upbringing. A.M. Henry, a Dominican, stresses Beauvoir's Christian heritage in his discussion of her writing. He notes that her paternal grandmother was a believer, that one of her maternal grandparents was brought up by Jesuits and that the other went to a convent and that her mother went to the Couvent des Oiseaux at Verdun.[62] Simone and her sister, Hélène, went to the Cours Désir, a Catholic private school. In the *Mémoires*, the rituals of religious observance are described:

J'étais très pieuse; je me confessais deux fois par mois à l'Abbé Martin, je communiais trois fois par semaine, je lisais chaque matin un chapitre de l'*Imitation*; entre les classes, je me glissais dans la chapelle de l'institut et je priais longtemps . . . souvent pendant la journée, j'élevais mon âme à Dieu.[63]

Simone also went on retreat once a year, decided to become a Carmelite nun, and played what her sister has described as 'des jeux catholico-sadico-masochistes'.[64] Relating these games in the *Mémoires*, the narrator explains that her childhood masochistic tendencies were satisfied by playing the victim. She would invent quasi-erotic games involving her physical humiliation because 'dans mon univers, la chair n'avait pas droit à l'existence'.[65]

These games may be interpreted as an ironic representation of religious practice through which the child, as performer, attempts to regain a measure of control over the religious values with which she is inculcated. The notion of 'jeu', as Dorothy Kaufmann has noted, is a key feature of both the *Mémoires* and Sartre's *Les Mots*, although it is Sartre rather than Beauvoir 'who plays the *enfant rangé* to perfection'.[66] For both Beauvoir and Sartre, religion as 'jeu' and as ritual will subsequently be replaced by literature as salvation.[67]

In the *Mémoires*, religion as ritual and as 'jeu' works through a psychological and physical disciplining of the child, which is reinforced by bourgeois gender codes to produce a 'corps docile' if not 'un esprit docile'.[68] Religion and bourgeois gender codes act as a 'technologie politique du corps',[69] so that the body is represented as a disciplined space. Moreover, the disciplined body is reflected in the ordered body of the text.

Very early in the *Mémoires*, the narrator relates the daily drama of being fed by Louise the maid and her mother. Moi argues that knowledge is represented as eating, as Simone consumes the world and all it has to offer.[70] Yet this episode is also an early example of Simone's spatial education. Elizabeth Grosz argues, citing Richard Stern's work on child development, that:

the child's first notion of space is "buccal", a space that can be contained in or exploited by [the child's] mouth. Not only the mouth but the whole respiratory apparatus gives the child a kind of experience of space. After that, other regions of the body intervene.[71]

Yet, significantly, some viscous foods fill Simone with horror, such as 'le mystère gluant des coquillages'. Such early anxieties over food may be related to a fear of maternal engulfment as Alex Hughes has argued in a productive, Irigarayan reading of the *Mémoires*.[72] The point I want to make here, however, is that viscous foods also confuse the child's developing spatial identity. The viscous is an expression of the Kristevan abject; it is neither inside or outside and only highlights the precarious grasp which Simone has on the world. Kristeva explores her notion of the abject in *Pouvoirs de l'horreur*, namely abjection towards food and bodily incorporation, abjection towards bodily waste which culminates in the fear of corpses and abjection towards the signs of sexual difference.[73] The existence of the abject signals the impossibility of maintaining the boundaries of the subject-object dualism. The body perpetually processes objects by ingesting and expelling and so cannot remain distinct from these objects on which its existence depends. The abject, which includes all the viscous products of the body, can never be completely expelled and remains the necessary condition for corporeal existence.

In the *Mémoires*, Simone's violent outbursts are represented as her only possibility of revolt at the age of three-and-a-half against the tyranny of towering adults, seeking to contain her within the bourgeois, gendered identity of 'jeune fille rangée'. Vomiting with rage, Simone is locked in the broom cupboard, which she views as a welcome punishment because finally the abstract and incomprehensible constraints against which she rebels have assumed a material form, constituted by the walls of the cupboard.[74] Her corporeal rebellion is contained as she is shut away with the instruments of domestic drudgery to learn her gendered role better. As in *Le Deuxième Sexe*, here, spatial appropriation is linked closely to the emergence of gendered subjectivity.

In the *Mémoires* this domination of the child is, primarily, channelled locally through the mother. Hélène de Beauvoir has commented that Françoise de Beauvoir 'avait une conception totalement tyrannique de la maternité'.[75] Her authoritarianism nevertheless turns into submission to Georges de Beauvoir and bourgeois 'convenances', as Simone notes, for Françoise has been well-disciplined in her role as bourgeois mother. Françoise, like Zaza, is represented as a victim of the patriarchal bourgeoisie from which the narrator is at pains to show how she escaped.[76]

It can be argued that Françoise de Beauvoir's subjection to bourgeois gender codes, which resulted in her 'vie gâchée', had a lifelong, salutary impact on her daughter, Simone. Although the sadness of her mother's life is only sketched in the *Mémoires*, in *Une Mort très douce* (1964), Beauvoir elaborates on the tragic life of Françoise who, by this time, is reduced to a dying body in the text:

Penser contre soi est souvent fécond; mais ma mère, c'est une autre histoire: elle a vécu contre elle-même. Riche d'appétits, elle a employé toute son énergie à les refouler et elle a subi ce reniement dans la colère. Dans son enfance, on a comprimé son corps, son coeur, son esprit, sous un harnachement de principes et d'interdits. On lui a appris à serrer elle-même étroitement ses sangles. En elle subsistait une femme de sang et de feu: mais contrefaite, mutilée, et étrangère à soi.[77]

Georges de Beauvoir is represented rather more positively in the *Mémoires*, offering an early path to intellectual fulfilment for Simone, despite his ultra-conservative political views. In contrast, in *Une Mort très douce*, the relatively idealised father of the *Mémoires* is debunked as an habitual adulterer.[78] This raises a number of issues pertaining to the construction of Beauvoir's autobiography, such as whether she knew about her father's adultery at the time of writing, and if she did, why she omitted this information. She may have done so in order to spare her mother's feelings, albeit at the cost of idealising her father.[79] Whatever the reasons for these different representations of her father in the *Mémoires* and *Une mort très douce*, this episode stands as an example of the impossibility of autobiographical closure, despite Beauvoir's desire for such closure.

### DESIRING ZAZA AND THE SUBVERSION OF BOURGEOIS CONTROL

Three-quarters of the *Mémoires* relates Simone's relationship with Elisabeth Lacoin or 'Zaza', who mysteriously dies at the end of the text. It may appear that Zaza has a negligible role in challenging the bourgeois order of the *Mémoires* for she is represented in many ways as more of a 'jeune fille rangée' than Simone. However, it will be argued that as a result of Simone's erotic attraction for Zaza, the latter constitutes the means through which Simone escapes the bourgeois, patriarchal and heterosexist order represented in the text, only to be 'saved' for heterosexuality at the end of the text by Sartre and by Zaza's death. According to this reading, 'the Zaza story' within the *Mémoires* would constitute – along with *L'Invitée*, for example – another oblique attempt by Beauvoir to represent her erotic experience with women.

This argument must be situated in terms of two productive readings of the Zaza-Simone relationship in the *Mémoires*. In an interesting reading which views the text as predicated on matricide, Alex Hughes examines, within a psychoanalytic framework, how Simone seeks out doubles (her sister, God and in particular, Zaza) to combat maternal engulfment.[80] Hughes shows how the Freudian concept of the fetishistic phallic mother appears to operate as a strategy to deny sexual difference, and how the text can be viewed as an initial attempt on Beauvoir's part to liquidate a series of phallic mothers.[81] This discussion charts convincingly the anxiety and antagonism towards the figures of Zaza, Françoise, Poupette (Beauvoir's sister) and Sartre in the *Mémoires*.

In this reading of the role played by Zaza in the *Mémoires*, it will be argued however, that for Beauvoir, instead of representing a phallic mother to be liquidated, Zaza may constitute a lesbian Other. Zaza must then eventually be liquidated to enable the heterosexual matrix to continue to function and to facilitate the heterosexual recuperation of Simone by Sartre at the end of the *Mémoires*.

Catherine Portuges has argued, in another reading of the Zaza-Simone relationship in the *Mémoires*, that Zaza represents for Simone 'a *point de repère* able to repair the schisms within her, and for that matter, a way of interpreting and analysing the world imposed upon her since birth.'[82] However, the representation of Zaza is not merely a way out of the contradictions represented by her parents for Simone; in my view, she represents an unsuccesful attempt to establish what Judith Butler has termed 'the lesbian phallus' as 'a displacement of the hegemonic symbolic of heterosexist sexual difference' within the text.[83] For the erotic aspect of Simone's attachment to Zaza suggests that Zaza may represent both a lesbian Other and the lesbian phallus to be ultimately liquidated, rather than a phallic mother.

In *Bodies that Matter*, Judith Butler proposes the notion of the lesbian phallus as a resignifying of the Lacanian phallic imaginary. Butler argues:

if the phallus is a privileged signifier, it gains that privilege through being reiterated. And if the cultural construction of sexuality compels a repetition of that signifier, there is nevertheless in the very force of repetition, understood as resignification or recirculation, the possibility of deprivileging that signifier.[84]

According to Butler, the concept of the lesbian phallus opens the possibility 'for the phallus to signify differently, and in so signifying, to resignify, unwittingly, its own masculinist and heterosexist privilege'.[85] For the phallic mother can be viewed, in Marcia Ian's phrase, as 'the conflation, compaction and concretion of all the most primitive fears and desires of hegemonic heterosexist white bourgeois patriarchy'.[86] The lesbian phallus, however, disrupts the heterocentric alignment of masculinity with always having the phallus and femininity with always being the phallus.

If the relationship between Simone and Zaza is viewed as rooted in lesbian eroticism,[87] Beauvoir would not be liquidating Zaza as phallic mother, but rather as lesbian phallus/Other. Zaza would be punished for both having and being the phallus and challenging the heterosexual hegemony of the text. This heterosexual hegemony operates in Simone's gender-polarised world. Heterosexuality is repetitively performed in the *Mémoires*,[88] as she re-enacts her mother's failed liaison with Charles Champigneulles with his son, Jacques.[89] Initially Zaza seems to constitute a way of positively reworking Simone's difficult relationship with Françoise. Later, however, Zaza becomes a necessary sacrifice in the final restoration of the 'hegemonic symbolic of heterosexist sexual difference', achieved by the entry of Sartre at the end of the *Mémoires*.[90]

There is strong evidence for viewing Simone and Zaza's relationship in the *Mémoires* as an erotic attachment. Immediately prior to recalling her first meeting with Zaza, the narrator describes at some length the importance which Louisa Alcott's *Little Women* (1868–69) had for her, and her identification with Jo. Simone and Jo seem to have much in common: intellectual interests, their rejection of the domestic domain and an intensity and anger which they are both 'taught' to control. Jo's assertion that 'I want to do something splendid . . . I think I shall write books and get rich and famous' is echoed by Simone.[91] Her attachment to Jo March allows her to write and consider herself exceptional: 'Je me crus autorisée moi aussi à considérer mon goût pour les livres, mes succès scolaires, comme la gage d'une valeur que confirmerait mon avenir. Je devins à mes propres yeux un personnage de roman.'[92] Within her bourgeois, gender-differentiated milieu, she constructs an alternative fictional identity. One afternoon, playing croquet, Simone has a quasi-religious revelation that she is living through the first chapter of a novel, during the course of which her sister and cousins would marry, although she would not, because 'quelque chose arriverait, qui m'exalterait au-dessus de toute préférence; j'ignorais sous quelle forme et par qui, mais je serais reconnue'.[93]

Beauvoir's future intellectual celebrity and her meeting with Sartre are implied here, as we assume that the teleological narrative is conditioned by its end. However, the revelation is immediately followed by Simone's meeting with Zaza. She is therefore 'recognised' by Zaza. Simone is struck by Zaza's spontaneity and vivacity, and by the end of the following week, the narrator noted, 'elle acheva de me séduire'. They become 'les deux inséparables', as they rehearse their roles in a play together – Simone playing Madame de Sévigné as a child and Zaza, 'un jeune cousin turbulent', whose 'costume garçonnier lui seyait'.[94] Zaza is an intellectual companion: 'avec Zaza, j'avais de vraies conversations, comme le soir papa avec maman'.[95] Zaza and Simone perform different gender roles together, experimenting with identities as various heterosexual and homosexual couples, even while addressing each other as 'vous' and avoiding physical contact, thereby observing bourgeois gender codes circumscribing 'appropriate' corporeal interaction.[96]

Reunited with Zaza after the holidays, Simone relates her joy at their reunion in erotic terms. She is initiated into the complexities of previously-unexperienced emotion and affective need, and accordingly, expresses her desire for Zaza in (rather banal) erotic imagery:[97]

Nous nous sommes mises à parler, à raconter, à commenter; les mots se précipitaient sur mes lèvres, et dans ma poitrine tournoyaient mille soleils; dans un éblouissement de joie, je me suis dit: "C'est elle qui me manquait!" Si radicale était mon ignorance des vraies aventures du coeur que je n'avais pas songé à me dire: "Je souffre de son absence". Il me fallait sa présence pour réaliser le besoin que j'avais d'elle. Ce fut une évidence fulgurante. Brusquement, conventions, routines, clichés volèrent en éclats et je fus submergée par une émotion qui n'était prévue dans aucun code. Je me laissai soulever par cette joie qui déferlait en moi, violente et fraîche comme l'eau des cascades, nue comme un beau granit.[98]

Her relationship with Zaza is described here as outside the signifying economy of the patriarchal bourgeoisie. Simone's passion for Zaza 'n'était prévue dans aucun code', as lesbian desire is, in psychoanalytic terms, beyond the phallus or beyond representation. Lesbian desire, according to most psychoanalytic theory, can only be an imitation of masculinity or evidence of pre-oedipal immaturity.[99] Henceforth, Simone realises that 'je ne peux plus vivre sans elle' and simply wishes 'd'être moi-même et d'aimer Zaza'.[100]

The affective importance of Zaza and Simone's relationship is further endorsed by entries in Beauvoir's currently unpublished journal of 1928–29, and Zaza's published correspondence. There are many references to Zaza in this journal. On 24 September, for example, Beauvoir notes: 'je pense à Zaza avec une tendresse infinie et j'ai aussi le goût de sa présence dans mon coeur'; on 2 October, she notes: 'en descendant je trouve une lettre de Zaza, d'une Zaza qui m'aime et à qui ma tendresse a apporté quelque douceur.' As Zaza becomes increasingly subjected to the demands of her bourgeois family, Simone attempts to extricate herself from her own family, with the help of Stépha (Awdykovicz, later Gerassi) and Lisa (José Le Core). The journals kept by Beauvoir between 1928–29 demonstrate the complexity of her emotional life with these women. In the *Mémoires*, however, the erotic content of these friendships is muted, and Simone is portrayed as prudish and more sexually inhibited than her journals of this period suggest. As Margaret Simons notes: 'judging from the journals, Beauvoir's lesbian connections were evident in her student days'.[101]

In Zaza's correspondence (despite the fact that both Simone and Zaza knew that their mothers read their letters, and adjusted the content accordingly) her love for Simone is equally evident.[102] In a letter dated 13 April 1927, she writes:

Cette grande amitié qu'il y a entre nous, je m'en sens si peu digne; je la sens tellement plus grande que moi que je me demande tous les jours comment elle peut exister. Votre intelligence est tellement supérieure à la mienne, vous êtes tellement plus riche, tellement plus ouverte, tellement plus vivante que moi, que souvent, en réfléchissant sur notre amitié, je ne m'explique pas comment un sentiment pareil peut exister de vous à moi. Et c'est grâce à vous qu'il existe, c'est vous qui êtes venue à moi . . . tandis que je continuais à vivre tout près de vous sans vous connaître, sans vous comprendre et vous aimer profondément comme je vous aime maintenant . . . J'avais vécu depuis mes quinze ans environ dans une très grande solitude morale, je souffrais de me sentir isolée et perdue, vous avez rompu ma solitude, vous m'avez fait connaître la joie de retrouver dans un autre être l'écho de tout ce que l'on a en soi de plus profond et de plus cher.[103]

Yet in the *Mémoires*, Simone is represented as uncertain how Zaza feels about her, for their communication is governed by bourgeois 'convenances'. Bourgeois 'mythology', according to Barthes, is marked by tautologous communication.[104] In the *Mémoires* this type of communication is represented by tautologous phrases such as 'on m'avait appris combien la vanité est vaine et futile la futilité'.[105] If Simone's attraction to Zaza is so intense it is because the relationship opens up a possible alternative to the static, middle-class world which Simone inhabits. Zaza represents the possibility of narrating the bourgeois identity proposed to Simone differently. Paradoxically, however, Zaza eventually becomes a casualty of the Catholic bourgeoisie, while facilitating Simone's escape.

Considering the textual murder of Zaza in the *Mémoires*, one might question why Beauvoir chose 'to kill' Zaza a second time. One can argue firstly that Zaza's death functions as an indictment of the bourgeoisie which, as noted earlier, was an implicit objective for Beauvoir in writing her *Mémoires* during the Algerian War. Zaza is portrayed to some extent as 'collaborating' with the bourgeoisie (notably her mother) and so, one might conclude, she has to be killed off for betraying Simone. The death of Zaza serves also to magnify the achievement of Simone's escape, and positions her in the camp of enlightened 'ex-bourgeois' intellectuals. Simone came close to bourgeois 'collaboration' herself, because she almost married Jacques Champigneulles. By escaping from her class, Simone is represented in the *Mémoires* as not guilty of passively 'collaborating'. Class guilt and guilt about her political inaction appear to be closely imbricated for Beauvoir.

Secondly, Zaza represents a challenge to the necessary hetero-sexual recuperation of Simone by Sartre at the end of the *Mémoires*. Given the (constructed) importance of Sartre in the text's 'dénoue-ment' and his subsequent significance in Beauvoir's life, it becomes textually necessary to find an appropriate way of dissolving the Simone-Zaza couple. For Sartre (and not Zaza) to function as Simone's saviour, it is not only necessary to transform certain inconvenient facts,[106] but also to eliminate the challenge to Simone's heterosexuality and to patriarchal power which Zaza represents.[107] Clearly, if Beauvoir is to respect the historical facts of 1928–29, it would be impossible to avoid representing Zaza's death in some way; moreover, she may have achieved a certain catharsis in recording it. However, my point is that Beauvoir was not obliged to juxtapose the death of her beloved friend with the rather inaccurate representation of Sartre as a saviour figure, particularly since she acknowledges Zaza's role in her escape from the bourgeois identity with which she had been inculcated and in the construction of her future life: 'Ensemble nous avions lutté contre le destin fangeux qui nous guettait et j'ai pensé longtemps que j'avais payé ma liberté de sa mort.[108] There is evidently room for only one saviour-architect of Beauvoir's life – namely, Sartre – who, from the first volume of her autobiography, must be seen to vanquish his rivals and to enable the heterosexual economy of the text to function. This is partly, as we have seen, the result of Beauvoir's construction of Sartre as a mythological genius figure in her memoirs and also the result of her need to disavow her erotic attachments with women.

Christine Battersby has argued that Beauvoir operates with a Romantic notion of genius and creativity, which is evident in *Le Deuxième Sexe* and in her observations on 'La Femme et la création' in Japan in 1966.[109] Battersby contends that Romanticism linked success to a notion of a genius-personality, which was characterised in terms of male sexual energy. The genius-personality had to exhibit certain traits associated with women, such as sensitivity, inspiration and instinctiveness, yet not be a woman, for the driving force of the genius was his sexual vitality. As far as the representation of Beauvoir's intellectual 'double' is concerned, it would not be possible for her to share her desired intellectual symbiosis with a woman – for example, Zaza, if she had survived – because this would run counter to the heterosexualised Romantic mythology of genius and creativity which informs her writing.

Moreover, killing off the lesbian Other is a persistent theme in Beauvoir's fiction, much of which was written prior to her auto-biographical volumes.[110] By the time she began writing her auto-biography, Beauvoir had, it seems, acquired the habit of 'killing off' the characters who were based on women with whom she had been emotionally and/or sexually involved. Despite their affective and sexual importance, her relationships with women throughout most of her lifetime are always represented in her texts as secondary to her relationship with Sartre.[111] In excising the erotic nature of her relationships with women in the *Mémoires*, Beauvoir set an important precedent for the remaining volumes of her autobiography.

In conclusion, it has been argued in this chapter that in the *Mémoires*, Beauvoir constructs a self to subvert the bourgeois dis-courses of gender, religion and sexuality to which she was subjected. This self will then be 'saved' by literature and her 'apocalyptic' meeting with Jean-Paul Sartre at the end of the text. The creation of a narrative self serves also to stave off guilt which she experienced during the Occupation and the Algerian War related to her political inaction and to her membership of a privileged social class. In the next chapter, the three remaining volumes of her memoirs will be examined as texts in which Beauvoir bears witness to personal and collective history.

# CHAPTER 6

# *Bearing witness with the Other, bearing witness for the Other*

In the previous chapter, it was argued that in *Mémoires d'une jeune fille rangée* Beauvoir constructs a narrative self in opposition to the patriarchal bourgeoisie of the 1950s and of her childhood, primarily through her attachment to Zaza. However, Zaza is sacrificed to the heterosexual recuperation and path to intellectual development constituted by the apocalyptic meeting with Sartre. In the *Mémoires*, a transition therefore exists from the narrative representation of a solipsistic 'je' who, although disciplined by the bourgeoisie, relates herself to herself (for the reader is envisaged as a benevolent other self), to the representation of a self who is formed in opposition to her class and constructed as a 'being-with-the Other' or 'Mitsein'.[1]

This construction of the past self as a 'being-with-the Other' is initially represented in the *Mémoires* as the female couple of Simone and Zaza, followed by the heterosexual couple of Simone and Jean-Paul Sartre.[2] Both these couples are represented as standing in different degrees of opposition to the bourgeoisie. Beauvoir constructs her autobiographical representation of selfhood, then, through two different relations to the Other: reciprocity (with Zaza and Sartre) and conflict (in opposition to the bourgeoisie).

Beauvoir had already examined these two forms of alterity in *Pour une morale de l'ambiguïté* and *Le Deuxième Sexe*. In *La Force de l'âge* and *La Force des choses*, this 'being-with-the-Other' also assumes a historical and ethical significance, for it comes to involve bearing witness *for* the Other. In her memoirs, reciprocity assumes a new, testimonial dimension.

By the end of *La Force des choses*, this 'being-with the Other', as a privileged 'nous' relationship to the world, reverts to the 'je' of 'j'ai été flouée'. Here the narrator assumes personal responsibility for her experience of being cheated. At this point, Beauvoir is alienated from the reader, her class and her life in what can be viewed as a crisis in the autobiographical subject's relationship to the Other. The collapse of her autobiographical methodology is imminent. This crisis coincides with two important changes in Beauvoir's life: her growing intimacy with Sylvie Le Bon during the autumn of 1963 and the death of her mother at the end of that year.

*Tout compte fait*, the final volume of memoirs, is dedicated to Sylvie Le Bon, who plays the role of final privileged Other in Beauvoir's autobiographical project. In this volume, material from the earlier volumes is reworked thematically. 'La boucle' appears to be 'bouclée', as the 'je' of *Tout compte fait* is represented as both co-extensive to the life related and consistent with the ambitions of the self represented in the *Mémoires*. This is an autobiographical device which seeks to establish consistency between the first and last volumes, for there is no definitive return to the narrative solipsism represented in the *Mémoires*.

In this chapter, it will be argued that the circular movement which can be traced in Beauvoir's project of self-narration relies to a large extent on the Other's presence, and that the narrative solipsism of the *Mémoires* is an aberrant, cathartic episode in her autobiographical project. This circuit begins with the representation of a disciplined self in the *Mémoires*, and continues with a narrative of experience, in which the narrator uses memoirs as testimony in her representation of her life and the lives of others. Finally, the autobiographical subject subverts the discourses which silence her, and writing memoirs becomes an act of speaking out which will serve as a means to political and social change. Before tracing these stages in more detail, the construction of this privileged 'nous' as 'Mitsein' in the couple Simone-Sartre at the end of the *Mémoires* and the beginning of *La Force de l'âge* will be examined. Analysing the construction of this privileged 'nous' is important because it is represented as a pivotal autobiographical 'event' and is, to some degree, at the expense of Beauvoir's own autonomy and the development of her individual intellectual project.

The construction of this privileged 'nous' can be examined first by comparing Beauvoir's unpublished diaries of the time with the published volumes of memoirs. Such an examination offers a valuable insight into her autobiographical methodology. It will not be argued that the diary account can be viewed as 'truer' than the memoir account; rather that as Beauvoir used her diaries extensively in the writing of her memoirs, one can observe how she reworked this diary material and notice features of her autobiographical methodology evident in these diaries.

Second, the cost of the narrative 'Mitsein' of Beauvoir and Sartre represented in the memoirs and of their intellectual collaboration will be demonstrated by the analysis of a disagreement between them at Saint-Cloud over the function of language and writing in *La Force de l'âge*. This event can be viewed as a continuation of the Luxembourg Gardens débâcle, analysed by Michèle Le Doeuff and Toril Moi, during which Sartre demolished Beauvoir's nascent ideas on ethics.[3] The later scene at Saint-Cloud is similarly pivotal for it established that the Beauvoir-Sartre intellectual symbiosis operated as a temporary discursive colonisation by Sartre of Beauvoir's literary 'voice' at a time when she was seeking to develop her individual vision of literature. First, however, it is necessary to look at Beauvoir's diaries of 1928–30 which offer an alternative account to the published memoirs of the formation of the Simone-Sartre couple as a privileged 'being-with the Other'.

### BEAUVOIR'S DIARIES 1928–30[4]

At the end of the *Mémoires* Sartre is represented as the ideal Other, 'le double' with whom Simone can share everything, replacing Zaza as Beauvoir's former privileged other self.[5]

Then, in the early part of *La Force de l'âge*, which is dedicated to Sartre, the narrator explains the terms of the Simone-Sartre relationship.[6] However, events represented in Beauvoir's diaries between 1928–30 are recast in the *Mémoires* and *La Force de l'âge* to represent Sartre as this absolute, ideal Other.

The 'casualties' at the end of the *Mémoires* are numerous, for Beauvoir reworks her relationships with René Maheu, Zaza, Stépha and Maurice Merleau-Ponty. The relationship between Beauvoir and Sartre, as recorded in her diaries, appears by no means as clear-cut, either emotionally or intellectually. As already noted in the context of her relationship with Zaza, Beauvoir's intimate relationships with women, such as Stépha and José [sic], are recorded allusively in her diaries of this period and omitted from the *Mémoires*.[7] Additionally, these diaries represent a rather more complex picture of her heterosexual attachments than the *Mémoires* and *La Force de l'âge* might suggest.

Firstly, as Kate and Edward Fullbrook have noted in their

discussion of this period,[8] Beauvoir was sexually involved with René Maheu (Herbaud in the *Mémoires*). This was a complicated relationship for her because he was married. Secondly, a diary reference to Maurice Merleau-Ponty (Jean Pradelle in the *Mémoires*) on 28 May 1929 suggests that Beauvoir's relationship with Merleau-Ponty was rather more intense than is implied in the *Mémoires*. At the time she was involved with Maheu and not yet involved with Sartre, and she notes: 'Maheu ou Merleau-Ponty? Vraiment de ces deux sentiments je ne saurais choisir.' This implies that Beauvoir may have had some romantic involvement with Merleau-Ponty, although this has not been confirmed elsewhere. If it were the case, it would be significant in terms of the representation of Zaza and Merleau-Ponty in the *Mémoires*. Much is made both by Beauvoir in the *Mémoires* and by critics of the Sartre-Beauvoir intellectual 'match'; however, it is important to remember that Merleau-Ponty was also an intellectually brilliant figure of his generation and was, for a time, Beauvoir's close friend. Philosophically, Merleau-Ponty was at least Sartre's and Beauvoir's equal; apart from *Phénoménologie de la perception*, he produced several important philosophical works, and was 'widely regarded as France's most brilliant and most profound philosopher' when he died in 1961.[9] Moreover, he worked with them in 'Socialisme et Liberté', a short-lived Résistance group, edited *Les Temps modernes* (until he resigned in 1952), and was involved in the RDR (Rassemblement Démocratique Révolutionnaire) with Sartre.[10] René Maheu and Paul Nizan, who followed a similar educational trajectory to Sartre and whom Beauvoir also knew very well, were highly talented. Maheu was later director-general of UNESCO.[11] Nizan was a member of the (parti communiste français) PCF, and wrote two polemical essays, *Aden Arabie* (1931) and *Les Chiens de garde* (1932), three novels, and other writings, before he died in 1940 at the age of thirty-five. It is therefore not plausible that in 1929 Beauvoir considered Sartre to be the unique intellect and love match portrayed in the *Mémoires*, even though he came to acquire such significance for her later.

Thirdly, the diaries offer a different account of the beginning of Beauvoir's relationship with Sartre. For example, on 27 July 1929, after several months of entries relating to her involvement with Maheu, Beauvoir notes 'Quand ils sont ensemble, Sartre et le Lama [Maheu], pourquoi le premier perd-il ainsi son importance?' In her summary of the year's events, she notes: '15 avril au 15 juin Maheu:

le long désir, la lente approche, l'espoir chaque jour confirmé . . .
J'apprends la douceur d'être femme.' Beauvoir continues to see
Maheu 'le plus possible' in October, according to a block entry at
the end of her diary for the year 1928–29. However, she is also
increasingly emotionally involved with Sartre. During the summer of
1929, both Sartre and Maheu visited Beauvoir in the Limousin,
where she was on a family holiday. Sartre visited her from 21 August
to 1 September, Maheu from 6 to 8 September.[12] In diary entries
between 6 to 10 September, Beauvoir comments on her liking for the
mornings she spends with Maheu in his blue pyjamas and eau de
cologne. In a long entry dated 10 September, she writes 'Je l'aime
aussi profondément qu'à Paris . . . où j'en suis avec Sartre, ça c'est
une autre question'.[13]

Her emotional confusion is indicated by her diary declarations of
love for Maheu, then Sartre and then Jacques. For example, on 16
September 1929 she notes that she no longer loves Jacques and that
she loves Sartre; two days later, she notes that she does not want
dishonesty with Jacques because she loves him too much and
simultaneously records 'amour immense pour Sartre'. On 21 September, she notes that 'je ne sais plus ce que je désire . . . J'aime
Jacques, j'aime Jacques, j'aime Jacques'. On 29 September, she notes
that Maheu tells her to marry Jacques. Yet, two weeks later on 14
October, Beauvoir becomes Sartre's lover.[14] On 24 October, she
talks with Maheu about Jacques, and he comments that he does not
want her to be 'une vieille fille' or 'passer d'homme en homme'. At
this time, Beauvoir was evidently confronted by the social constraints
on women's sexual freedom and was under pressure to attach herself
to a single man. She was also perhaps torn between the prospects of
illicit sexual passion with Maheu and a potentially innovative
partnership with the charismatic and intellectual Sartre who would
support her in her ambition of becoming a writer. By Christmas
1929 her attachment to Sartre has grown further, and diary entries
reflect her love for him. They also reflect her continuing deep
distress over the death of Zaza, and her anxiety over not being able
to write.

Therefore Beauvoir's diaries of this period tell a different story to
her published memoirs. The comparison between the published
memoirs and unpublished diaries highlights the nature of inevitable
autobiographical selectivity and shows how the passage of time
transforms the autobiographer's perspective on his or her life. More-

over, the 'contingent' detail of the choices facing Beauvoir at this time is simplified in her evocation of this period to harmonise with her overall autobiographical strategy of self-representation as an intellectual and a writer at the expense of the representation of her personal life. Such a strategy may be explained – at least in part – by the existence of socio-political constraints on (the representation of) women's sexual freedom and Beauvoir's recognition of the need for representations of female intellectuals, given their restricted number in the public forum and collective consciousness in France in the 1950s.[15]

Moreover, diaries are also highly individual documents, which are used in different ways by the individual concerned at different times in his or her life. In her discussion of the 'journal intime', Béatrice Didier notes this variety of uses of diary writing, that 'la périodicité est pourtant la seule loi ressentie comme telle par l'auteur' and that the most frequent reason for keeping diaries is to have a record of one's time: 'le temps transcrit sur la feuille blanche semble moins irrémédiablement perdu.'[16]

In an interview with Deirdre Bair, Beauvoir talked at some length about her diary writing.[17] She said that, around the age of seventeen, she began to write a diary in which she could confide and that she kept diaries consistently from the ages of eighteen to twenty-two. She claimed that she had felt 'hostile to a milieu that had become hostile to me' at that time and wrote mostly about her states of mind.[18] Beauvoir noted that, unlike her published writing, her diaries reflected her moods. She said that she stopped writing diaries (probably at the end of 1930)[19] and when she resumed 'much later' she began to record items of interest.[20] The Algerian War was one such period of interest because in *La Force des choses* she includes extracts from a diary she kept during that time.[21] Beauvoir also commented in the interview with Bair on this use of excerpts from her diaries in her published texts. She said that she included diary extracts:

when I thought they were lively or amusing, or when I thought it best not to try and recreate how I felt about something or someone, but to give instead the exact words I wrote at the time. I also quoted a few sections here and there when I thought they were more appropriate than anything I could invent at the time I was writing.[22]

These remarks are interesting because the entries from her Second

World War diary which she includes in *La Force de l'âge* are not only abbreviated but different from entries for the same days in the *Journal de guerre*.[23] Beauvoir also emphasised in this interview that her diary 'had no literary value whatsoever' and that 'it was a private record', which she did not want to survive her.[24] Perhaps she thought that the publication of her diaries might diminish the testimonial authority of the memoirs. This is understandable because a comparison between the *Journal de guerre* and the memoirs does indeed highlight the constructed nature of the memoir account of the same period. These different accounts need not, however, diminish Beauvoir's testimonial authority because testimony always takes place within a given context. She might reasonably have a different perspective on these events twenty years later. However, these different diary accounts of the same period in the *Journal de guerre* and *La Force de l'âge* are problematic because, as Terry Keefe argues, Beauvoir does not acknowledge in *La Force de l'âge* that she has altered the war diary entries included in the text.[25] These competing versions of autobiographical 'truth' offer much opportunity for speculation and illustrate the construction involved in the production of autobiographical texts; there is, therefore, no reason to suppose that the diary account is 'truer' than the later memoir account, particularly as Beauvoir did not apparently intend to publish it and may not have been completely rigorous in her record-keeping of factual details.[26]

Between 1928–30, Beauvoir seems to have used her diaries to record her emotional confusion, her work activities and details of her income and expenditure. In terms of the later construction of her memoirs, it is interesting to note that she does not write her diary every day. There are frequent gaps and the missing periods are sometimes, but not always, related in block form. This technique of often recording events several days later necessarily reduces her account to a representation of events rather than a record of her transient emotional states, because it is probably easier to remember facts rather than emotions experienced several days earlier. Combined with Beauvoir's method of researching her past by reading newspapers of the particular era, the use of this summarising technique in her diary contributes to the production of an 'événe-mentiel' effect in her memoirs.[27]

In her diaries, Beauvoir also uses organising strategies such as writing year summaries and projected schedules for the coming year, illustrating a strict temporal disciplining of her existence acquired during her childhood and adolescence. Her diary covering the period from 24 September 1928 until 12 September 1929 contains many entries which are marked in the margin in black pen (probably at a later date, because the ink is of a different colour), as if these were entries which Beauvoir marked up later for inclusion in some form in either fiction or memoirs. In particular, many entries pertaining to Zaza are highlighted in this way, suggesting Beauvoir's desire to tell the 'Zaza story'. The diary of the following year is not marked in this way and certain parts are simply underlined.

In summary, this reading of Beauvoir's diaries in the context of her memoirs demonstrates the reworking and the nature of selectivity involved in evoking the beginning of her almost lifelong relationship with Sartre. That relationship is presented as a pivotal episode in the memoirs yet, as we have seen, it was simplified and reworked from her diary account written approximately thirty years earlier.

### DEBATING THE ROLE OF LANGUAGE AT SAINT-CLOUD

In *La Force de l'âge*, in a scene as important as the Luxembourg Gardens débâcle in the construction of the Beauvoir-Sartre intellectual collaboration in the memoirs, Sartre and Beauvoir discuss the roles of language and writing in representing experience. Looking out over the view from the hills of Saint-Cloud,[28] Beauvoir reproaches Sartre for his indifference to his surroundings, and he explains that a writer has to dominate his emotional and bodily responses to the world in order to write about it:

Il se défendit. Qu'est-ce au juste que sentir? Il n'était pas enclin aux battements de coeur, aux frissons, aux vertiges, à tous ces mouvements désordonnés du corps qui paralysent le langage: ils s'éteignent et rien ne demeure; il accordait plus de prix à ce qu'il appelait "les abstraits émotionnels"; la signification d'un visage, d'un spectacle l'atteignait, sous une forme désincarnée, et il en restait assez détaché pour tenter de la fixer dans des phrases. Plusieurs fois, il m'expliqua qu'un écrivain ne pouvait pas avoir d'autre attitude; quiconque n'éprouve rien est incapable d'écrire; mais si la joie, l'horreur nous suffoquent sans que nous les dominions, nous ne saurons pas non plus les exprimer.[29]

However, Beauvoir is not convinced:

Parfois je lui donnais raison; mais parfois je me disais que les mots ne retiennent la réalité qu'après l'avoir assassinée; ils laissent échapper ce qu'il y a en elle de plus important: sa présence. J'étais amenée à me demander avec un peu d'anxiété ce qu'il convenait de leur accorder, de leur soustraire.[30]

Sartre explains further that in his view,

L'erreur se situait au départ, dans l'énoncé de la question. Il pensait lui aussi que tout récit introduit dans la réalité un ordre fallacieux; même si le conteur s'applique à l'incohérence, s'il s'efforce de ressaisir l'expérience toute crue, dans son éparpillement et sa contingence, il n'en produit qu'une imitation où s'inscrit la nécessité. Mais Sartre trouvait oiseux de déplorer cet écart entre le mot et la chose, entre l'oeuvre créée et le monde donné; il y voyait au contraire la condition même de la littérature et sa raison d'être; l'écrivain doit en jouer, non rêver de l'abolir: ses réussites sont dans cet échec assumé.[31]

As she developed her ideas, Beauvoir was influenced by Virginia Woolf's writing, which she obtained through Sylvia Beach's English language bookshop in Paris, Shakespeare and Company.[32] She alighted on Woolf's fourth novel, *Mrs Dalloway* (1925), to provide answers to her own questions concerning language and the novel:[33]

Je me sentis très concernée par les réfléxions de Virginia Woolf sur le langage en général et sur le roman en particulier. Soulignant la distance qui sépare les livres de la vie, elle semblait escompter que l'invention de nouvelles techniques permettrait de la réduire; je souhaitais la croire. Mais non! Son plus récent ouvrage, *Mrs Dalloway*, n'apportait nulle solution au problème qu'elle soulevait.[34]

At this point it is useful to consider briefly some of Woolf's ideas about literature prior to 1925, and one of her most important statements is to be found in the essay 'Modern Fiction', to which Beauvoir is probably referring here.[35] In this essay, Woolf criticises her predecessors – Arnold Bennett, John Galsworthy and H.G.Wells – for their 'materialism', namely that 'they spend immense skill and immense industry making the trivial and the transitory appear the true and the enduring'. These writers seek to make their novels correspond to life using plot and character as fixed formulae, whereas Woolf doubts whether life and art can be contained in this way:

Look within and life, it seems, is very far from being "like this". Examine for a moment an ordinary mind on an ordinary day. The mind receives a myriad impressions – trivial, fantastic, evanescent, or engraved with the sharpness of steel. From all sides they come, an incessant shower of innumerable atoms; and as they fall, as they shape themselves into the life of Monday or Tuesday, the accent falls differently from of old; the moment of importance came not here but there; so that, if a writer were a free man and not a slave, if he could write what he chose, not what he must, if he could base his work upon his own feeling and not upon convention, there would be no plot, no comedy, no tragedy, no love interest or catastrophe in the accepted style . . . Life is not a series of gig lamps systematically arranged; life is a luminous halo, a semi-transparent envelope surrounding us from the beginning of consciousness to the end. Is it not the task of the novelist to convey this varying, this unknown and uncircumscribed spirit, whatever aberration or complexity it may display, with as little mixture of the alien and the external as possible?[36]

From *Jacob's Room* (1922) onwards, Woolf had begun to write experimentally and it is this break with realism and the exploration of aesthetic form which appealed to Beauvoir.[37] While Woolf was writing *Jacob's Room*, she was also reading her friend, Roger Fry's influential collection of essays, *Vision and Design* (1920).[38] It is widely accepted that Fry's aesthetic theories influenced Woolf's conception of the novel at this time, and it is worth giving brief consideration to some of his observations on the relationship between art, imagination and emotion because they answer, to some degree, Sartre's objections to Beauvoir's desire to write experimentally.

In his 'An Essay in Aesthetics', Fry argues that the graphic arts (by which he appears to mean writing and painting) need to be concerned with the expression of the imaginative life rather than the imitation of nature. In real life, our vision becomes over-specialised, able only to read the 'labels' of reality, and our emotions become numbed, because these faculties are necessarily channelled to supply our everyday needs. Emotions experienced are unintelligible to us because we lack distance from them and to some degree, these emotions are channelled towards useful action. Thus, according to Fry, 'morality, then appreciates emotion by the standard of resultant action. Art appreciates emotion in and for itself.'[39] Moreover, Fry argues that art arouses emotion by playing on our primary physical needs so that, for example, rhythm appeals to physical sensations accompanying muscular activity, or light to our sensitivity to changes in light intensity and so on. Art which mimics nature cannot contain this emotional and corporeal appeal which, in experimental art, is arranged by the writer or artist so that the reader or viewer can contemplate the aesthetic object in an appropriate way. Although mimetic art might also be able to inspire disinterested contemplation on occasions, in the case of objects created to arouse aesthetic feeling, the reader or viewer has an additional sense of the creator's aesthetic purpose and hence an expanded appreciation of life.

Sartre, however, in contrast to Beauvoir, Woolf and Fry, argues that the emotional and corporeal demands that real life and experimental art makes upon us should be mastered. As he would argue in *L'Etre et le néant*, he maintains in his disagreement with Beauvoir that the body must be 'dépassé' for the writer to exercise his discourse of mastery and appropriate the world. For Sartre, there appears to be no alternative to linguistic representation as an act of appropriation and, although he rejects the omniscient, 'objective' narratives of the French realist tradition exemplified by Balzac, he nevertheless contends that language is a tool of discursive mastery which guards against the dissipation of the subject's reality and possession of the world.[40] Yet, it was precisely literature's ability to express this fragmented, disparate reality which interested Beauvoir and Woolf.[41]

Allied to this rather masculinist notion of language as a tool of discursive mastery are Sartre's views on the work of art in his second study of the imagination, *L'Imaginaire* (1940).[42] Here he argues that the imaginary and real worlds are always distinct from each other: 'le monde imaginaire est entièrement isolé, je ne puis y entrer qu'en me irréalisant'.[43] Moreover, to imagine is an act of appropriation:

L'acte d'imagination . . . est un acte magique. C'est une incantation destinée à faire apparaître l'objet auquel on pense, la chose qu'on désire, de façon qu'on puisse en prendre possession. Il y a dans cet acte, toujours quelque chose d'impérieux et d'enfantin, un refus de tenir compte de la distance, des difficultés.[44]

Moreover, the acts of imagining and of aesthetic appreciation acquire a sexualised significance for Sartre, because he implies that they have an emasculating force:

L'extrême beauté d'une femme tue le désir qu'on a d'elle. En effet nous ne pouvons à la fois nous placer sur le plan esthétique où paraît cet "elle-même" irréel que nous admirons et sur le plan réalisant de la possession physique.[45]

As the ending of *La Nausée* demonstrates, the realms of the imaginary and the aesthetic can act as alternative refuges from our awareness of the contingency and absurdity of life, but are always nevertheless dependent on consciousness and its apprehension and appropriation of the world. In the 1930s and early 1940s, Sartre appears to argue that art could not offer an expanded appreciation of life or an alternative affective experience of the world, because it was the product of the imagination and the imagination always involves a negation or an abandonment of the real.

Beauvoir, however, was keen to explore an experimental use of language and literature. Echoing Woolf and Fry, she explains in *La Force de l'âge* that,

Evidemment, je savais qu'une oeuvre forgée sur terre ne peut jamais parler qu'un langage terrestre; mais certaines me semblaient avoir échappé à leur auteur et résorbé en elles le sens dont il avait voulu les charger; elles se tenaient debout, sans le secours de personne, muettes, indéchiffrables, pareilles à de grands totems abandonnés: en elles seules, je touchais quelque chose de nécessaire et d'absolu.[46]

This disagreement is represented as a major difference between Sartre and Beauvoir and the issue remains unresolved, for two years (and roughly a hundred pages) later, on a visit to England, Sartre and Beauvoir resume the same argument:

Nous reprîmes, avec plus d'acharnement, la discussion qui nous avait opposés deux ans plus tôt sur les hauteurs de Saint-Cloud et qui s'était plus d'une fois répétée. Je soutenais que la réalité déborde tout ce qu'on peut en dire; il fallait l'affronter dans son ambiguïté, dans son opacité au lieu de la réduire à des significations qui se laissent exprimer par des mots. Sartre répondait que si on veut, comme nous le souhaitions, s'approprier les choses, il ne suffit pas de regarder et de s'émouvoir: il faut saisir leur sens et le fixer dans des phrases . . . Cette divergence entre nous devait se perpétuer longtemps; je tenais d'abord à la vie, dans sa présence immédiate, et Sartre d'abord à l'écriture. Cependant, comme je voulais écrire et qu'il se plaisait à vivre, nous n'entrions que rarement en conflit.[47]

In *La Force de l'âge*, Beauvoir is represented as conceding to Sartre's view expressed at Saint-Cloud, for she has no viable alternative to his ready-made, masculinist theories about language and writing. This was the second 'defeat' of her nascent theories by Sartre following the 'débâcle' at the Luxembourg Gardens and she conceded reluctantly. Yet this experience of discursive colonisation by Sartre at Saint-Cloud helps explain why she came to view language as a form of Trojan horse which women have to steal from men. In an interview in 1979 with Alice Jardine, Beauvoir talked at some length on her views on women's relationship to language. She commented for example: 'Women simply have to steal the instrument; they don't have to break it, or try, a priori, to make of it something totally different. Steal it and use it for their own good.'[48]

Beauvoir's formulation here of the roles of language and of writing is close to her comments about the roles of speech and silence in her negotiations of autobiography with the reader, and gestures towards the concepts of the 'nouveaux romanciers'. Her readiness to embrace more experimental techniques later in her writing career may be explained by the fact that they had formed part of the vision of writing which she expressed in her early debate with Sartre about language's ability to represent experience. Her adoption of his notion of language as an instrument and as a 'discourse of mastery',[49] rooted in corporeal disavowal and a masculinist appropriation of the world, can be viewed as an expedient measure, while Beauvoir works out a strategy 'to steal the instrument', as she put it, and express her own particular vision.

Mary Evans reads this same disagreement between Beauvoir and Sartre as concerning a difference in their individual philosophical perspectives. She argues that it indicates Beauvoir's reluctance to accept Sartre's search for a single epistemology to explain the world, and suggests that Beauvoir may be articulating a postmodernist critique of Sartre's ideas.[50] Evans contends that Beauvoir appears to be arguing for the philosophical validity of a subjective view of an always ambiguous world. In short, in her writing project, she prioritises describing a subjective experience of 'situation' over establishing abstract principles of knowledge about that 'situation'. However, in addition to its epistemological dimension, my point here is that this was a significant disagreement between Sartre and Beauvoir about the subject's relationship to language, literature, imagination and emotion, and how she might communicate her individual vision of the world. Beauvoir abandoned experimental literature because of her disagreement with Sartre and because she had no viable alternatives to pursue at that time. Later, as a result of her realisation of the importance of 'situation' and the role of the Other, she decided to pursue a literary project which was rooted in the recognition of her own experience and a testimonial obligation to the Other. It would only be in her later fiction, such as *Les Belles Images* and *La Femme rompue*, that Beauvoir would make a sustained attempt to experiment with linguistic form to communicate diverse subjective experiences and abandon language as a mimetic instrument of mastery.

In summary, the cost of the construction of the Simone-Sartre collaboration in the *Mémoires* and *La Force de l'âge* is considerable. It entails the reworking of the representation of her relationships with other people, the loss of some measure of her intellectual autonomy and of her own notions of language and writing. This cost may have encouraged Beauvoir to explore the domain of autobiographical writing (in which Sartre apparently did not have much interest), for autobiography could be viewed as a means of investigating a subjective experience of the world, which became a testimony to her life conceived within a historical and political framework. By undertaking a multi-volume autobiographical project, Beauvoir was establishing beyond doubt the importance of herself and her experience as her literary capital even if, until the 1960s, she largely abandoned attempts to write experimentally.

The multiple auto/biographical forms used by Beauvoir bear witness to her desire to record her life, as a life experienced with and for others. From *La Force de l'âge* onwards, collective history takes on an increasingly important role in the representation of Beauvoir's personal story. The testimonial quality of Beauvoir's memoirs is a major reason for their success, and the remainder of this chapter is devoted to examining how several types of testimony are operative in her autobiographical project.

### BEAUVOIR AND TESTIMONY: SOME PRELIMINARY REMARKS

Shoshana Felman, citing Elie Wiesel, has argued that 'testimony is the literary – or discursive – mode . . . of our times, and that our age can precisely be defined as the age of testimony'.[51] Wiesel suggests that since the Second World War the event of the Holocaust has continued to shape the discursive space, and that creative artists continually have to address the question of how to bear witness to it. Although Beauvoir was not directly implicated herself in the Holocaust, she nevertheless responded to this need for testimony.

However, since the 1960s, the authority of the writer or artist to speak as witness has been substantially challenged in the intellectual critical climate generated by structuralist, feminist, psychoanalytic and post-structuralist critiques of truth and identity, which have radically questioned the concept and parameters of agency. In such a critical climate, Beauvoir's testimonial autobiographical project may appear naïve and anachronistic for a number of reasons: her reliance on the presence and integrity of the autobiographical 'je', her mimetic use of language and her adoption of a linear, teleological narrative which, from *La Force de l'âge* onwards, foregrounds the experience of subjective presence within a collective historical framework.

One might argue that the testimonial and 'événementiel' form of Beauvoir's memoirs and the prescriptive stance she sometimes takes in her negotiations with the reader positions him or her to seek truth and identity in her texts. This often results in two responses to her memoirs, particularly since the publication of the *Lettres à Sartre* and the *Journal de guerre* in 1990: the charge of mythologisation and selectivity and, to a lesser extent, the assertion that Beauvoir was not an active participant in the events that she recounts (for example during the Second World War) and so her testimonial authority is questionable.

Examples of the first critical tendency are numerous. For example, in 1989, Jane Heath observes that it might not be coincidental that Beauvoir's name suggests 'seeing it beautiful' and 'seeing in vain' ('avoir beau voir') because her mythologising memoirs give us 'a rosy picture'.[52] Marianne Alphant, reviewing the *Lettres à Sartre* and *Journal de guerre* in 1990, notes: 'Que nous apprennent-ils? . . . que *La Force de l'âge* est un récit truqué.'[53] Recently, Mary Evans argues in a similar vein that '[Beauvoir's] autobiography. . . had been extremely selective in its revelations'.[54] These writers, acting as arbiters of autobiographical 'truth', all imply that it might have been possible for Beauvoir to write an unselective autobiography.

Alphant also falls into the second category of critics who question Beauvoir's memoirs for their authority because she is deemed not to have been an active participant in the historical events to which she bears witness – a position which implicitly prescribes appropriate forms of political action. Gilbert Joseph's sensationalist *Une si douce occupation. Simone de Beauvoir et Jean-Paul Sartre 1940–44* similarly condemns Beauvoir and Sartre for their wartime inactivity and accuses them of being uniquely preoccupied with their literary careers and personal lives.

These reader responses mobilise specifically disciplinary notions of truth and testimony, at the heart of the juridical and Christian discourses shaping subjectivity which have traditionally been prominent in autobiography reception. Such notions of truth and testimony involve an expectation that the autobiographical account should be mimetically truthful or provide a scientific truth of correspondence with the object/events described. Yet, crucially, this notion of mimetic truth is not a form of truth which can be communicated in autobiography, for the self who narrates is always separated from, and yet irremediably imbricated with, the self observed. Instead, a 'truth of coherence' seems more relevant to the understanding of self-representational narratives. According to Charles Hanly:

> The coherence theory of truth is compatible with the theory that there is more than one true description of the world . . . The coherence theory abandons objects as they actually are as the ground of truth for objects as they are constructed or constituted by the belief and theory investments that govern their observation and the way in which they are experienced by observers.[55]

The autobiographical narrative may then be judged 'true' as 'an interpretation that coheres with the beliefs and theories of the observer and with his "belief-and-theory-invested" experience of the object described'. It may also be judged 'true' according to the way in which it is broadly accepted by other observers and coheres roughly with their descriptions of the same events, as a narrative among other narratives.[56] Yet the conflation of mimetic truth and truth of coherence has been common in autobiography reception and particularly prevalent in the reception of Simone de Beauvoir's auto/biographical project.

Wider notions of truth can operate in her memoirs, then, if they are interpreted as a narrative of experience, and as 'témoignage engagé'. According to this notion of testimony, rooted in a notion of truth as coherence, an individual can bear witness on the basis of having been actively involved in the events related or because he or she has been present as an observer of those events. An observer can be as deeply affected by events as a participant, as Anne observes in *Les Mandarins*: 'les vrais malheurs ce n'est pas à moi qu'ils étaient arrivés, et pourtant ils avaient hanté ma vie'.[57] The testimonies of both active participants and observers are necessary to provide a range of perspectives on the events witnessed, as Claude Lanzmann's film *Shoah* (1985) demonstrates.[58] Lanzmann refused to use archive footage in his nine-hour record of the Holocaust. He conducted interviews with three categories of witnesses: Nazi perpetrators, victims who have survived, and observers (or pejoratively, onlookers or bystanders). As Shoshana Felman has argued, Lanzmann's approach to filming these testimonies of the Holocaust constantly questions the meaning of the act of 'bearing witness'.[59] Similarly, Beauvoir's memoirs, straddling historical and autobiographical discourse, the collective and the subjective, question what it means to be a witness to history. Both Lanzmann and Beauvoir, in their different ways, attempt to refine our notions of what it means to act as a witness to history. Beauvoir's literary project was shaped in wartime, in the discursive space of the events of the Second World War. Her testimonial project can be viewed as an affirmation of history and as an attempt to respond to an important ethical problem of her time: how to bear witness for the Other.

First, however, it is necessary to investigate further the operation of different forms of testimony before we assess how it functions in Beauvoir's memoirs.

### WHAT IS TESTIMONY?

Shoshana Felman says that 'to testify – to vow to tell, to promise and produce one's own speech as material evidence for truth – is to accomplish a speech act, rather than to simply formulate a statement'.[60] In *How To Do Things with Words*, J.L. Austin has argued that 'I testify' is a performative speech act, that 'it indicates that the issuing of the utterance is the performing of the action'.[61] He clarifies that although 'I testify' can be considered to function as an expositive or as having an explanatory or descriptive function, we may interpret it as a commissive or as a declaration which commits the speaker to a certain course of action.[62]

Commissive testimony is routinely employed in juridical and religious ritual. Felman describes how this 'most traditional, routine use' of legal testimony works in a courtroom scenario:

Testimony is provided, and is called for, when the facts upon which justice must pronounce its verdict are not clear, when historical accuracy is in doubt and when both the truth and its supporting elements of evidence are called into question. The legal model of the trial dramatizes, in this way, a contained, and culturally channelled, institutionalised, crisis of truth. The trial both derives from and proceeds by, a crisis of evidence, which the verdict must resolve.[63]

In this situation the testimony is preceded by the affirmation that it is 'the whole truth and nothing but the truth' and delivered in support of the case which is being argued and is then judged by an authority, who has already been judged as competent to judge.

Michel Foucault has argued in *Surveiller et punir* that legal judgement involves more than the localised judgement of a specific action. It entails the production of the biography of the accused or witness on which judgements are made as to how the individual has acted and will act in the past, present and future.[64] The judgement is passed on the individual's biography as well as on the specific action involved, and so serves to prescribe and produce forms of sanctioned subjectivity.

An important factor in the notion of testimony as commissive is that it works as a ritualised activity which takes place before the authority which requires the act of testimony. In religious and legal contexts, both parties have specific roles: the authority has to be present or virtually present, and then to pardon, console or punish and the confessing subject to articulate the confession, to receive the judgement of the authority and to be transformed by the cathartic process. In summary, testimony as a commissive activity functions as a speech act and involves the production of biographical and autobiographical material for the Other in response to a crisis of truth. The judgement which resolves this crisis of truth can then serve to elaborate sanctioned forms of subjectivity.

The notion of testimony as a response to a crisis of truth is pertinent in the case of Beauvoir and creative writers and artists of her generation. For writers who had experienced the Second World War as active participants or observers, two key questions were how literature might be possible after the atrocities committed during the war and how to represent that wartime experience. In her reading of Camus's *La Chute*, published in 1956 (the year Beauvoir began writing her memoirs), Shoshana Felman identifies a circumlocutionary structure in the text which, she argues, is organised around the Holocaust as the unspeakable centre of the novel.[65] For Felman, one of the implicit questions of *La Chute* is 'what does it mean to inhabit history as crime, as the space of the annihilation of the other?' Beauvoir's project of testimonial autobiography was similarly shaped in the discursive space of the events of the Second World War and by her notion of the intellectual as a witness for the Other. Her testimony to personal and collective history can be viewed as produced by what Felman describes as 'the silent absence of the

Holocaust' and as an attempt to respond to the historical crisis of testimony which it triggered.

A second notion of testimony, as expositive and descriptive, has a very broad application for it can refer to a narrative produced by anyone based on their experience of 'being there'. In this case, there is less concern with factual accuracy for there is no legal or religious sanction attached to the process. Expositive testimony is not produced in a crisis of truth in order to supply a single truth of correspondence, but rather to multiply truths, to disrupt a univocal, hegemonic, congealed truth. As noted earlier, Beauvoir's debate with Sartre at Saint-Cloud concerned her belief in the validity of subjective experience or first-hand testimony and her rejection of a universal epistemology. Both commissive and expositive testimony require presence or virtual presence of the testimonial subject and his or her interlocutor. However, the operation of power within the commissive testimonial relationship is disciplinary – both parties are bound to play their respective roles in order to produce a disciplined truth. Within the scenario of the expositive testimony, the narrative of experience is shared with the interlocutor who offers the speaker an opportunity to bear witness to his or her experience.

If these two concepts of testimony are considered in relation to Beauvoir's memoirs, it can be observed that reading them uniquely as commissive testimony positions her as an authoritative subject who is bound to tell the whole truth. When she is judged not to have provided a 'whole' truth, she is viewed as a selective, mythologising autobiographer. Her 'authority' as witness may also be deemed questionable because patriarchy has traditionally positioned women as unreliable witnesses in relation to truth-telling, and constituted masculine truths as universally valid. Beauvoir's use of diverse autobiographical forms (memoirs, diary, letters) may also be a reason to question her status as witness because the 'truth' of the self is not expressed in a coherent, homogeneous, autobiographical whole. Foucault's point in *Surveiller et punir* that juridical judgement disciplines the subject as well as judging his or her actions is useful here. For Beauvoir is judged an unsuitable witness when judgement is passed on her testimonial autobiography.

Reading Beauvoir's autobiography as expositive testimony – as a narrative of experience – produces a number of different tensions. The narrative appears too authoritative and self-assured, too linear. Published after *Le Deuxième Sexe*, Beauvoir's autobiographical self-portrait seems both exemplary and individualistic. Writing her narrative as a success story, she does not dwell on the episodes during which she may have experienced marginalisation and alienation as a female intellectual in a predominantly masculine environment.[66] She refuses to occupy the position of Other, instead she bears witness for the Other. The difficulties which she experienced as a woman seeking to explore her sexuality in heterosexual and homosexual relationships are only implied, if they are mentioned at all.[67] On occasions, this is not a narrative of experience, but a narrative of silence, in which 'l'indicible' is produced by the guilt-saturated, discursive space constructed from the annihilation of Others.

Both forms of testimony operate at various points in Beauvoir's memoirs and furthermore, she maps a third position of 'témoignage engagé' in a cyclical process of testimony. In her writing, although the self is constituted 'en situation' and in this instance, 'en situation autobiographique', agency is a key factor to be retained for Beauvoirian ethics. As noted in Chapter 2 in relation to *Le Deuxième Sexe*, Sonia Kruks has argued that Beauvoir's notion of the self is that of a situated subjectivity, who is both constituted, as a product of her/his situation, and constituting.[68] In her memoirs, it can be argued that to preserve agency and yet to represent the subject as a discursive production, a route is mapped through a cycle of testimony working from the disciplined self to the situated testimonial subject. In Beauvoir's project of testimonial autobiography, the self is represented 'en situation' by the agential 'je' who drives the narrative onward through a cycle of testimony.

To argue for intentionally multiple forms of testimony in Beauvoir's autobiography is not necessarily to play the dutiful, disciplined reader who believes each and every statement of autobiographical intention. For, as will be argued, these multiple forms of testimony function cyclically and they exceed Beauvoir's intentions and control.

## THE FUNCTION OF TESTIMONY IN THE MEMOIRS

In this cycle of testimony in the memoirs, although the Beauvoirian self is initially represented as shaped by discourses of gender, class, sexuality, race and nationalism, a route of resistance is sketched in *Mémoires d'une jeune fille rangée* for the not-so-dutiful daughter to follow.

Testimony takes place 'en situation' and sometimes the constraints of that situation dictate that only presence or simply 'being there' for the Other is possible. At the first stage in the testimonial cycle of the memoirs, the Beauvoirian autobiographical subject functions as a narrating 'attente'.

Although this disciplined self, who is able only to 'be there' but not able to act, appears chiefly in the *Mémoires*, it re-emerges in *La Force des choses* during the early years of the Algerian War, when Beauvoir represents herself as involuntarily re-assimilated into the conservative bourgeoisie as a result of her political inactivity. The disciplined self is also evident in the crisis of 'j'ai été flouée' at the end of the volume. She is 'flouée' not only by the discrepancy between her early bourgeois apolitical idealism and life's harsh realities, such as the atrocities of war and the ageing process, but also by the chronological and teleological structure of the autobiographical narrative which does not enable her to recapture her life.

This first stage can be viewed as analogous with Murielle's monologue in the eponymous second story of *La Femme rompue*. This monologue is discourse marked by repetition, threatening anarchy and violence, contesting bourgeois reason and order. The autobiographical subject is thoroughly disciplined at this point, locked in passivity and discursive subjection. She is a physical presence, although her corporeality is produced as a Foucauldian 'corps docile', contained in gendered space, subjected to gendered discourses which produce a gendered body in the autobiographical text.

Nevertheless, the autobiographical narrative can also operate as expositive testimony and as a narrative of experience. The cycle of testimony shifts to a second stage as the speaking subject gradually works out possibilities of agency through analysis of her experience.

At the third stage of the testimonial cycle, the active subject has subverted discourses which silenced her and autobiography becomes an act of speaking out, an act of ethical testimony which aims to produce political and social change. This autobiography of praxis, articulated by a 'témoin engagé', is accompanied by Beauvoir's active subversion of the juridical system in the 'real', demonstrated by her defence of the Other through the signing of petitions and appearances as a defence witness in court cases, as in the case of Djamila Boupacha. The best-known manifestos signed by Beauvoir were the 1960 'Manifeste des 121' against the Algerian War and the pro-abortion 'Manifeste des 343' in 1971. Between 1958–69, of the 488 manifestos which were published in *Le Monde*, Beauvoir ranked as the third most frequent signatory, having signed 72 manifestos. Jean-Paul Sartre ranked first, with 91 manifestos signed. During this period Beauvoir was by far the most frequent female signatory, followed a long way behind by Marguerite Duras, the next most frequent, who signed 37 manifestos. However, women represented only 11.1 per cent of the total number of signatories of manifestos published in *Le Monde* during this period.[69] One might question whether the signing of manifestos is an appropriate arbiter of intellectual activity. One might also question the efficacy of intellectuals signing manifestos at all. Beauvoir's frequent signing of manifestos is, however, an important indicator of *her* notion of intellectual activity as testimonial. At this stage, words are action, as Sartre writes in *Qu'est-ce que la littérature?* (1948): 'parler, c'est agir: toute chose qu'on nomme n'est déjà plus tout à fait la même'.[70] This literature of praxis is a call to action to the reader:

Il n'est plus temps de décrire ni de narrer; nous ne pouvons pas non plus nous borner à expliquer. La description, fût-elle psychologique, est pure jouissance contemplative; l'explication est acceptation, elle excuse tout; l'une et l'autre supposent que les jeux sont faits. Mais si la perception même est action, si, pour nous, montrer le monde c'est toujours le dévoiler dans les perspectives d'un changement possible, alors, dans cette époque de fatalisme, nous avons à révéler au lecteur, en chaque concret, sa puissance de faire et de défaire, bref, d'agir.[71]

Beauvoir speaks out on the major events of her time – the Occupation, the Holocaust, the Cold War, the Vietnam War, the Algerian War, May '68, the women's movement, and AIDS, in autobiography, in fiction, in prefaces, in petitions and by testifying in court cases. In this third stage, autobiography cannot contain Beauvoir's testimonial project.

If we relate this cycle of testimony more closely to her autobiographical production, it appears that the dynamic testimonial figure which she represents from the late 1950s onwards has little connection with Murielle, the ranting narrator of 'Monologue'. The ordered text of the memoirs appears quite removed from Murielle's anarchic discourse. Beauvoir is in her late forties, a Goncourt prize winner, an international intellectual celebrity, and outraged by the French government's policy in Algeria. She is poised to denounce the bourgeois values to which she was subjected during her

childhood, and assumes her long overdue project of autobiography
as a subversive witness who undertakes an act of speaking out.
Murielle, on the other hand, appears locked in the first stage of the
testimonial cycle in discursive subjection, inaction, guilt and in
conflict with the Other.

A closer examination of the situations of Beauvoir, the successful
autobiographer, and Murielle in 'Monologue' nevertheless demonstrates the proximity of the first and final stages in the testimonial
cycle evident in Beauvoir's autobiographical project. In 1956, during
the Algerian War, she embarks on autobiography at a time when she
is also locked in silence, inaction and guilt. Although Murielle is
attempting to escape *from* the past in which she is locked, whereas
Beauvoir escapes *into* her childhood past from the present of the
Algerian War, both are trying to recreate their past with varying
degrees of success. In Murielle's case, enforced silence produces
interior monologue as revenge, whereas for Beauvoir, writing her
autobiography is a further opportunity for dialogue with her readers,
which nevertheless begins as a revenge on the bourgeoisie of her
childhood.

Both narrators claim to be motivated by lucidity and a search for
truth. Murielle claims 'je ne joue pas le jeu' and that 'dès l'enfance
j'ai eu ça dans le sang: ne pas tricher'.[72] In the prologue to *La Force
des choses*, the narrator similarly asserts 'Je répète que jamais je n'ai
délibérément triché'. The key difference is that Murielle, as Elizabeth Fallaize has pointed out, uses monologue 'to provide her with
an erroneous and self-justified reading of her situation'.[73] Murielle
only dreams of writing her autobiography as revenge, to tell 'la
vérité, la vraie', which, in her view, would be far more interesting
than the 'conneries' of other women's autobiographies, as she
describes them. She fantasises about seeing her photo and name in
bookshop windows – her identity disciplined by these talismanic
symbols of identity – and having scores of men at her feet, drawn by
this apparent evidence of her celebrity.[74]

Beauvoir's memoirs, however, function to a large extent dialogi-
cally, for she engages continually with the Other as reader and bears
witness for the Other. At times, in the third stage of the testimonial
cycle, her memoirs assume an ethical function, silencing Murielle's
repetitive, raging monologue which hovers at the margins of the
autobiographical text. 'Monologue' ends with Murielle banging her
head against the wall, imploring God to reunite her with her

children so that she can enact her revenge and watch her enemies burn in hell. Does this bear any resemblance to the 'j'ai été flouée' crisis at the end of *La Force des choses*? It can be argued that, in some respects, it does, for both Murielle and the narrator of *La Force des choses* are alienated and in conflict with the Other. However, unlike Murielle, Beauvoir does not blame other people for being 'flouée'. In her memoirs, as in her philosophy, she rejects this conflictual relationship with the Other and advocates reciprocity instead. At the end of *La Force des choses*, this alienation can be viewed as a temporary state for, in the final volume of her memoirs, Beauvoir ends on a collaborative note:

Je voulais me faire exister pour les autres en leur communiquant, de la manière la plus directe, le goût de ma propre vie: j'y ai à peu près réussi. J'ai de solides ennemis, mais je me suis aussi fait parmi mes lecteurs beaucoup d'amis. Je ne désirais rien d'autre. Cette fois, je ne donnerais pas de conclusion à mon livre. Je laisse au lecteur le soin d'en tirer celles qui lui plairont.[75]

To summarise, there are several stages in the testimonial cycle in Beauvoir's memoirs. First, there is a juridical and commissive notion of testimony, in which the autobiographical subject is represented as a narrating 'attente', a disciplined presence, existing in discursive subjection. In the second stage, testimony functions expositively, as a narrative of experience, in which the subject uses testimony to make sense of her life in relation to the lives of others, thereby seeking a truth of coherence. In the final stage, testimony takes on an ethical function as the autobiographical subject subverts the disciplinary discourses which have shaped her speech, silence and style of embodied subjectivity. These stages of testimony are interwoven and can be viewed as in operation throughout Beauvoir's autobiography. However, on certain aspects of certain issues, such as her experiences of sexuality and embodiment, her autobiography remains largely silent and the testimonial process hardly moves beyond its first stage.

Are we to conclude that Beauvoir's writing practice in her memoirs is locked in this testimonial cycle?[76] In so far as the notion of 'témoignage' remained central to Beauvoir's vision of writing, the answer must be 'yes'. However, in so far as the various forms of testimony in her memoirs operate as discourses specifying variable forms of knowledge and truth, it is notable that Beauvoir continually negotiates her engagement with testimonial autobiography with the reader. As noted above, although there are crises in the relationship with the Other, there is no definitive return to the narrative solipsism of the *Mémoires* because from the end of this text Beauvoir's memoirs become a continuing dialogue with the Other. In her negotiation of testimony as discourse, she avoids being locked in any particular stage of the cycle. As Foucault describes the operation of discourse in *La Volonté de savoir*:

Il ne faut pas imaginer un monde du discours partagé entre le discours reçu et le discours exclu ou entre le discours dominant et celui qui est dominé; mais comme une multiplicité d'éléments discursifs qui peuvent jouer dans des stratégies diverses . . . Les discours pas plus que les silences, ne sont une fois pour toutes soumis au pouvoir ou dressés contre lui. Il faut admettre un jeu complexe et instable où le discours peut être à la fois instrument et effet de pouvoir, mais aussi obstacle, butée, point de résistance et départ pour une stratégie opposée. Le discours véhicule et produit du pouvoir; il le renforce mais aussi le mine, l'expose, le rend fragile et permet de le barrer.[77]

It could be argued that the use of the term 'testimonial cycle' does suggest a certain stasis, for it implies that whatever stage Beauvoir occupies in her negotiation of autobiography, she nevertheless does not or cannot move out of the cycle. In a sense this is valid, for what is at issue here is the continuing, guilt-ridden obligation – itself a form of stasis – to bear witness in Beauvoir's writing.

In her memoirs, whether we are offered a disciplined monologue, a narrative of experience or a 'témoignage engagé', the notion of presence, of being there in the world for the Other, is consistently important. In Beckett's *En attendant Godot* (1952), proclaiming the importance of presence while waiting for the absent Godot, Vladimir says: 'Nous sommes au rendez-vous, un point, c'est tout. Nous ne sommes pas des saints, mais nous sommes au rendez-vous. Combien de gens peuvent en dire autant?' Estragon replies: 'Des masses'.[78] Although presence is sometimes all that is possible in our relationship with the Other, Beauvoir represents her project of testimonial autobiography as a means of reaching these others whose testimonies are silenced in order to break down our common existential isolation.[79] Living with others in 'the real', resisting the Disneyland hyperreality parodied by Beauvoir in the mid-1960s in *Les Belles Images*, may seem an increasingly remote option at the end of the second millenium. Before we learn to live with the 'loss of the real',[80] Beauvoir's testimonial autobiographical project alerts us to the continuing importance of being there and bearing witness.

# CHAPTER 7

# Writing the Other

In this final chapter, Beauvoir's negotiation of biography will be considered initially as a corporeal encounter with the Other, focusing on *Une Mort très douce* (1964) and *La Cérémonie des adieux* (1981).[1] The subsequent focus for discussion will be Beauvoir's reworking of prior autobiographical self-representations in these biographical texts and her attempt to convey the lived experience of the Other. For Beauvoir, writing autobiography was, as we have seen, an intersubjective testimonial enterprise and a continuing exploration of the parameters of alterity. In these Other-oriented texts, although the apparent focus is the representation of the ailing Other's situation, they cast crucial light on Beauvoir's auto-biographical self-representation, developing her concern with inter-subjectivity in new directions.[2]

Before considering *Une Mort très douce* and *Adieux*, it should be noted that these texts are not the only examples of biographical writing in Beauvoir's corpus. There are also short biographical portraits in her memoirs, some of which may be described as psychologically-oriented case studies.[3] This juxtaposition of the auto/biographical and the perpetual imbrication of self and Other in Beauvoir's philosophy suggests that, although this chapter focuses on her Other-oriented texts, it will be more productive to consider *Une Mort très douce* and *Adieux* as auto/biographies.[4]

The first of these, *Une Mort très douce*, was written after the first three volumes of Beauvoir's memoirs and is concerned with the illness and death of her mother. *Adieux* is the final, major text which was published in Beauvoir's lifetime. The first part is a chronological narrative in which she relates the last ten years of Sartre's life (1970–80); the final part of the text is a series of thematically-oriented interviews with Sartre conducted by Beauvoir in 1974.

Unlike the bodily containment evident in the memoirs, both these texts are concerned with what Geneviève Idt has termed 'the primacy of the corporeal', and it is this concerted attempt on Beauvoir's part (albeit partly circumstantial) to engage here with issues of embodied alterity which will be the preliminary focus for discussion.[5]

## THE BIOGRAPHICAL BODY

As we have seen in Chapter Five, to write autobiography is also in some way to write the body. Sidonie Smith has argued:

The autobiographical subject carries a history of the body with her as she negotiates the autobiographical "I", for autobiographical practice is one of those cultural occasions when the history of the body intersects with the deployment of subjectivity.[6]

If Simone de Beauvoir as autobiographer negotiates the historical terrain of the body, how does she represent the body of the Other in biography – the body as perhaps radically other to her, to her history and experience of corporeality? In what ways does Beauvoir carry 'a history of the [Other's] body' with her as she writes biographies of her mother and Sartre, who are, for her, both long-alienated bodies?

In *Une Mort très douce* and *Adieux*, it will be argued that although the body of the Other is initially deployed and disciplined in these texts as radically Other, the events of illness and death force a confrontation between Beauvoir and her embodied biographical subject. She will confront the history of her relationship with the embodied Other, and the deaths of Françoise de Beauvoir and Sartre, like the death of Zaza in *Mémoires d'une jeune fille rangée*, will serve to author-ise Beauvoir, who survives to bear witness to the events of their lives and deaths.

*Une Mort très douce* is, like *L'Invitée*, an overtly cathartic text which emerges from a guilt-ridden crisis – the death of Beauvoir's mother. Similarly, *Adieux* deals with the monumental crisis in her life represented by the illness and death of Sartre. As *cathartic* texts, both *Une Mort très douce* and *Adieux* enable Beauvoir to encounter and to purge/excrete the abject corpse, which Julia Kristeva describes in *Pouvoirs de l'horreur*:

Le cadavre (*cadere*, tomber), ce qui a irrémédiablement chuté, cloaque et mort, bouleverse plus violemment encore l'identité de celui qui s'y confronte comme un hasard fragile et fallacieux . . . tel un théâtre vrai, sans fard et sans masque, le déchet comme le cadavre m'indiquent ce que j'écarte en permanence pour vivre . . . J'y suis aux limites de ma condition de vivant.[7]

Beauvoir's encounters with the abject corpse can be interpreted as occasions for a confrontation with the limits of her subjectivity, for the abject threatens the identity and order of her former auto/biographical (self-)representations:

Ce n'est donc pas l'absence de propreté ou de santé qui rend abject, mais ce qui perturbe une identité, un système, un ordre. Ce qui ne respecte pas les limites, les places, les règles. L'entre-deux, l'ambigu, le mixte.[8]

Yet, this encounter with corporeal excess will ultimately affirm Beauvoir's subjectivity and testimonial stance as she confronts her own abjection:

S'il est vrai que l'abject sollicite et pulverise tout à la fois le sujet, on comprend qu'il s'éprouve dans sa force maximale lorsque, las de ses vaines tentatives de se reconnaître hors de soi, le sujet trouve l'impossible en lui-même, découvrant qu'il n'*est* autre qu'abject. L'abjection de soi serait la forme culminante de cette expérience du sujet auquel est dévoilé que tous ses objets ne reposent que sur la *perte* inaugurale fondant son être propre. Rien de tel que l'abjection de soi pour démontrer que toute abjection est en fait reconnaissance du *manque* fondateur de tout être, sens, langage, désir.[9]

In these texts, Beauvoir is forced to confront – through the recognition of her own abjection – her experience of lack, desire, and the ultimate impending annihilation of her own subjectivity (the end of desire) at the heart of her literary project through the staging of the long-postponed encounter with the abject bodies of Françoise de Beauvoir and Sartre.

In *Une Mort très douce* and *Adieux*, sexuality, ageing, illness and death are represented as brutal reminders of human corporeality and, unlike maternity, experienced by both women and men. Beauvoir attempts to decipher some of the meanings which the aged body has accumulated throughout a lifetime, which have hitherto been concealed from her.

Describing this Kafkaesque inscription of the body by history,[10] Foucault has argued in his important essay, 'Nietzsche, Genealogy and History' that:

The body manifests the stigmata of past experience . . . [It is] the inscribed surface of events (traced by language and dissolved by ideas), the locus of a dissociated self (adopting the illusion of a substantial unity), and a volume in perpetual disintegration.[11]

The task of Foucauldian genealogy or the study of history through discourses of power, is:

To expose a body totally imprinted by history and the process of history's destruction of the body.

Following Nietzsche, Foucault argues that the body does not escape history:

We believe . . . that the body obeys the exclusive laws of physiology and that it escapes the influence of history, but this too is false. The body is molded by a great many distinct regimes; it is broken down by the rhythms of work, rest, and holidays; it is poisoned by food or values, through eating habits or moral laws; it constructs resistances . . . Nothing in man – not even his body – is sufficiently stable to serve as the basis for self-recognition or for understanding other men.[12]

The body cannot be a stable guide to self-knowledge or to knowledge of others for it is imprinted with the discontinuities of history. The knowledge of history written/read through the body of the Other is therefore potentially discovered every time as historical narratives come into being. However, the knowledge acquired is not knowledge as a perpetual re(dis)covery of the body, rather it is knowledge 'made for cutting' 'the consoling play of recognitions' found in the necessary continuity of historical narratives, rooted in corporeal abnegation.[13] In this way, gaining self/other-knowledge through the moribund bodies of her mother, Françoise and Sartre, Beauvoir will not recognise, repeat and appropriate their life narratives, she will be forced to discover aspects of her desires, her life and those of her mother and her life partner anew.

To some degree, *Une Mort très douce* and *La Cérémonie des adieux* seem to constitute an attempt on Beauvoir's part to rescue the lost Other from the 'scandale' of physical disintegration and death, through the process of writing the Other's body. Her singular life as an intellectual had distanced her from her mother's banal life; distinct intellectual and political interests separated her from Sartre in the 1970s, so that, in these texts, the body acts as a point of contact with the intellectually alienated Other. Moreover it will constitute a focus, in its own right, for Beauvoir's intellectual and moral preoccupations.

In both *Une Mort très douce* and *Adieux*, Beauvoir usurps the doctor's privilege by appropriating the role of medical discourse and attempting to render the 'lived experience' of the other's dying. In her bedside testimony, speaking candidly of the bodily decay and death of her biographical subjects, Beauvoir aligns herself with the body of the Other, thereby resisting the discourses of gender and class which would silence and separate her from the moribund Other. For Beauvoir, illness and death are occasions for solidarity with the Other, rather than an opportunity to subject the Other's body to the disciplinary incisions of medical discourse.

Critical reception of both *Une Mort très douce* and *La Cérémonie des adieux* has included accusations of voyeurism and an excessive concern on Beauvoir's part for the physical disintegration of her subjects.[14] Yet, if these texts have shocked by their attempt to represent the disintegrating body, it is, as Elaine Marks has noted of *Adieux*, because they are 'situated at a crossroads' of various discourses of the body, sexuality and sexual difference which circumscribe the unsaid, the private and the taboo. Marks writes: 'it is as if the "real" had overwhelmed the reviewers . . . It is as if [Beauvoir] had made dirty, had sullied the white page.'[15] For Marks, Beauvoir transgresses the parameters of textual form and content, as the bodies of her abject biographical subjects seep through the textual body. This transgression may also be viewed as a reworking of the Foucauldian 'corps docile' of the memoirs through an exploration of the viscous as the site of the irreducible corporeality of Beauvoir's bio-subjects. Moreover, these encounters with corporeality represent an opportunity for her to rewrite her relationship with the female body.

Beauvoir began writing *Une Mort très douce* quickly after her mother's death of intestinal cancer in 1963, and it depicts the final month of her mother's life, interspersed with reflections on the complexities of the mother-daughter relationship. Over four weeks, she is brutally confronted with the reality of her mother's life as she attempts to decipher the meanings of her mother's body-as-text. In the second, untitled chapter of *Une Mort très douce*, in a micro-biography of her mother, Beauvoir sketches Françoise's unhappy early life and the disappointments of her marriage with the adulterous Georges – a portrait which, although it might explain Beauvoir's mother's situation for the reader, nevertheless contrasts sharply with the voluntaristic self-determination of her daughter's life in her multi-volume autobiography. In later life, however, Françoise is represented as refusing to assume the constraints imposed by her ageing body, much to the admiration of Simone.

The death of Georges de Beauvoir back in 1941 had constituted for her mother 'une page à tourner' and, 'avide de vivre enfin à sa guise', Françoise takes on part-time library work, learns German and Italian, improves her English and travels widely in Europe, in a Lilliputian adaptation of her celebrated daughter's life as intellectual and writer. Unfortunately, increasing abdominal pain and a fractured femur result in her hospitalisation, initially in the nearest hospital and then, in an expensive Paris clinic.

When she visits her mother, Beauvoir is struck by the contrast between the class prejudices emanating from her mother's mouth as she relates her night in a state hospital and 'la vérité de son corps souffrant'.[16] Unable to communicate with her mother, Beauvoir seeks knowledge of her mother's life and the maternal body becomes a theatrical space for her mother's 'situation'. In a pivotal early scene, she is confronted abruptly by Françoise de Beauvoir's naked body as the physiotherapist conducts a pelvic examination. Beauvoir is shocked by her mother's physical frailty and her oblivious attitude towards the exposure of her sexual body:

Voir le sexe de ma mère: ça m'avait fait un choc. Aucun corps n'existait moins pour moi – n'existait davantage. Enfant je l'avais chéri; adolescente, il m'avait inspiré une répulsion inquiète; c'est classique, et je trouvai normal qu'il eût conservé ce double caractère répugnant et sacré: un tabou. Tout de même je m'étonnai de la violence de mon déplaisir.[17]

In *Une Mort très douce*, her mother's body soon assumes new meaning – no longer sacred or repulsive, it becomes 'une dépouille: une pauvre carcasse sans défence, palpée, manipulée par des mains professionnelles'.[18]

For Beauvoir, a turning point is constituted by the sight of her mother's frailty, the diagnosis of her mother's intestinal cancer and her realisation of her own alienation from the female body – rooted in bourgeois gender codes and her disavowed experience of lesbian corporeal pleasure. Thereafter, Beauvoir and her mother attempt to build a relationship of solidarity in the last month of her life. This solidarity is rooted in an attempt on Simone and Hélène de Beauvoir's part to protect their mother's body from a condescending bourgeois doctor who is 'ivre de technique'.

Abstract knowledge of the human body may be the preserve of the medical professionals in *Une Mort très douce*, but when the cancer is finally diagnosed, the widespread ethical dilemma of whether to inform the patient and to assume the human cost of that knowledge or 'trahison' (as it is termed) falls upon Beauvoir and her sister. This dilemma arises again for Beauvoir as far as Sartre is concerned and is debated in *La Cérémonie des adieux*. In both cases, fatal illness is presented as an epistemological problem and a moral issue, on the grounds of the biographical subject's prerogative to direct his/her existential, corporeal fate. When the biographer possesses privileged knowledge of the biographical subject's body, does she tell? Beauvoir decides not to inform her mother and Sartre of the imminence of their death, in her mother's case because she needed to live in hope, and in Sartre's case, because his situation was 'ambiguous' – having been ill intermittently for several years, he might have lived on. Beauvoir explains in *Adieux* that he also needed to live in hope and asserts that her silence did not separate them.[19]

In both texts there is much detail about the fluctuating medical conditions of Françoise and Sartre, conveyed in the terse, testimonial style of Beauvoir's memoirs. She acts as a privileged witness who transgresses by breaking the silence surrounding the corporeal experience of the dying. As Nancy Miller has argued: 'if the ultimate commandment of filiality is to not forget, then what can be more seemly than the will to record?'[20] Indeed, in *Une Mort très douce*, Beauvoir relinquishes her distancing irony of the memoirs and represents herself here as the 'truly' dutiful daughter in her commitment to record and analyse the situation and death of her mother.

This testimonial act also implicates Beauvoir corporeally, which is illustrated by two striking examples in *Une Mort très douce*. In the first, she relates her 'crise de nerfs' following a visit to her mother at the clinic. Relating this visit to Sartre, Beauvoir is unable to control her despair. Involuntarily, she begins to mime her mother's facial movements – movements which encapsulate Françoise de Beauvoir's lifetime of servility, despair and solitude:

Je parlai à Sartre de la bouche de ma mère, telle que je l'avais vue le matin et de tout ce que j'y déchiffrais: une gloutonnerie refusée, une humilité presque servile, de l'espoir, de la détresse, une solitude – celle de sa mort, celle de sa vie, qui ne voulait pas s'avouer. Et ma propre bouche, m'a-t-il dit, ne m'obéissait plus: j'avais posé celle de maman sur mon visage et j'en imitais malgré moi les mimiques. Toute sa personne, toute son existence s'y matérialisaient et la compassion me déchirait.[21]

In this example, the corporeal expression of her mother's 'vie gâchée' is channelled through Beauvoir's own adult body, recalling the infant's early experience of body image as confused with the mother as Other. Here, in the phenomenon of appersonisation, in which the meaning expressed by her mother's body is transferred to Beauvoir's current body image, the act of witnessing her mother's suffering involves an involuntary enactment of corporeal solidarity.

In the second example in *Une Mort très douce*, Beauvoir relates how her mother often became confused with Sartre in her dreams, until the dreams became a nightmare in which she believed herself to be subjugated by her mother once more, as in her childhood. As Alice Jardine and Alex Hughes have argued in convincing feminist psycho-analytic readings of this passage, there is an evident violence in Beauvoir's treatment of her mother and in the feminisation of Sartre here and in *La Cérémonie des adieux* which entails that Françoise and Sartre, representing the all-powerful, pre-Oedipal phallic mother must be killed off to enable Beauvoir to write.[22] In an alternative reading, Marks has argued that if such episodes always already constitute re-runs of the Oedipal romance, how is it then possible to write about *adult* experiences of illness, ageing, death and the material impact of such experiences?[23] As Marks notes, Beauvoir's writing project is transgressive and, in its commitment to the real, challenges the hyperreality of poststructuralist and psychoanalytic theory. In both *Une Mort très douce* and *La Cérémonie des adieux*, Beauvoir confronts the reader with the abject materiality, the perpetual excess of the adult body which, elsewhere in her textual corpus, is usually channelled through discourses of disavowal. Such abject materiality therefore appears violent and shocking – particularly because this confrontation with corporeal abjection has long been staved off in Beauvoir's writing.

In *Adieux*, Sartre's physical fragility is established very early in the text; moreover, it is made clear that his health is not a source of recent concern but rather had been a cause for Beauvoir's anxiety since 1954, following Sartre's first bout of hypertension: 'en dépit de mon apparente tranquillité je n'avais pas cessé depuis plus de vingt ans d'être sur le qui-vive'.[24] Her entire autobiographical project has therefore been undertaken in the shadow of Sartre's anticipated decline and death, which may partly explain the idealised represen-tation of him in the memoirs.

As Sandra Beyer argues, in the first half of the decade related in *Adieux*, much of '[Beauvoir's] concern for Sartre's health is secondary to her interest in his political activities . . . as time went by, the balance of these themes was reversed.'[25] The corporeal abnegation of the Cartesian ego is abandoned, and where once Sartre was represented as the consummate, yet disembodied, intellect in the earlier volumes of memoirs, by the late 1970s, he is represented as faulty intellect reduced to failing flesh. Beyer notes that although Beauvoir continues to chronicle Sartre's intellectual activities, she stops analysing their importance to him. Her narrative lapses into enumeration, indicating her anxiety to record the events relating to Sartre's diminishing presence.

In the latter half of the 1970s, Beauvoir's relationship to Sartre is a (re-)discovery of his physicality, as she records the fluctuating medical condition of the body of her former and long-alienated lover. Elsewhere in Beauvoir's autobiography, Sartre's intellect appears to function synecdochically for his corporeality and sexuality so that his intellect – acting as a metaphor for male sexual energy – replaces his physical relationship with Beauvoir.

In *Adieux* and in the accompanying 1974 interviews, Beauvoir's relationship to Sartre's body – like her relationship to her mother's body – is represented as a 'double-bind' which has 'ce double caractère répugnant et sacré: un tabou'.[26] The double-bind is characterised by Beauvoir's represention of the conflicting messages communicated to her initially by her mother's and then her lover's bodies.[27] The possibility of corporeal reciprocity – or the mutual recognition of the Other as an *embodied* freedom – with Françoise de Beauvoir and with Sartre is passed over in silence and fraught with conflict in *Mémoires d'une jeune fille rangée* and *La Force de l'âge*.[28] Then, as they become ill and die, Beauvoir's attention to their corporeality is demanded, once her desire for corporeal reciprocity with them has been abandoned. In this way, the double-bind established in relation to the maternal body in *Mémoires d'une jeune fille rangée* is repeated in the representation of Beauvoir's corporeal relationship with Sartre, for once the double-bind structure is established – here, in relation to the Other's body – it functions as 'an habitual expectation'.[29]

Simultaneously in *Adieux*, Beauvoir watches over Sartre's intellectual legacy, establishing the record of his final activities and attempting to preserve the patrimony intact, despite her dispute with Benny Lévy.[30] The Sartrian intellectual corpus becomes co-extensive with the failing body of the 70–year-old, as Beauvoir attempts to manage their respective viscous seepages.

The final tableau in the encounter with the body of Sartre takes place just after his death. Beauvoir lies down next to his corpse and falls asleep, as if miming, rehearsing her own death, which will take place six years later:

A un moment, j'ai demandé qu'on me laisse seule avec Sartre, et j'ai voulu m'étendre près de lui sous le drap. Une infirmière m'a arrêtée: "Non. Attention . . . la gangrène." C'est alors que j'ai compris la vraie nature de ses escarres. Je me suis couchée sur le drap et j'ai un peu dormi.[31]

She represents herself here as oblivious to the decay of Sartre's body, to the seepage of necrotic tissue which, although not contagious, is usually abject, taboo.

This attempt to perform the autobiographically and existentially impossible – namely Beauvoir's representation of her own (idealised) death – is itself a 'live', uncanny repetition and 'la boucle est bouclée' as literature produces life, which in turn produces literature.[32] As Geneviève Idt notes in her reading of *Adieux*, this death tableau is represented on at least two occasions in Sartre's and Beauvoir's texts. In *Le Diable et le bon dieu* (1951), Hilda tells Goetz:

Je t'ai soigné, lavé, j'ai connu l'odeur de ta fièvre. Ai-je cessé de t'aimer? Chaque jour tu ressembles un peu plus au cadavre que tu seras et je t'aime toujours. Si tu meurs, je me coucherai contre toi et je resterai là jusqu'à la fin, sans manger ni boire, tu pourriras entre mes bras et je t'aimerai charogne: car l'on n'aime rien si l'on n'aime pas tout.[33]

In *La Force de l'âge*, the communal death tableau is anticipated again:

Cette mort qui nous est commune à tous, chacun l'aborde seul. Du côté de la vie, on peut mourir ensemble; mais mourir, c'est glisser hors du monde, là où le mot "ensemble" n'a plus de sens. Ce que je souhaitais le plus au monde, c'était de mourir avec qui j'aimais; mais fussions-nous couchés cadavre contre cadavre, ce ne serait qu'un leurre, de rien à rien, il n'existe pas de lien.[34]

An additional example is Beauvoir's anticipation of Zaza's death in *Mémoires d'une jeune fille rangée*, which also prepares the reader for the textual dénouement. Having realised her love and affective need for Zaza, she comments:

Quelques jours plus tard, j'arrivai au cours en avance, et je regardai avec une espèce de stupeur le tabouret de Zaza: "Si elle ne devait plus jamais s'y asseoir, si elle mourait, que deviendrai-je?" Et de nouveau une évidence me foudroya: "Je ne peux plus vivre sans elle". C'était un peu effrayant: elle allait, venait, loin de moi, et tout mon bonheur, mon existence même reposait entre ses mains. J'imaginai que Mlle Gontran allait entrer, balayant le sol de sa longue jupe, et elle nous dirait: "Priez, mes enfants: votre petite compagne, Elizabeth Mabille, a été rappelée par Dieu la nuit dernière." Eh bien, me dis-je, je mourrais sur l'heure! Je glisserais de mon tabouret, et je tomberais sur le sol, expirante. Cette solution me rassura. Je ne croyais pas pour de bon qu'une grâce divine m'ôterait la vie; mais je ne redoutais pas non plus réellement la mort de Zaza. J'avais été jusqu'à m'avouer la dépendance où me mettait mon attachement pour elle: je n'osais pas en affronter toutes les conséquences.[35]

Moreover, this repetitive quality of observing the rites of the Other's death is recognised in *Une Mort très douce*, when Beauvoir describes her mother's funeral as 'la répétition générale de notre propre enterrement'.[36]

Following the failed staging of the death tableau à la *Romeo and Juliet* in *Adieux* (Beauvoir survives Sartre as she survived Zaza), all that remained to Beauvoir was to replicate Sartre's death uncannily in 1986, when she died almost to the day of almost identical symptoms: severe cirrhotic damage and pulmonary oedema. In its almost flawless pre-enactment of Beauvoir's own death in 1986, the death tableau in *Adieux* is therefore uncanny, for her long-repressed fear of mortality recurs through this compulsive re-staging of this and other death tableaux.[37]

In the representation of ageing embodiment in these later texts, in contrast to the relative self-disembodiment of her memoirs, Beauvoir takes up her theorisation of embodied existence which is first articulated in her philosophy of the 1940s. Her focus in *Une Mort très douce* and *Adieux* on the ageing body may be explained by an attempt to represent the materiality of the body without recourse to the gendered example of maternity. The ageing, illness and death of the human body is presented as an irreducible and largely democratic event which affects women and men, whatever their social and economic status. Moreover, in their representation of the lived experience of illness and dying, both these texts constitute 'cas particuliers' of the generalised arguments advanced in *La Vieillesse*.[38]

As the mother of an intellectual celebrity, Françoise de Beauvoir's final days are lived out in the privileged surroundings of an expensive Paris clinic; Sartre, despite his monumental renown, is nevertheless reduced to incontinence, bedsores and gangrene – a somewhat ironic fate given his phobic attitude towards viscosity. The event of death is represented as merciless, yet also democratising, bringing totalisation for Françoise de Beauvoir and Sartre – despite their privileged, bourgeois status which allows them to experience death supported by friends and family in comfortable surroundings.

Yet, a significant difference between the two texts' presentations of the experience of dying is at the level of textual form which demonstrates a difference in Beauvoir's attitude towards her bio-graphical subjects. Although *Une Mort très douce* and the first part of *Adieux*, relating Sartre's last ten years, are narrated in broadly chronological fashion, Beauvoir exploits narrative form differently in each text. In *Une Mort très douce*, labelled a 'récit', the reader is initially given precise dates and times of events (except in the second chapter – a micro-biography of Françoise de Beauvoir's life). As the narrative develops, dates become infrequent and the focus narrows to a daily and hourly record of the last days of Beauvoir's mother. Following her death, there are four brief chapters relating the funeral arrangements and analyses of the impact of her mother's death and the moral questions it raised for Beauvoir.

In *Adieux*, the same period – approximately one month prior to the biographical subject's death – is covered in less than ten pages, while the earlier part of the text offers a year-by-year account of the last decade of Sartre's life. Yet in contrast to *Une Mort très douce*, the account in *Adieux* appears excessively factual and enumerative, with only occasional glimpses of Beauvoir's attitude towards the events related. In *Adieux*, there is a lack of concern for rhetorical strategies, as if Sartre's absence as privileged reader of the text necessarily entails Beauvoir's disappearance from the narrative and a lack of concern for the text's reception. Michel Contat has noted this absence of style and the repetitive, brooding quality of the first part of *Adieux*:

un livre qui se veut pur compte rendu des dernières années de Sartre, qui est donc écrit dans un style qui se donne de façon presque provocante comme refus du style, non pas degré zéro de l'écriture ou écriture mate, mais écriture dépouillée de toute séduction, jusqu'à la négligence, au ressassement et à la platitude.[39]

The difference in the treatment of the two deaths can partly be explained by circumstances: Françoise de Beauvoir's decline and death took place quite rapidly and Beauvoir swiftly composed her account. She was therefore still immersed in grief and probably confused because of the 'rapprochement' with her mother prior to her death. In *Tout compte fait*, Beauvoir provides a vivid description of the genesis and the cathartic value of *Une Mort très douce*:

Quelques jours après son enterrement la décision de les raconter s'est brusquement imposée à moi, ainsi que le titre de mon récit, l'épigraphe et la dédicace. J'ai passé l'hiver à l'écrire. Presque toutes les nuits je voyais ma mère en rêve. Elle était vivante et parfois je m'émerveillais qu'on eût réussi à la sauver; le plus souvent je la savais condamnée et j'avais peur . . . Je n'avais pas prémédité d'écrire *Une Mort très douce*. Dans les périodes difficiles de ma vie, griffoner des phrases – dussent-elles n'être lues par personne – m'apporte le même réconfort que la prière au croyant: par le langage je dépasse mon cas particulier, je communie avec toute l'humanité; mais les lignes que j'ai tracées alors, si elles m'ont aidée à retrouver certains détails, ne m'étaient pas nécessaires pour évoquer les journées que je venais de vivre: elles s'étaient gravées en moi à jamais.[40]

Sartre's decline, however, took place over several years during which Beauvoir could repeatedly imagine and rehearse her reaction to her partner's death. Her account of this period in *Adieux*, in much the same way as her memoirs, was composed from several different sources, such as diaries which she kept during 1970–80, accounts which referred to Sartre's final years and the recollections of friends and acquaintances in the Sartre-Beauvoir entourage.[41]

Moreover, *Une Mort très douce* can be described, to some extent, as a conversion narrative in that it relates – at least as far as Beauvoir is concerned – a process of enlightenment, as she comes to understand the significance of her mother's life and situation. Accordingly, in comparison with the representation of Françoise de Beauvoir in *Mémoires d'une jeune fille rangée*, the reader is offered a more sympathetic portrait, which is informed by Beauvoir's adult appraisal of the complexities of her mother's life and her analysis of gender in *Le Deuxième Sexe*.

In *Adieux*, Beauvoir does not retouch her autobiographical representation of Sartre, she dutifully completes her chronological account. If there is any reworking of the representation of her relationship with Sartre, it is the distance between them which becomes increasingly evident – on intellectual, political and material levels – as Beauvoir is forced to compete daily with Benny Lévy, Arlette Elkhaïm, Liliane Siegel, Michèle Vian and Wanda Kosakievicz among others for Sartre's time. Moreover, *Adieux* appears to have been written for a different purpose, according to Beauvoir's explanation or biographical 'pact' in the 'Préface':

En vérité, c'est aux amis de Sartre que je m'adresse: à ceux qui souhaitent mieux connaître ses dernières années. Je les ai racontées, telles que je les ai vécues. J'ai parlé un peu de moi, car le témoin fait partie de son témoignage, mais je l'ai fait le moins possible. D'abord parce que ce n'est pas mon sujet; et puis, comme je le notai en réponse à des amis qui me demandaient comment je prenais les choses: "Ça ne peut pas se dire, ça ne peut pas s'écrire, ça ne peut pas se penser; ça se vit, c'est tout".[42]

In short, unlike *Une Mort très douce*, the reader apparently cannot share the emotional journey that Sartre's death represents for Beauvoir – because it is 'indicible', beyond representation. Consequently, in *Adieux*, she resorts to compiling an amalgam of accounts of Sartre's last decade and, although the text's concern with abject physicality gives it literally a cathartic content, she achieves only a minimal *affective* catharsis in writing *Adieux*.

The chronological and 'événementiel' quality of *Adieux* moreover constitutes a rejection of the largely thematic presentation adopted in *Tout compte fait*, which covers most of the decade (1962–71) immediately prior to the years recorded in *Adieux*. The reversion to a chronological presentation in *Adieux* is partly the result of the method of its composition, although it also suggests other elements at work in Beavoir's negotiation of the auto/biographical. Firstly, the chronological presentation of *Adieux* may serve as a means to stave off the representation of Sartre's death. As noted in Chapter 3, Beauvoir's chronological method employed in autobiography can be frustrating for both author and reader, for it appears to defer meaning and avoid conclusion.Yet, it was also argued that a chronological presentation of auto/biography, in its ability to render 'la déception ontologique', was particularly apt for representing the decline of the ageing self. The reversion to a chronological presentation in *Adieux* suggests that Beauvoir was able and prepared to confront Sartre's ageing (if not his death) in a way that she could not write about her own. Second, the chronological and factual presentation enables Beauvoir to avoid having to represent Sartre's affective experience of ageing, for this would demand both a high level of intimacy between them for that experience to be communicated (which did not necessarily exist in the 1970s) and Sartre's consent for such an intimate portrait to be revealed.

Aware perhaps that this affective 'lived experience' of ageing and Sartre's 'voix vivante' was lacking in her account in *Adieux*, Beauvoir appended a series of interviews to the text, which provided not only the Sartrian imprimatur to her decadal account, but also a portrait of the Sartre-Beauvoir couple in the mid-1970s. More importantly for this discussion of Beauvoir's auto/biographical project, these interviews offer a further glimpse of different aspects of Beauvoir's life.

### ENTRETIENS AVEC JEAN-PAUL SARTRE, 1974

The project to conduct a series of interviews with Sartre was mooted by Beauvoir in mid-1974:

Au début de juin, Sartre allait vraiment bien. Je le trouvais même "transformé". Il ne somnolait plus, il réfléchissait à un livre qu'il voulait écrire sur lui-même. Nous causions, comme autrefois . . . Un jour, j'ai suggéré que pendant les vacances nous enregistrions des entretiens sur lui: littérature, philosophie, vie privée. Il a accepté. "Ça remédiera à *ça*", m'a-t-il dit en désignant son oeil d'un geste bouleversant.[43]

These interviews with Beauvoir, the film, *Sartre par lui-même*, and other lengthy interviews which Sartre gave during the 1970s such as Michel Contat's 'Autoportrait à soixante-dix ans', can be seen to constitute a form of oral autobiography and sequel to *Les Mots*, although he does not uniquely determine the focus of the conversations.[44] The 1974 interviews are not the only occasions on which Beauvoir interviewed Sartre, as Terry Keefe and Jean-Pierre Boulé note for, approximately six months later, in May 1975, *L'Arc* published another thematically-oriented interview with Sartre in which he expresses his views on the situation of women and the feminist movement.[45]

In the preface to the 1974 interviews, Beauvoir explains that she organised the interviews thematically and that she re-wrote the recorded text, but without any overt literary intention – 'je n'ai pas tenté de les écrire au sens littéraire du mot: j'ai voulu en garder la spontanéité'.[46] Moreover, she explains: 'parfois Sartre était fatigué et me répondait mal; ou c'était moi qui manquais d'inspiration et posais des questions oiseuses: j'ai supprimé les conversations qui m'ont paru sans intérêt'. She concludes:

On y trouvera des passages décousus, des piétinements, des redites, et même des contradictions: c'est que je craignais de déformer les paroles de Sartre ou d'en sacrifier des nuances. Elles n'apportent sur lui aucune révélation inattendue, mais elles permettent de suivre les méandres de sa pensée et d'entendre sa voix vivante.

In fact, as the above quotations indicate, far from being 'témoignage brut' in which the reader has access to the 'voix vivante' of the now-defunct Sartre, the text is, inevitably, highly-constructed. In an oblique renunciation of the value of Sartre's controversial interviews with Benny Lévy which had recently taken place, Beauvoir tells the reader that she does not intend to offer any new perspectives on Sartre's life.[47] Yet the purpose here is not to speculate on the possible lacunae in these interviews, but rather to analyse their representation of Beauvoir in conversation with Sartre.

The reader learns a plethora of detail which is not necessarily present in the earlier autobiographical texts.[48] In the first interview, for example, when Sartre is relating how he used to steal money from his mother to buy cakes for his schoolfriends and thereby ingratiate himself with them, Beauvoir comments that she would not have been able to do such a thing and implies that her own mother was far more watchful.[49] Later we learn that Beauvoir initiated Sartre into the appreciation of modern painting and that from around 1952, when he became less inclined to read literature, they no longer shared the same reading tastes.[50] The different personalities of Sartre and Beauvoir emerge in these interviews, unlike the harmonised representation of the couple in the memoirs. For example, Beauvoir enjoyed friends confiding in her, whereas Sartre claims here that he disliked being confided in because it created inequality in his relationship with the person in question. Nevertheless, these scruples appear only to apply to his relationships with men, for he apparently readily solicited women's confidences.[51] In this interview, which is concerned with what one might loosely term, 'les relations avec autrui', Beauvoir probes Sartre and in the ensuing discussion they demonstrate quite distinct ways of relating to the Other:

SdeB: Vous avez à l'égard des hommes et des femmes, du genre humain en général, une double attitude qui est le contraire de la mienne, d'ailleurs, c'est peut-être pour ça que je la trouve si curieuse. C'est-à-dire que vous êtes très ouvert quand quelqu'un vient vous parler. . . moi je suis chameau, j'ai toujours envie d'envoyer les gens balader. . . et cependant quand vous avez un renseignement à demander dans une rue, c'est épouvantable; si moi je vous dis: je vais demander un renseignement, nous sommes perdus dans Naples, je vais demander où est telle rue, ça, vous ne voulez pas, vous vous raidissez. Pourquoi cette attitude d'accueil, et en même temps cette attitude de refus presque haineux?[52]

Sartre explains that engaging with someone in the street entails 's'adresser à la subjectivité d'un autre' which involves – to his dismay – that he has to depend on the other person and he adds: 'surtout la subjectivité d'autrui ne me plaît guère'.[53]

Beauvoir continues to probe Sartre about his relations with others, likening him to Henri Michaux's comic character M. Plume, from *Un certain Plume* (1930), who is 'perpétuellement agacé, inquiété par les autres', and Sartre explains that his Other-related anxiety was linked to his sense of his own physical ugliness. Beauvoir concludes by contrasting her own sense of being physically attractive with Sartre's inability to feel 'bien dans sa peau devant autrui'. Through these perhaps seemingly trivial instances of self-Other relationships, the reader is offered sharply differentiated pictures of Beauvoir and Sartre's modes of engagement with the Other and with the world.

In the following two interviews, Beauvoir questions Sartre about his attitudes towards women and his relationship to his own body – the latter forming an interesting personal commentary on the account of Sartre's physical decline in the first part of *Adieux*. Once more, distinct aspects of their subjective, corporeal engagements with the world and with others emerge. Beauvoir does not baulk at questioning Sartre about his various relationships with women, including those by which she had felt personally threatened, although here she is relatively silent on the detail of their lifelong partnership and her own relationship to him, commenting brusquely, 'ne parlons pas de moi'. The first part of the subsequent interview is concerned with 'la saisie subjective du corps', and again, Beauvoir and Sartre emerge as having distinct experiences of corporeality. Beauvoir reflects how she enjoyed physical fatigue, whereas Sartre could not yield to any form of physical abandon – be it sexual pleasure, acceptance of his own tiredness, physical limitations or need for comfort.[54] The only exception to this refusal to abandon himself to physical sensation was in his attitude towards illness.[55]

In later interviews, certain intellectual differences emerge, such as a disagreement regarding their awareness of the class struggle in the 1930s. Beauvoir contests Sartre's view that their awareness was limited and that they had not really intellectually assimilated the concept of class struggle. Beauvoir comments briefly on her attitude towards socialism, then swiftly reverts to questioning Sartre:

J'ai toujours été assez vague là-dessus. J'étais tout de même assez gagnée par l'idée de socialisme. Il y avait un côté d'égalité dans la pénurie qui me plaisait beaucoup pendant l'Occupation. Et je pensais qu'un vrai socialisme, qui aurait des raisons positives, constructives, ce serait très bien. Mais restons sur votre lancée à vous.[56]

In the second interview about Sartre's political involvement, Beauvoir overtly directs the content of the interview, referring to her memoirs:

Il ne faut pas refaire toute l'histoire chronologique de votre vie politique jusqu'en '62, parce que, ça, je l'ai écrit en partie sous votre dictée dans *La Force des choses*.[57]

The phrase, 'sous votre dictée', is perhaps not particularly surprising because, as Beauvoir has often explained, her method of research for her memoirs was to collate various accounts – including accounts from people in her entourage such as Sartre – in her representation of a specific period.[58] In the case of Beauvoir and Sartre, this remark and her research methodology seem to me to be unrelated to questions of authority and authorship, and concerned rather with Beauvoir's purpose of providing a factually accurate account of Sartre's political trajectory with an awareness of his political adversaries and with the practical considerations of having shared many life experiences.

Approximately fifteen years earlier, Beauvoir had written in the prologue to *La Force de l'âge*:

Ma vie a été étroitement liée à celle de Jean-Paul Sartre; mais son histoire, il compte la raconter lui-même, et je lui abandonne ce soin. Je n'étudierai ses idées, ses travaux, je ne parlerai de lui que dans la mesure où il est intervenu dans mon existence.[59]

The question of what constitutes 'une intervention dans l'existence d'autrui' is a complex one. It subsumes not only some of the key issues of Beauvoirian philosophy relating to the ethics and parameters of self-Other relations, but also wider concerns relating to gender and auto/biographical self-representation in which the representation of the lives of intellectual and creative women is elided in favour of the celebration of male lives. Consequently, in Beauvoir's auto/biographical project, there is a perpetual tension between representing the 'radicale entente' experienced with Sartre and her experience of (the parameters of) subjectivity. In the quotation from *La Force de l'âge* cited above, Beauvoir appears keen to avoid acting as 'sage-femme' to the delivery of Sartre's auto-biography. She therefore attempts to direct the reception of her text so that her life is not elided in favour of his.

In the 1974 interviews in *Adieux*, Beauvoir exercised a high degree of control over Sartre's self-representation, both at the time the interviews were conducted and then published in 1981 with an account of Sartre's last decade. Why? In part, this need for control is the hallmark of Beauvoir's publication strategy as a woman writer attempting to safeguard her future in the marketplace and, as such, is quite comprehensible. Furthermore, her need for control has to be understood in the context of the dispute with Lévy over Sartre's intellectual corpus and legacy and Beauvoir's need to assert her authority over the future reception of Sartre's work, as noted earlier.

Finally, *La Cérémonie des adieux* constitutes Beauvoir's attempt to bear witness to the life and work of one of France's most famous intellectuals – a task for which not only was she uniquely suited but one which she probably also perceived as a moral and intellectual duty by the end of the 1970s. In *Tout compte fait*, Beauvoir's explanation of her fascination for biography may shed some light on her own role as biographer in *Adieux*:

Un genre qui me séduit parce qu'il se situe à l'intersection de l'histoire et de la psychologie, c'est la biographie. Comme dans toutes les monographies, je suis renvoyée à travers un cas singulier à la totalité du monde . . . La biographie de Proust par Painter ne m'a pas aidée à mieux le connaître: son oeuvre permet de l'approcher de bien plus près. Mais en indiquant quels paysages, quels visages, quels événements l'ont inspiré, elle m'a renseignée sur son travail créateur. C'est ce qui m'intrigue le plus: quel lien – pour chacun d'eux si différent – existe entre la vie quotidienne d'un écrivain et les livres où il s'exprime.[60]

There are two key issues here which are significant for Beauvoir's engagement with auto/biography. Firstly, the link between the singular and the universal is crucial for literature to function intersubjectively, and auto/biography seems to be an appropriate mode of writing to explore intersubjective experience.[61] Beauvoir recognised that the success of *Une Mort très douce* was indeed its universal appeal:

Quand, récemment j'ai écrit sur la mort de ma mère, j'ai réçu des quantités de lettres me disant: "En parlant de la mort de votre mère, vous avez parlé de la mort de la mienne, de celle de ma femme, de mon mari, et curieusement vous m'avez aidé à la supporter; bien que votre livre soit très sombre, vous m'avez aidé." Pourquoi? C'est que quand on traverse une expérience douloureuse, on souffre de deux manières; d'abord du malheur qui vous frappe; mais aussi la douleur vous isole et vous êtes séparé parce que vous êtes malheureux. Si vous pouvez écrire, le fait même d'écrire brise cette séparation; si les écrivains décrivent souvent des expériences douloureuses ce n'est pas parce qu'ils font de la littérature avec n'importe quoi, d'une manière sacrilège, comme on le dit quelquefois; c'est parce que pour eux il y a là une manière de dépasser leur douleur, leur angoisse, leur tristesse en en parlant. Et de même pour les gens qui lisent, du fait qu'ils ne se sentent plus isolés dans leur tristesse, dans leur angoisse, ils la supportent mieux . . . Parler des expériences les plus intimes que nous pouvons avoir comme la solitude, l'angoisse, la mort des gens que nous aimons, notre propre mort, c'est au contraire une manière de nous rapprocher, de nous aider et de rendre le monde moins noir. Je crois que c'est là une des tâches absolument irremplaçables et essentielles de la littérature: nous aider à communiquer les uns avec les autres en ce que nous avons de plus solitaire et par quoi nous sommes liés le plus intimement les uns aux autres.[62]

Secondly, in Beauvoir's explanation of her interest in literary biography, she emphasises the importance of the link between a writer's daily life and the books s/he writes. In the *Adieux* interviews, although there is no extensive discussion of Sartre's writings, the reader is offered an opportunity to understand the link between the writings and the man, because of Beauvoir's privileged position as witness to Sartre's life and lifelong reader of his work. Without lapsing into hagiography, few have been able to question Sartre about his relationship to his own corporeality, sexuality and other people – aspects of his daily life which have an immediate interface with his philosophy, but which tend to be elided.[63]

In these body-oriented auto/biographical texts, written in the latter stages of her literary career, Beauvoir addresses the abject Otherness of intersubjective relations. Through the representation of the Other's decline and death, she is able both to confront certain aspects of her own subjectivity which remained opaque in the memoirs and explore possibilities of reciprocity at a time when the Other is potentially most distant from the self – at the end of his/her life. Yet the dilemma which runs through Beauvoir's auto/biographical writing and which she is forced to confront as a woman writer and intellectual partner of Jean-Paul Sartre is aptly expressed by Goetz to Hilda in *Le Diable et le bon dieu*:

*Tu n'es pas* moi, c'est insupportable. Je ne comprends pas pourquoi nous faisons deux et je voudrais devenir toi en restant moi-même.[64]

# Epilogue

In this study, it has been argued that Simone de Beauvoir's testimonial autobiographical project developed from her Other-oriented philosophy of the 1940s, in which she argued that subjectivity must always be a subject-in-the-world and a subject-for-others.

Beauvoir said in the final volume of her memoirs that 'écrire est demeuré la grande affaire de ma vie'.[1] Her notion of literature, from the beginning of her writing career, was concerned with bearing witness to her own experience and engaging with alterity. Writing was an opportunity to create a 'rapprochement' between people, as she explained in 1966:

Je pense qu'une des tâches des écrivains, c'est de briser la séparation au point où nous sommes le plus séparés, au point où nous sommes le plus singuliers.[2]

To some extent, it can be argued that this concern for others was rooted in the Christian values of her bourgeois background, against which she struggled for much of her life. More important, perhaps, is the fact that much of her life and her writing project was affected by war.

Her knowledge of the different 'situations' of other people's lives was also decisively influential in shaping her testimonial writing project. Moreover, her friendships with Nelson Algren, Richard Wright and Claude Lanzmann confirmed her belief in the importance of testimony. For these men were all concerned with bearing witness in their writing for society's 'others' – be they Chicago drug addicts, the disfranchised black population of America during the late 1930s and 1940s or Holocaust survivors – and bearing witness to the collective psycho-social cost of conflictual self-Other relationships.

In Beauvoir's writing, her concern for the marginalised Other and the damaging consequences of oppression is evident across the range of her work. In her fiction, she offers a critique of the French middle-class and explores the constraints and realities of gendered identity as well as the parameters of our responsibility to the Other. In her philosophy, she offers a theoretical analysis of intersubjective relations and how marginalised identity is constructed and how women, especially, might accede to subjecthood. In this respect, her memoirs acts as a case study in female subjectivity, assumed in the mainstream of the French intelligentsia. Her political activism, at the time of the Algerian War and in the French feminist movement, during which she exploited her celebrity as 'Simone de Beauvoir' to represent marginalised others and to help effect social change, bears witness to her solidarity with the disfranchised.

Throughout her life, Beauvoir found herself fighting against the masculinism of French intellectual and political life despite, and perhaps also because of, her collaboration with Jean-Paul Sartre. Her solution was always to fight in the mainstream, to be engaged with 'the real'. By constructing herself as witness to the twentieth century and writing herself into the male-constructed French auto-biographical tradition, by writing philosophy almost 'à son insu' and by espousing an unpopular, anti-essentialist, materialist feminism at a time when psychoanalysis was a dominant discourse in French feminism, Beauvoir assumes the role of a survivor within the French intellectual field.

This is a difficult role because survivors of all kinds often experience a self-inflicted sense of shame. In the aftermath of the Second World War, Beauvoir reflects on the shame she felt having lived through some of the worst traumas of history: 'ce passé brutalement dévoilé me rejetait dans l'horreur; la joie de vivre cédait à la honte de survivre'.[3] Her shame at having survived Zaza, at having lived through the Second World War as a witness rather than an active participant, at having survived in the mainstream as a female intellectual, writer and philosopher, may explain her ambivalence to her own status and towards other women.[4] Yet the role of survivor is also rooted in a potentially productive consciousness of the Other, which in Beauvoir's case, shaped her entire literary project.

Survivors of any kind are rarely welcome because they force a confrontation with guilt and responsibilty for the past, at the expense of relinquishing the novelty of the present: 'insofar as they bear witness to our own historical disfiguration, survivors frighten us. They pose for us a riddle and a threat from which we cannot turn away.'[5] Embracing Beauvoir's intellectual project, we are forced to confront her particular role as a survivor and witness to many of the vicissitudes, injustices and traumas of recent intellectual, social and political history. Yet, by confronting these various histories and assuming the past, we are able to face the future as 'solidaires' rather than 'solitaires'.[6]

# Notes

INTRODUCTION

1 Toril Moi, *Simone de Beauvoir: The Making of an Intellectual Woman* (Oxford: Blackwell, 1994), p. 1.

2 *Le Deuxième Sexe* (Paris: Gallimard, 1949).

3 *Lettres à Sartre*, Vols 1 and 2 (Paris: Gallimard, 1990); *Journal de guerre* (Paris: Gallimard, 1990); *Lettres à Nelson Algren, un amour transatlantique*, trans. Sylvie Le Bon de Beauvoir (Paris: Gallimard, 1997). The English version of Beauvoir's letters to Algren has been published as *Beloved Chicago Man: Letters to Nelson Algren 1947–64* (London: Victor Gollancz, 1998).

4 Deirdre Bair, *Simone de Beauvoir, A Biography* (London: Jonathan Cape, 1990).

5 Margaret Crosland, *Simone de Beauvoir: The Woman and Her Work* (London: Heinemann, 1992).

6 Eva Lundgren-Gothlin, *Sex and Existence, Simone de Beauvoir's The Second Sex* (London: Athlone, 1996), first published in Sweden in 1991.

7 Ruth Evans (ed.), *Simone de Beauvoir's The Second Sex, New Interdisciplinary Readings* (Manchester University Press: 1998).

8 Kate and Edward Fullbrook, *Simone de Beauvoir and Jean-Paul Sartre, The Remaking of a Twentieth-Century Legend* (Hemel Hempstead: Harvester Wheatsheaf, 1993).

9 Karen Vintges, *Philosophy as Passion, The Thinking of Simone de Beauvoir* (Bloomington and Indianapolis: Indiana University Press, 1996), originally published in the Netherlands in 1992.

10 Kate and Edward Fullbrook, *Simone de Beauvoir: A Critical Introduction* (Cambridge: Polity Press, 1998).

11 Joseph Mahon, *Existentialism, Feminism and Simone de Beauvoir* (Basingstoke: Macmillan, 1998).

12 Elizabeth Fallaize, *The Novels of Simone de Beauvoir* (London: Routledge, 1988) and (ed.) *Simone de Beauvoir, A Critical Reader* (London: Routledge, 1998).

13 In *L'Amérique au jour le jour* (Paris: Morihien, 1948), Beauvoir recounts her four- month visit to America in 1947 (from 25 January to 20 May).

14 See Margaret A. Simons, 'Beauvoir and Sartre: The Philosophical Relationship', *Yale French Studies* 72 (1986), 165–79 (p. 166).

15 The Simone de Beauvoir Society publishes an annual journal and a biennial newsletter, holds an annual conference and sponsors sessions at the annual *Modern Language Association of America* convention.

16 'Simone de Beauvoir: Witness to a Century', *Yale French Studies* 72 (1986) (special issue).

17 Judith Butler, *Gender Trouble, Feminism and the Subversion of Identity* (London: Routledge, 1990).

18 Several essays on Beauvoir's philosophy were collected in Azizah Y. al-Hibri and Margaret Simons (eds.) *Hypatia Reborn, Essays in Feminist Philosophy* (Bloomington and Indianapolis: Indiana University Press, 1990), pp. 227–335.

19 *Feminist Interpretations of Simone de Beauvoir*, (ed.) Margaret A. Simons (Pennsylvania State University Press, 1995) and *Beauvoir and The Second Sex: Feminism, Race and the Origins of Existentialism* (Lanham, MD: Rowman & Littlefield, 1999).

20 Debra B. Bergoffen, *The Philosophy of Simone de Beauvoir, Gendered Phenomenologies, Erotic Generosities* (New York: SUNY, 1997).

21 Moi, *Simone de Beauvoir, The Making of an Intellectual Woman*, pp. 11–12.

22 Nevertheless, Beauvoir's contribution to French feminism is still recognised in France and in January 1999 a major international conference took place organised by *Nouvelles Questions Féministes* and the Festival International de Films de Femmes de Créteil to mark the 50th anniversary of *Le Deuxième Sexe*.

23 Gilbert Joseph, *Une si douce Occupation . . .: Simone de Beauvoir et Jean-Paul Sartre 1940–1944* (Paris: Albin Michel, 1991).

24 Bianca Lamblin, *Mémoires d'une jeune fille dérangée* (Paris: Balland, 1993).

25 Jean-Pierre Saccani, *Nelson et Simone* (Monaco: Du Rocher, 1994).

26 Claudine Monteil, *Simone de Beauvoir, Le Mouvement des femmes, Mémoires d'une jeune fille rebelle* (Monaco: Du Rocher, 1996).

27 'Dossier critique: *L'Invitée* et *Les Mandarins*', études réunies et présentées par Jacques Deguy, *Roman 20–50*, 13 (1992), 5–188.

28 Michèle Le Doeuff, *L'Etude et le rouet: des femmes, de la philosophie, etc* (Paris: Seuil, 1989).

29 Michèle Le Doeuff, 'Simone de Beauvoir, les ambiguïtés d'un ralliement', *Magazine littéraire*, April 1994, pp. 58–61.

30 Mona Ozouf, *Les Mots des femmes, essai sur la singularité française* (Paris: Fayard, 1995).

31 Geneviève Gennari, *Simone de Beauvoir* (Paris: Editions Universitaires, 1958).

32 Octave Mannoni, 'Relation d'un sujet à sa propre vie', *Les Temps Modernes*, 528 (July 1990), 57–77. I am grateful to Michel Contat for alerting me to the existence of this article.

33 Francis Jeanson, *Simone de Beauvoir ou l'entreprise de vivre* (Paris: Seuil, 1966), p. 195.

34 Jane Heath, *Simone de Beauvoir* (Hemel Hempstead: Harvester Wheatsheaf, 1989).

35 Leah D. Hewitt, *Autobiographical Tightropes* (Lincoln and London: University of Nebraska Press, 1990).

36 Terry Keefe, 'Autobiography and Biography: Simone de Beauvoir's Memoirs, Diary and Letters' and Emma Wilson, 'Daughters and Desire: Simone de Beauvoir's *Journal de Guerre*' in Terry Keefe and Edmund Smyth (eds.) *Autobiography and the Existential Self* (Liverpool University Press, 1995), pp. 61–81 and pp. 83–98 respectively.

37 Valérie Baisnée, *Gendered Resistance, The Autobiographies of Simone de Beauvoir, Maya Angelou, Janet Frame and Marguerite Duras* (Amsterdam and Atlanta GA: Rodopi, 1997).

38 For example, Toril Moi, 'Power, Sex and Subjectivity: Feminist Reflections on Foucault', *Paragraph* 5 (1985), 95–102; Isaac D. Balbus, 'Disciplining Women, Michel Foucault and the Power of Feminist Discourse', in Seyla Benhabib and Drucilla Cornell (eds.) *Feminism as Critique* (Cambridge: Polity Press, 1987), pp. 110–27; Lois McNay, *Foucault and Feminism: Power, Gender and the Self* (Cambridge: Polity Press, 1992); Caroline Ramazanoglu (ed.) *Up Against Foucault* (London: Routledge, 1993).

39 Vintges explains her Foucauldian methodology on pp. 6–9 of *Philosophy as Passion*.

40 Michel Foucault, *L'Usage des plaisirs* (Paris: Gallimard, 1984) and *Le Souci de soi* (Paris: Gallimard, 1984).

41 Kate Soper, 'Forget Foucault?' in *Michel Foucault: J'Accuse*, special issue of *New Formations* 25 (1995), 21–7 (pp. 26–7).

42 Soper, 'Forget Foucault', p. 27.

43 Jean Grimshaw, 'Practices of Freedom' in Ramazanoglu (ed.) *Up Against Foucault*, pp. 51–72 (pp. 65–9); Terry Eagleton, *The Ideology of the Aesthetic* (Oxford: Blackwell, 1990) pp. 391–95.

44 See also Sandra Lee Bartky, 'Foucault, Femininity, and the Modernization of Patriarchal power' in I.Diamond and L.Quinby (eds.), *Feminism and Foucault: Reflections on Resistance* (Boston: NorthEastern University Press, 1988), pp. 61–86, in which Bartky examines within a Foucauldian critical perspective how the female body is physically disciplined by the regime of femininity.

45 Eagleton, *The Ideology of the Aesthetic*, p. 393.

46 Philippe Lejeune, *Moi aussi* (Paris: Seuil, 1986), p. 16.

47 Interview with Hélène de Beauvoir on 13 September, 1993, in Goxwiller, France.

48 Beauvoir explains the 'transparency' of her early relationship with Sartre in *FA*, pp. 31–4.

49 Elie Wiesel, cited by Shoshana Felman, 'Education and Crisis or the

Vicissitudes of Teaching' in Shoshana Felman and Dori Laub, *Testimony, Crises of Witnessing in Literature, Psychoanalysis and History* (New York and London: Routledge, 1992), pp. 1–56 (p. 5)

50 *Pyrrhus et Cinéas* (Paris: Gallimard, 1944); *Pour une morale de l'ambiguïté* (Paris: Gallimard, 1947).

51 Having lost contact with Jacques Champigneulles for approximately twenty years, Beauvoir met up with him again by chance in March 1950; he had become alcoholic and empoverished, see *LNA*, p. 362. Deirdre Bair claims that Jacques died shortly after a final meeting with Beauvoir in 1950, see Bair, *Simone de Beauvoir*, p. 420.

1 *PYRRHUS ET CINEAS AND POUR UNE MORALE DE L'AMBIGUÏTÉ*

1 Recent studies have convincingly demonstrated the specificity of Beauvoir's philosophy and exposed the sexism involved in the dismissal of her philosophy as merely derivative of Sartre's, see for example: Michèle Le Doeuff, *L'Etude et le rouet: des femmes de la philosophie, etc.* (Paris: Seuil, 1989), Toril Moi, *Simone de Beauvoir: The Making of an Intellectual Woman* (Oxford: Blackwell, 1994), Eva Lundgren-Gothlin, *Sex and Existence, Simone de Beauvoir's The Second Sex* (London: Athlone, 1996) and Margaret Simons, 'Beauvoir and Sartre: The Philosophical Relationship', Yale French Studies 72 (1986). See also Sonia Kruks's chapter on Beauvoir in *Situation and Human Existence* (London: Unwin Hyman, 1990) and the following articles by Kruks: 'Simone de Beauvoir: Teaching Sartre about Freedom' in Ronald Aronson and Adrian Van Den Hoven (eds.) *Sartre Alive* (Detroit: Wayne State University Press, 1991) and 'Gender and Subjectivity: Simone de Beauvoir and Contemporary Feminism' in *Signs: Journal of Women in Culture and Society*, Vol. 18, no.1, (1992), pp. 89–110, which was published as 'Genre et subjectivité: Simone de Beauvoir et le féminisme contemporain' in *Nouvelles Questions Féministes*, Vol. 14, no.1 (1993); see finally Kate and Edward Fullbrook, *Simone de Beauvoir and Jean-Paul Sartre, the Remaking of a Twentieth-Century Legend* (Hemel Hempstead: Harvester Wheatsheaf, 1993) and *Simone de Beauvoir: A Critical Introduction* (Cambridge: Polity Press, 1998); Karen Vintges, *Philosophy as Passion, The Thinking of Simone de Beauvoir*, (Bloomington and Indianapolis: Indiana University Press, 1996); Debra Bergoffen, *The Philosophy of Simone de Beauvoir, Gendered Phenomenologies, Erotic Generosities* (New York: SUNY, 1997); Joseph Mahon, *Existentialism, Feminism and Simone de Beauvoir* (Basingstoke: Macmillan, 1998) and Margaret A. Simons (ed.) *Feminist Interpretations of Simone de Beauvoir* (Pennsylvania State University Press, 1995).

2 For discussions of the divergences between Beauvoir's and Sartre's work in the 1940s, see Kruks, 'Simone de Beauvoir', Lundgren-Gothlin, *Sex and Existence* and Simons' 'Beauvoir and Sartre', above.

3 See Kruks' chapter on Beauvoir in *Situation and Human Existence*, her 'Gender and Subjectivity: Simone de Beauvoir and Contemporary Feminism' and 'Teaching Sartre about Freedom'; see also Moi, *Simone de Beauvoir*, pp. 169–71.

4 This position is taken by Kate and Edward Fullbrook in *Simone de Beauvoir and Jean-Paul Sartre* and *Simone de Beauvoir: A Critical Introduction*.

5 Margaret Simons has noted that 'Beauvoir was the first one to address herself to the problem of the Other, a concern which later became so prominent in Sartre's work'. Simons bases her generalised discussion in this article on Beauvoir's fiction, autobiography and *Le Deuxième Sexe*; see Simons, 'Beauvoir and Sartre: The Philosophical Relationship', p. 169.

6 *FCII*, p. 62.

7 *FA*, p. 626.

8 *FA*, p. 625.

9 *FA*, p. 627. Michèle Le Doeuff argues that Beauvoir's double negative here – 'Je ne désapprouve pas' – highlights her uneasy relationship to the existentialist camp. Le Doeuff argues that for Beauvoir

> 'son vrai point de redémarrage fut Hegel, bien plus que Sartre [. . .] Car, pour écrir son oeuvre, elle avait besoin d'une philosophie de la conscience qui s'ouvre d'emblée et radicalement sur une problématique de la pluralité des consciences, en lutte les unes avec les autres, donc existant les unes et les autres, dans une extériorité réciproque. Or une telle idée n'est pas au travail dans l'existentialisme de Sartre; tout au plus apparaît-elle comme un horizon menaçant et comme non thématisable: dire que "l'enfer, c'est les autres" [. . .] revient à reconnaître que le rapport des diverses personnes entre elles dépasse l'ordre du pensable.'

See Le Doeuff, 'Simone de Beauvoir: les ambiguïtés d'un ralliement', pp. 60–1.

10 In *Huis Clos* (1944) and *Les Mains sales* (1948) Sartre similarly used the devices of recollection and flashback. Used in theatre, rather than in narrative prose fiction such as *Le Sang des autres*, these devices constitute a more direct method of conveying several vantage points and existential dilemmas simultaneously.

11 Fallaize, *The Novels of Simone de Beauvoir*, 1988), p. 47.

12 Kruks, 'Gender and Subjectivity: Simone de Beauvoir and Contemporary Feminism', pp. 99–100.

13 These questions are raised in a slightly different form by Catherine in *BI*, pp. 29–30.

14 *PC*, p. 244.

15 *Ibid.*, p. 370.

16 G.W.F. Hegel, *Phenomenology of Spirit*, trans. by A.V. Miller (OUP, 1977), p. 308; see also p. 395.

17 Jean-Paul Sartre, *L'Etre et le néant* (Paris: Gallimard, 1943), collection 'tel' 1995, p. 404.

18 Sartre's view of the conflictual nature of self-Other relations is also demonstrated in his theatre and fiction of this period, notably *Huis-Clos* (1944) and *L'Age de raison* (1945). In these texts, the Other constitutes an obstacle to the characters' transcendence.

19 *PC*, p. 300.

20 *Ibid.*, p. 302.

21 This is demonstrated by Françoise's crisis at Sacré-Coeur in *L'Invitée*; her dilemma is how to live authentically with the Other while safeguarding her independent projects (see *L'Invitée*, pp. 215–17).

22 *PC*, p. 323.

23 *Ibid.*, p. 331.

24 Laurie Spurling, *Phenomenology and the Social World, The Philosophy of Merleau-Ponty and its Relation to the Social Sciences* (London: Routledge, 1977), pp. 180–1.

25 *PC*, p. 339.

26 *PC*, p. 341.

27 See Bair, *Simone de Beauvoir, A Biography*, pp. 293–4.

28 *MJFR*, pp. 184–5.

29 *Ibid.*, p. 185.

30 The dilemma of whether to use violence is demonstrated by Jean Blomart's predicament in *Le Sang des autres*, in which he has to decide whether to sanction further Resistance actions, which will entail bloodshed.

31 *FA*, p. 627.

32 *Ibid.*, pp. 627–8.

33 Beauvoir's dating of this event is inaccurate here because, according to the dates of the letters which she received from Sartre, he was on leave from 28 March 1940 until 8 or 9 April, see *Lettres au Castor 1940–1963*, p. 153.

34 *FA*, pp. 498–9.

35 Kruks, 'Simone de Beauvoir: Teaching Sartre about Freedom', p. 288.

36 Moi, *Simone de Beauvoir, The Making of an Intellectual Woman*, pp. 253–4.

37 Kruks, 'Teaching Sartre about Freedom', and Terry Keefe, 'The Other in Sartre's Early Concept of "Situation"', *Sartre Studies International* 1, Nos.1/2 (1995), pp. 95–113.

38 Keefe, 'The Other', p. 109.

39 In June 1946, *Labyrinthe* published Beauvoir's 'Introduction à une morale de l'ambiguïté', which can be found in Francis and Gontier, *Les Ecrits de Simone de Beauvoir*, pp. 337–3. As this is an extremely truncated version of what later became *Pour une morale de l'ambiguïté*, I will pass over this text and examine the subsequent full-length version.

40 *PMA*, p. 53.

41 Simons, 'Beauvoir and Sartre: The Philosophical Relationship', pp. 173–7.
42 Terry Keefe, one of the few to discuss this essay in detail, does not engage with Beauvoir's description of childhood at any length, see *Simone de Beauvoir, A Study of Her Writings* (Totowa, New Jersey: Barnes and Noble, 1983), p. 80.
43 *PMA*, pp. 54–5.
44 *Ibid.*, pp. 58–9.
45 Beauvoir claims that her use of these portraits was influenced by Hegel (*FCI*, p. 99).
46 *PMA*, p. 186.
47 *Ibid.*, pp. 103–4.
48 *Ibid.*, p. 110.
49 *Ibid.*, p. 112.
50 *Ibid.*, p. 120.
51 Kruks, 'Gender and Subjectivity', p. 100.
52 *EN*, p. 485.
53 *Ibid.*, p. 534.
54 *Ibid.*, p. 569.
55 Kruks, 'Gender and Subjectivity', p. 97.
56 Keefe, *Simone de Beauvoir, A Study*, p. 84.
57 Interview with Claude Lanzmann cited in Felman, 'The Return of the Voice: Claude Lanzmann's Shoah' in Felman and Laub, *Testimony, Crises of Witnessing in Literature, Psychoanalysis, and History*, p. 244.
58 *PMA*, p. 60.

### 2 LE DEUXIÈME SEXE

1 Toril Moi, 'An Intellectual Woman in Postwar France', in Denis Hollier (ed.) *A New History of French Literature* (London and Cambridge, MA.: Harvard University Press, 1989), p. 984.
2 Toril Moi, *Simone de Beauvoir*, pp. 186–9; Dorothy Kaufmann, 'Simone de Beauvoir: Questions of Difference and Generation', p. 124; Elizabeth Houlding 'Simone de Beauvoir: From the Second World War to The Second Sex', *L'Esprit créateur* 33, (1993), 39–51, and Lundgren-Gothlin, *Sex and Existence, Simone de Beauvoir's The Second Sex* (see especially Chapter 1 for historical background to *Le Deuxième Sexe*).
3 Houlding, 'Simone de Beauvoir', p. 41.
4 The recent publication of a French translation of Beauvoir's letters (in English) to Nelson Algren, some of which were written during the period when she was writing *Le Deuxième Sexe*, may encourage future biographical readings of Beauvoir's pioneering work, see Simone de Beauvoir, *Lettres à Nelson Algren, Un Amour Transatlantique 1947–64*, trans. Sylvie Le Bon de Beauvoir (Paris: Gallimard, 1997), hereafter abbreviated to *LNA*.

5 Houlding, 'Simone de Beauvoir', p. 41.
6 *FA*, p. 654.
7 Mary Evans, *Simone de Beauvoir, A Feminist Mandarin* (London and New York: Tavistock, 1985), p. 59. Francis Jeanson also makes a similar point, although in relation to Beauvoir's childhood, in an interview in 1965. Beauvoir replied that in her opinion 'cette espèce de neutralisation des inconvénients de la condition féminine' occurred later. See Jeanson, *Simone de Beauvoir ou l'entreprise de vivre*, p. 253.
8 Lundgren-Gothlin, *Sex and Existence*, pp. 15–17.
9 *Ibid.*, pp. 245–6.
10 The information in this section on the condition of women in France has been taken from Lundgren-Gothlin, *Sex and Existence*, Chapter 1, unless otherwise noted.
11 Antony Copley, *Sexual Moralities in France 1780–1980* (London: Routledge, 1989), pp. 201–2.
12 According to Catherine van Casselaer, it was possible to obtain a 'permission de travestissement' and both Rachilde and Rosa Bonheur benefited from this special dispensation. Bonheur applied for a 'permission de travestissement' to facilitate her work as an artist at the horse market in Paris. Ironically, once when she was dressed 'en femme' she was arrested by a policeman believing her to be a man dressed as a woman. He became further convinced of Rosa Bonheur's masculine identity when she hit him in indignation. See Catherine van Casselaer, *Lot's Wife, Lesbian Paris 1890–1914* (Liverpool: Janus Press 1986), pp. 39–40.
13 Christopher Robinson, *Scandal in the Ink, Male and Female Homosexuality in Twentieth-Century French Literature* (London: Cassell, 1995), p. 2.
14 A number of documents relating to this investigation are cited by Gilbert Joseph in his sensationalist *Une si douce Occupation*, pp. 199–222.
15 Olga Kosakievicz and Bianca Bienenfeld were similarly legally under age at the time of their relationships with Beauvoir. However, Olga's father defended Beauvoir in a letter to the officer investigating Mme Sorokine's complaint; see Joseph, pp. 213–14.
16 In 1946, Christopher Robinson notes that employment legislation which was passed stating that those who worked in the public sector must have 'good morals' was easy to use against lesbians, gay men and anyone considered to lead an 'immoral' lifestyle (see Robinson, *Scandal*, p. 3). By 1946, both Beauvoir and Sartre had given up teaching for writing, which was fortuitous because clearly they would have been affected by this legislation.
17 The critical neglect of Beauvoir's lesbian experiences may in part be attributed to their omission in her autobiography and Beauvoir's denial in interviews of having had sexual relationships with women. Several critics (Moi, Marks, Simons, Ferguson and Card, for example) do, however, consider Beauvoir's discussion of lesbianism in *Le Deuxième Sexe*.

18 Shari Benstock, *Women of the Left Bank 1900–1940* (London: Virago, 1987), p. 47.
19 For information on the lesbian community in Paris at the turn of the century, see Benstock, *Women of the Left Bank*, and van Casselaer, *Lot's Wife*.
20 Michel Foucault, *La Volonté de savoir, Histoire de la sexualité 1* (Paris: Gallimard, 1976), p. 137.
21 *Ibid.*, p. 139.
22 *Ibid.*, p. 143.
23 *Ibid.*, p. 159.
24 *Ibid.*, p. 193.
25 For surveys of the material produced by sexologists at the end of the nineteenth century and early twentieth century, see Jeffrey Weeks, *Sexuality and its Discontents, Meanings, Myths and Modern Sexualities* (London and New York: Routledge, 1985) Chapter 4, pp. 61–95 and Lilian Faderman, *Surpassing the Love of Men* (London: The Women's Press, 1985), pp. 239–53.
26 Noreen O'Connor and Joanna Ryan, *Wild Desires and Mistaken Identities, Lesbianism and Psychoanalysis* (London: Virago, 1993), p. 48.
27 Hélène V. Wenzel, 'Interview with Simone de Beauvoir', *Yale French Studies* 72, p. 7. This interview is published in English translation.
28 Judith Okely, *Simone de Beauvoir, a Re-Reading* (London: Virago, 1986), p. 72.
29 Alice Schwarzer, *Simone de Beauvoir Today* (London: Chatto and Windus, 1978), pp. 84–5.
30 *FCI*, pp. 135–6.
31 *Ibid.*, p. 136.
32 Ian Birchall has argued that Audry abandoned this project because of lack of time resulting from her 'frenetic political commitment' and notes the many political and philosophical discussions Beauvoir, Audry and Sartre were likely to have had together – particularly about Heidegger and German phenomenology – in the early 1930s, see Ian Birchall, 'Prequel to the Heidegger Debate, Audry and Sartre', *Radical Philosophy* 88 (1998), 19–27.
33 Richard Wright, 'How Bigger was Born', (New York: Harper Brothers, 1940) published in the restored edition of *Native Son* (New York: Harper Collins, 1993), p. 539. Wright's interest in the situation of women is rather paradoxical, however, given that in *Native Son*, *Black Boy* and *The Outsider* for example, women are portrayed very negatively – either as blind (literally or metaphorically) to the plight of the male protagonist, in the case of women within the family unit (Wright's mother, grandmother, Mrs Dalton, Bigger's mother, Cross's mother) or, in the case of Mary Dalton, Bessie Mears and Dot, as 'bodies' which threaten Bigger's and Cross's precarious situations as alienated black men in a racist society. In *Native Son*, the murders of Mary Dalton and Bessie Mears

cause Bigger's final downfall at the hands of the white supremacist patriarchy. Beauvoir's letters to Nelson Algren indicate her knowledge of the Wrights' troubled marriage and refers to Wrights' persistent pursuit of women (which does not indicate a very advanced understanding of sexual politics on Wright's part). See the abstracted versions of Beauvoir's letters to Algren (for example, 9 January 1952 and the following undated letter, probably written about the end of January 1952) in Lauren Pringle Delavers, 'An Annotated and Indexed Calendar and Abstract of the Ohio State University Collection of Simone de Beauvoir's Letters to Nelson Algren', Vols. i and ii (unpublished doctoral thesis, Ohio State University, 1985), pp. 473–4, rather than the *LNA*, from which these references to the Wrights' marriage are omitted.

34 According to Deirdre Bair, Sartre was involved with Dolores Ehrenreich between 1945–50, (see Bair, *Simone de Beauvoir*, pp. 300–4, p. 414). Beauvoir conducted an intense relationship with Algren from 1947–51 and continued to correspond with him after 1951 until their relationship foundered in the mid-1960s. This estrangement occurred because Algren objected to the fact that Beauvoir had used his letters and spoken openly about their relationship in *La Force des choses*, in an article in *Harper's* (December 1964), as well as in earlier slightly disguised accounts in *Les Mandarins* and *L'Amérique au jour le jour*.

35 In an interview with Michel Fabre, Wright's principal biographer, on 24 June, 1970, Beauvoir said that Sylvia Beach had introduced her to Wright's work in 1940 (Michel Fabre, 'An Interview with Simone de Beauvoir' in Michel Fabre, *The World of Richard Wright* (Jackson: University Press of Mississippi, 1985), pp. 253–5. I am grateful to Frank McMahon for alerting me to the existence of this interview.

36 In addition, Algren's *Never Come Morning* (New York: Harper Row, 1942) and *The Man with the Golden Arm* (New York: Doubleday, 1949) demonstrate certain interests and priorities shared by Beauvoir and Algren, such as the representation of the material aspects of oppression and the testimonial use of literature to represent the experience of that oppression. They held similar views on prostitution and on the notion of the individual as a product of irrepressible social forces, although Algren's social pessimism and commitment (at great personal cost) to representing the experience of terminal social outcasts was not shared by Beauvoir. Algren was not a supporter of feminism yet consistently prioritised the theme of social injustice in his writing.

37 See Sylvie Le Bon's comments on this correspondence in my 'Entretien avec Sylvie Le Bon de Beauvoir' in *Simone de Beauvoir Studies* 12 (1995), 10–16 (pp. 13–14).

38 Cf. the account of *Le Deuxième Sexe* given in *FCI*, pp. 257–68.

39 *LNA*, p. 40.

40 *LNA*, p. 119.

41 Margaret Simons, 'The Second Sex: From Marxism to Radical

Feminism' in *Feminist Interpretations of Simone de Beauvoir*, p. 247; Alva Myrdal, 'A Parallel to the Negro Problem' in Gunnar Myrdal, *An American Dilemma, Vol. II, The Negro Social Structure* (New York: McGraw-Hill, 1964), pp. 1073–8.

42  *AJLJ*, p. 233–4.

43  *Le DSI*, p. 25.

44  Margaret Atack, 'Writing from the centre: ironies of otherness and marginality', in Evans (ed.) *Simone de Beauvoir's The Second Sex, New Interdisciplinary Essays*, pp. 31–58 (pp. 41–2).

45  *AJLJ*, pp. 231–2.

46  *Ibid.*, p. 231; Myrdal argued that black culture was a 'pathological condition' of American culture, which emerged in reaction to white racism – a view that was rejected by Ralph Ellison in a 1944 review and by black nationalists in the 1960s, see David W. Southern, *Gunnar Myrdal and Black-White Relations, The Use and Abuse of An American Dilemma, 1944–69* (Baton Rouge and London: Louisiana State University Press, 1987), pp. 67–8 and p. 94.

47  Southern, *Gunnar Myrdal*, pp. 44–5.

48  *LNA*, p. 141 and p. 169 respectively. *Native Son* (1940) is a novel about Bigger Thomas, a young black living in Chicago who goes to work as a chauffeur for a millionaire who has a philanthropic interest in the plight of the black population. Thomas accidently kills his boss's daughter and then incriminates her Communist boyfriend because he has heard that Communists are evil. He inveigles his girlfriend into blackmailing the millionaire, and then feels obliged to kill her to prevent her from talking. He is arrested and sentenced to death, realising he is being punished for the murder of the white woman, while the black woman's death is 'merely evidence' (p. 383). *Black Boy* (1945) is an autobiographical account of the first nineteen years of Richard Wright's life, growing up in the southern states of America. Both texts examine the material and psychological impact of oppression. It is significant in terms of Beauvoir's work and friendship with Wright that, from 1941, Wright was increasingly interested in the psychoanalytical dimensions of oppression (Richard Wright, *Native Son*, New York: Harper Collins, 1993, Chronology pp. 556–57). There has been little critical interest in looking at Wright's work on black identity in relation to Beauvoir's work, and this angle is briefly considered in this chapter.

49  Beauvoir told Michel Fabre that she and Wright were especially close between 1947–55 (see Fabre, 'An Interview with Simone de Beauvoir', in *The World of Richard Wright*, p. 254); Ellen Wright was also Beauvoir's literary agent, see Bair, *Simone de Beauvoir*, p. 389.

50  *AJLJ*, p. 234, p. 236 and p. 241; *Le DSII*, p. 47 and p. 540.

51  Interestingly, reviewers of Wright's autobiography, *Black Boy*, hailed it as 'a supplement to the Myrdal report', see Southern, *Gunnar Myrdal*, p. 108.

52 *LNA*, p. 182.

53 *LNA*, p. 210.

54 *LNA*, pp. 213–14.

55 In *FCI*, Beauvoir discusses the safety problems women faced in Tunisia, with an account of her visit there in 1946, which includes a reference to herself being attacked (*FCI*, p. 83).

56 *LNA*, pp. 229–30.

57 *LNA*, p. 230.

58 *LNA*, p. 239.

59 Kinsey described male sexual activity rather bizarrely as 'sexual outlets' (perhaps because he was a zoologist, like H.M. Parshley, the US translator of *Le Deuxième Sexe*) and noted that men reached a sexual peak in adolescence. He also showed that men were more easily psychologically conditioned to respond sexually than women and that 37 per cent of men had had a homosexual experience, which he demonstrated using a continuum method of measuring sexual experience. In general, men reported greater sexual activity and satisfaction than women. The Kinsey reports were groundbreaking in the late 1940s and 1950s because they demonstrated the wide range of human sexual activities which existed and because, as Jeffrey Weeks has observed, Kinsey abstained from moral judgements on sexuality. Kinsey's *Sexual Behaviour in the Human Female* was published in 1953, and argued that women's sexuality functioned differently, stressing its clitoral dimension. He also argued that lesbian experience was far more widespread than previously assumed, and questioned the notion of heterosexuality as the only 'normal' sexual behaviour. According to Kinsey's research, women experienced a sexual peak in their late twenties which was maintained until their fifties. Religion was the most important factor in inhibiting women's sexuality whereas for men it was negligible. Cultural attitudes also influenced the expression of female sexuality. This information on the Kinsey reports is taken from John Archer and Barbara Lloyd, *Sex and Gender* (Harmondsworth: Penguin, 1982), pp. 81–3.

60 Curiously, Beauvoir did not read Margaret Mead's *Male and Female*, which came out in 1949, although Mead had used the research in lectures in 1946. She did, however, share a platform with Mead in Paris on 3 February, 1950 to debate gender; Mead was also a member of the panel who reviewed *Le Deuxième Sexe* for *The Saturday Review of Literature* (see Bair, *Simone de Beauvoir*, p. 418 and p. 438). Although Mead's work is heavily criticised today, Jeffrey Weeks has praised it for highlighting the cultural relativity of Western sexual behaviour and questioning received beliefs about sexuality (see Weeks, *Sexuality and its Discontents*, pp. 104–8). Betty Friedan has also described Mead as 'the most powerful influence on modern women, in terms of both functionalism and the feminine protest' and says that Mead had a profound effect on three generations

of women; see Betty Friedan, *The Feminine Mystique* (Harmondsworth: Penguin, 1979), p. 120.

61 Emmanuel Levinas, *Le Temps et l'Autre* originally published in Jean Wahl (ed.) *Le Choix – Le Monde – l'Existence* (Grenoble-Paris: Arthaud, 1947); *Le DSI*, p. 15. As regards Beauvoir's criticisms of Levinas's masculinist perspective, Seán Hand has argued that Levinas 'emphasizes the formal and cultural nature of the difference between the sexes' and questions Beauvoir's assertion that Levinas attributes a secondary derivative status to woman because 'the Other has a priority over the subject' in Levinas's philosophy; see Seán Hand (ed.) *The Levinas Reader* (Oxford: Blackwell, 1989), p. 38 and p. 57. Despite their different views of the relation between gender and alterity, Beauvoir's and Levinas's respective critiques of existentialism were nevertheless somewhat similar because, like Beauvoir, Levinas criticised phenomenology on the grounds that it attributed too much importance to ontology, at the expense of ethics and the primordial relationship of responsibility between self and Other.

62 *Le DSI*, p. 25.

63 Le Doeuff, 'Simone de Beauvoir: les ambiguïtés d'un ralliement', p. 58; according to the *Journal de guerre*, Beauvoir began reading *Phenomenology of Spirit* on 6 July 1940; see *JG*, pp. 339–40 (this diary entry also appears in abbreviated form in *FA*, pp. 523–4).

64 *LSII* (Paris: Gallimard, 1990), p. 155.

65 Sartre and Beauvoir also draw on Husserl's concept of 'intentionality' (which Husserl originally derived from Brentano), according to which consciousness is always of something and is directed towards objects in the world, see Laurie Spurling, *Phenomenology and the Social World*, pp. 16–21.

66 See 'Independence and Dependence of Self-Consciousness: Lordship and Bondage' in Hegel's *Phenomenology of Spirit*, pp. 111–19.

67 Kruks, 'Gender and Subjectivity', p. 97.

68 See Lundgren-Gothlin's Chapter 4, 'The Master-Slave Dialectic in *The Second Sex*' in *Sex and Existence*, pp. 67–82.

69 *Le DSI*, p. 232.

70 *Ibid.*, p. 72.

71 *Le DSI*, p. 19.

72 Elaine Hoffman Baruch, 'Simone de Beauvoir: Feminism and Biology', unpublished paper given at colloquium on Simone de Beauvoir at Columbia University, New York, 4–6 April 1985. I am grateful to Margaret Crosland for making this available to me.

73 *Le DSI*, p. 75.

74 The intellectual proximity of Beauvoir and Merleau-Ponty concerning their respective accounts of the body is increasingly recognised, for example by Kruks, Moi, Bergoffen and Vintges.

75 Sonia Kruks, 'Simone de Beauvoir: Teaching Sartre about Freedom',

p. 287; Moi, *Simone de Beauvoir, The Making of an Intellectual Woman*, pp. 169–70; Simone de Beauvoir, 'La Phénoménologie de la perception', *Les Temps modernes* 2 (1945), 363–67.

76 Beauvoir, 'La Phénoménologie de la perception', p. 364.

77 See Kruks, 'Simone de Beauvoir: Teaching Sartre about Freedom', p. 287.

78 Sartre, *EN*, p. 366.

79 Maurice Merleau-Ponty, *Phénoménologie de la perception* (Paris: Gallimard, 1945), collection 'tel', 1994, p. 97.

80 Merleau-Ponty, *Phénoménologie*, p. 162.

81 As Toril Moi has noted, from 1945–52 Merleau-Ponty was Beauvoir's and Sartre's closest collaborator, and 'in the politically beleaguered position in which the existentialists found themselves at this time, she would be unlikely to signal any kind of public disagreement with him'; see Moi, *Simone de Beauvoir*, p. 283n. Nevertheless, Beauvoir seemed unwilling to acknowledge any intellectual proximity with Merleau-Ponty either.

82 Bair, *Simone de Beauvoir*, pp. 152–3; in her letter to Nelson Algren of 11 December 1947, Beauvoir describes Merleau-Ponty as: 'un vieil ami, mon plus vieil ami, je le connais depuis vingt ans, il travaille dur avec nous aux *T.M.*, à la radio, partout. Comme personne, je ne l'aime pas trop, je vous expliquerai pourquoi au printemps'; Sylvie le Bon de Beauvoir adds in an Editor's note that Beauvoir primarily blamed Merleau-Ponty for Zaza's death at that time, *LNA*, p. 123.

83 *Le DS1*, p. 66.

84 *Ibid.*, p. 165.

85 Charlene Haddock Seigfried, 'Second Sex: Second Thoughts', in al-Hibri and Simons (eds.) *Hypatia Reborn, Essays in Feminist Philosophy*, p. 319.

86 Elizabeth Fallaize, 'A Saraband of Imagery: the uses of biological science in *The Second Sex*' in *The Existential Phenomenology of Simone de Beauvoir* (Boston and London: Kluwer Academic Publishers) (forthcoming).

87 Bergoffen, *The Philosophy of Simone de Beauvoir*, p. 21.

88 Moi, *Simone de Beauvoir, The Making of an Intellectual Woman*, p. 280n.

89 *Le DS1*, pp. 82–4.

90 See *EN*, pp. 283–4, where Sartre discusses these terms used by Heidegger in *Being and Time* to describe human reality.

91 Sartre, 'Sartre par Sartre', *Situations IX* (Paris: Gallimard, 1972), p. 105.

92 *Ibid.*, pp. 106–7.

93 'Simone de Beauvoir, féministe', une entrevue de Hélène Pedneault et Marie Sabourin, *La Vie en rose* (March 1984), p. 34.

94 Jacques Lacan, *Les Complexes familiaux dans la formation de l'individu: essai d'analyse d'une fonction en psychologie*, 1938 (Paris: Navarin, 1984); Havelock Ellis, *Studies in the Psychology of Sex* (Philadelphia: F. A. Davis, 1897–1928);

Helene Deutsch, *The Psychology of Women* (New York: Grune and Stratton, 1944).

95  Sartre, *Les Mots* (Paris: Gallimard, 1964), Folio 1990, pp. 86–7.

96  *Le DSI*, p. 17.

97  *Le DSII*, p. 17; Maurice Sachs, *Le Sabbat* (Paris: Gallimard, 1960), p. 26.

98  *Le DSII*, p. 38, and *Phénoménologie de la perception*, especially pp. 291–4.

99  *Le DSII*, p. 34.

100  See p. 193 and 'L'Espace', the second chapter of Part Two in Merleau-Ponty's *Phénoménologie de la perception*.

101  Merleau-Ponty, *Phénoménologie*, pp. 339–40.

102  *L'Invitée* (pp. 215–17), where Françoise experiences a crisis of identity at Sacré-Coeur; *Le Sang des autres* (p. 132), where Hélène is at the zoo with Jean and recalls earlier, discontented times when she used to come there alone and look out over Paris. The issue in the latter text is whether she will abdicate her sense of identity to Jean. On p. 144 of *Le Sang des autres*, Jean and Marcel look out over Paris towards Sacré-Coeur discussing their respective relationships and the effects of their behaviour on Hélène and Denise. Lastly, in *Les Belles Images* (p. 177), Laurence observes Sacré-Coeur from the restaurant terrace where she takes her mother after the latter has been left by Gilbert for a younger woman. In all these extracts, Sacré-Coeur seems to represent the constraints of the traditional female role, exemplified by the pious, self-sacrificing life of Françoise de Beauvoir, which Beauvoir rejected. Sacré-Coeur may therefore be viewed as a maternal symbol in Beauvoir's work, which at times she is able to resignify, so that the female protagonist assumes a vantage point from which Sacré-Coeur is absent. In her article, 'The City and the Female Autograph', Alex Hughes considers the issue of gender and spatiality in the context of the presence of Paris in Beauvoir's and Leduc's autobiographical writings. However, she argues that in Beauvoir's case, the city is predominantly gendered male, whereas I argue here that certain sectors of the city, such as Sacré-Coeur, can be read as female, see Hughes, 'The City and the Female Autograph' in Sheringham (ed.) *Parisian Fields*, (London: Reaktion, 1995), pp. 115–32.

103  *FA*, pp. 49–50; this passage is analysed in Chapter 6.

104  *FA*, p. 104.

105  *Le DSII*, p. 133.

106  Lundgren-Gothlin, *Sex and Existence*, pp. 207–10 and Moi, *Simone de Beauvoir, The Making of an Intellectual Woman*, p. 168; Margaret Atack argues that although one might deplore Beauvoir's representation of heterosexuality as an encounter between an active male and a passive female, it is important to note that Beauvoir is describing sexuality rather than female ontology and that the experience of passivity and shame can be shared by men in their experience of their sexuality, see Atack, 'Writing from the Centre: Ironies of Otherness and Margin-

ality', in Ruth Evans (ed.), Simone de Beavoir, *The Second Sex, New Interdisciplinary Readings* (MUP, 1998), pp. 31–58.

107 Judith Butler has noted the heterosexism of Merleau-Ponty's account of sexuality in *Phénoménologie de la perception*, arguing that he does not address gender sufficiently in his account and therefore genders the subject as male. The same charge has been levelled at Sartre's *L'Etre et le néant*, which is perhaps more actively misogynistic than Merleau-Ponty's *Phénoménologie*, see Judith Butler, 'Sexual Ideology and Phenomenological Description, A Feminist Critique of Merleau-Ponty's *Phenomenology of Perception*', in Jeffner Allen and Iris Marion Young (eds.) *The Thinking Muse, Feminism in Modern French Philosophy* (Bloomington and Indianapolis: Indiana University Press, 1989), pp. 85–100.

108 *Le DSII*, p.172.

109 *Le DSII*, p.173.

110 Ann Ferguson has noted that Beauvoir's notion of a continuum of female sexuality is developed by Adrienne Rich in her groundbreaking essay, 'Compulsory Heterosexuality and Lesbian Existence', see Ferguson, 'Lesbian Identity, Beauvoir and History' in al-Hibri and Simons (eds.) *Hypatia Reborn, Essays in Feminist Philosophy*, p. 281. In this essay Rich addresses a number of issues which are still pertinent: the marginalisation of lesbian existence in feminist theory and patriarchy's enforced heterosexualisation of women as a key site of control (heterosexuality as a political institution). She argues firstly for the reconceptualisation of the clinical term 'lesbianism' as 'lesbian existence', which embraces the historical presence of lesbians and the ongoing elaboration of lesbian existence. Secondly, she proposes the notion of a lesbian continuum which would include a wide range of woman-identified experience; see Rich, 'Compulsory Heterosexuality and Lesbian Existence', *Signs: Journal of Women in Culture and Society* 5, no.4 (1980), 631–60.

111 Foucault, *La Volonté de savoir*, pp. 55–9.

112 Moi, *Simone de Beauvoir*, pp. 199–203.

113 *Ibid.*, p. 203.

114 Ferguson, 'Lesbian Identity', p. 285.

115 Denise Warren, 'Beauvoir on Bardot: The Ambiguity Syndrome', *Dalhousie French Studies* 13 (1987), p. 40.

116 Foucault, 'Vérité et Pouvoir', p. 21.

## 3 NARRATIVES OF SELF-REPRESENTATION

1 Kate Millett, address to Simone de Beauvoir colloquium held at Columbia University, New York, April 4–6, 1985. A later version of this paper appeared in Elaine Marks (ed.) *Critical Essays on Simone de Beauvoir* (Boston: G.K. Hall, 1987), pp. 200–6.

2 In addition to Colette, Clara Malraux and Violette Leduc, one might

also mention Edith Thomas, whose journals were published in 1995; however, the scope of Beauvoir's project is considerably greater.

3 Jerry Aline Flieger, *Colette and the Fantom Subject of Autobiography* (Ithaca and London: Cornell University Press, 1992), p. 2.

4 Flieger uses these categories in *Colette and the Fantom Subject of Auto-biography*, p. 4.

5 Elaine Marks, 'I Am My Own Heroine: Some Thoughts About Women and Autobiography In France', in Sidonie Cassirer (ed.) *Female Studies IX: Teaching about Women in the Foreign Languages* (New York: Feminine Press, 1975), pp. 1–10 (pp. 3–4).

6 In *Le Pacte autobiographique*, Philippe Lejeune asserts that 'le sujet profond de l'autobiographie, c'est le nom propre' and that 'il est impossible que la vocation autobiographique et la passion de l'ano-nymat coexistent dans le même être'. Although Lejeune retracts these trenchant observations in *Moi aussi*, he does not address the relationship between naming, ideology and the representation of marginalised identities in autobiography, see Lejeune, *Le Pacte autobiographique* (Paris: Seuil, 1975), p. 28.

7 Louis Althusser, 'Ideology and Ideological State Apparatuses', in *Lenin and Philosophy and Other Essays*, trans. Ben Brewster (New York: Monthly Review Press, 1971), pp. 127–186; for an interesting analysis of the limitations of Althusserian interpellation, see Judith Butler, *Excitable Speech, A Politics of the Performative* (London and New York: Routledge, 1997).

8 I adapt here in the context of autobiography Judith Butler's interesting analysis of hate speech and the subject's potential reworking of the trauma of Althusserian interpellation; see Judith Butler, *Excitable Speech*, pp. 24–38, (pp. 32–4).

9 See Bair, *Simone de Beauvoir*, pp. 300–1, and p. 293, p. 641n. respectively.

10 This is an example of an ideological disciplining of identity, which was common during the Second World War. In a comparative article on the wartime writing of Beauvoir and Edith Thomas, Dorothy Kaufmann notes that Thomas refers in her diary to a number of false declarations she made about her identity which enabled her to work and to travel during wartime. Thomas notes that an official who administered these oaths joked with her about 'tous les faux serments qu'on fait journelle-ment dans cette pièce', which suggests that false declarations were frequent during the Second World War and that Beauvoir's declaration that she was not Jewish was not unusual, see Dorothy Kaufmann, 'Resistance and Survival: Edith Thomas: Simone de Beauvoir's Shadow Sister', *Simone de Beauvoir Studies* 12 (1995), pp. 35–6.

11 *PC*, p. 341.

12 *Simone de Beauvoir*, un film de Josée Dayan et Malka Ribowska (Paris: Gallimard, 1979), p. 17.

13 Nancy Miller, 'Writing Fictions: Women's Autobiography in France' in

Bella Brodzki and Celeste Schenck (eds.), *Life/Lines: Theorizing Women's Autobiography*, pp. 45–61 (p. 56).

14 *Ibid.*, pp. 59–60.

15 Leigh Gilmore, *Autobiographics; A Feminist Theory of Women's Self-Represen-tation* (Ithaca and London: Cornell University Press, 1994), p. xiii-xiv.

16 The coining of new terms to describe the textual variations of auto-biographical writing demonstrates the plurality of recent approaches. The terms 'nouvelle autobiographie', coined by Alain Robbe-Grillet, 'anti-autobiographie' coined by Germaine Brée and Serge Doubrovs-ky's 'autofiction' coined in response to his 'novel', *Fils* (1977) are recent examples.

17 'Witness to a Century' is the title of the edition of *Yale French Studies* 72 (1986), devoted to Beauvoir.

18 Sartre, 'Autoportrait à soixante-dix ans', in *Situations X* (Paris: Galli-mard, 1976), pp. 133–226 (p. 146).

19 In 'Les Enfances de Sartre' in *Moi aussi*, in his survey of Sartre's autobiographical trajectory, Philippe Lejeune describes *Les Mots* as 'un moment dans une entreprise autobiographique qui est coextensive à la vie de Sartre', Lejeune, *Moi aussi*, pp. 117–63 (p. 117). Although Sartre's autobiographical activity should indeed not be defined narrowly, the point made here is that Beauvoir's autobiographical project, in its vast scope, is an intentional attempt to write the self and the life and is, therefore, quite different to Sartre's autobiographical project; Vintges similarly describes Beauvoir's autobiography as 'the core of her oeuvre', whereas in *Les Mots*, Sartre sought 'to unmask systematically and demolish completely the young Poulou he once was', in *Philosophy as Passion*, p. 88.

20 Mary Warnock, *Memory* (London: Faber and Faber, 1987), p. 114–15.

21 Mary Evans has also noted the differential scopes of Beauvoir's and Sartre's autobiographical projects, although I question her assertion that Beauvoir neatly falls into the gendered behaviour of allowing Sartre to dominate her memoirs while the converse is not the case, because Sartre had not even met Beauvoir or many other people who would have significance in his later life by the time *Les Mots* ends and therefore they would not feature in his autobiography; moreover, Beauvoir's and Sartre's autobiographical methodologies are signifi-cantly different; see Evans, *Simone de Beauvoir* (London: Sage, 1996), p. 41.

22 *CDA*, p. 293.

23 Lejeune, *Le Pacte autobiographique*, pp. 207–9.

24 See for example, Mona Tobin Houston,'The Sartre of Madame de Beauvoir', *Yale French Studies* 30 (1962–63), 23–9 and Robert Kanters, 'De Sartre à de Beauvoir', *Le Figaro Littéraire* (23–29 January, 1964), p. 4.

25 For example, in the 'Prologue' to *La Force de l'âge*, Beauvoir says: 'Ma vie a été étroitement liée à celle de Jean-Paul Sartre; mais son histoire, il

compte la raconter lui-même, et je lui abandonne ce soin. Je n'étudierai ses idées, ses travaux, je ne parlerai de lui que dans la mesure où il est intervenu dans mon existence.'

26 *CDA*, p. 274

27 *CDA*, pp. 274–7.

28 *CDA*, p. 230.

29 Sheringham, *French Autobiography*, p. vii.

30 In *Qu'est-ce que la littérature?*, Sartre similarly talks of the relationship between the writer, the reader and the act of reading, although in her 1966 lecture in Japan, Beauvoir discusses the collaborative relationship between author and reader in the context of the representation of temporal experience in autobiography and thus, it is symptomatic of a much wider problem for her, (namely the subject's experience of time and temporal succession), cf. Sartre, *Qu'est-ce que la littérature?* (Paris: Gallimard, 1948) Folio, 1993, pp. 48–58.

31 'Mon expérience d'écrivain', in Francis and Gontier (eds.) *Les Ecrits de Simone de Beauvoir*, pp. 453–4.

32 'L'Existentialisme et la sagesse des nations' in *L'Existentialisme et la sagesse des nations* (Paris: Nagel, 1986), pp. 35–6.

33 Warnock, *Memory*, p. 138.

34 *La Nausée* (Paris: Gallimard, 1938), 1968 edn, pp. 117–33, especially pp. 118–19.

35 *La Vieillesse*, p. 389. The reference to 'les monuments funèbres' is a reference to Chateaubriand's *Mémoires d'outre-tombe* (1849–50).

36 In addition to explaining her use of a chronological autobiographical methodology in the memoirs, Beauvoir also discussed the disadvantages of her method with Francis Jeanson in one of two interviews in 1965, see Jeanson, *Simone de Beauvoir ou l'entreprise de vivre*, p. 294.

37 This refers to the temporally situated individual whose life assumes purpose through action, although the meaning of that life is always deferred until death. Sartre explains this in *L'Etre et le néant*, p. 185:

'Cette totalité n'est jamais achevée, elle est totalité qui se refuse et qui se fuit, elle est arrachement à soi dans l'unité d'un même surgissement, totalité insaisissable qui, au moment où elle se donne, est déjà par delà ce don de soi. Ainsi le temps de la conscience, c'est la réalité-humaine qui se temporalise comme totalité qui est à elle-même son propre inachèvement, c'est le néant se glissant dans une totalité comme ferment détotalisateur'.

38 Exceptions include Chantal Moubachir who briefly explores Beauvoir's notion of time in *Simone de Beauvoir* (Paris: Seghers, 1971), and a recent study which addresses the thematic of time and the transcendent in Beauvoir's writing, see Betty Halpern-Guedj, *Le Temps et le transcendant dans l'oeuvre de Simone de Beauvoir* (Tübingen: Gunter Narr Verlag, 1997).

39 Beauvoir examines the role of memory and our changing perception of time in the context of ageing in 'Temps, activité, histoire' in *La Vieillesse*, pp. 383–471.

40 *MJFR*, p. 287.
41 As far as I can ascertain, unlike Merleau-Ponty, Beauvoir did not attend Husserl's lectures in Paris in February 1929 and does not mention them in her memoirs. According to these memoirs and to her biographer, Deirdre Bair, Beauvoir had 'flu which developed into a severe bronchial infection in February which obliged her to curtail her teaching practice at the Lycée Janson-de-Sailly begun in January 1929, so illness probably prevented her from attending. However, as she was close friends with Merleau-Ponty at this time and was on teaching practice with him and Claude Lévi-Strauss, it is very likely that she talked about Husserl's 1929 Paris lectures with Merleau-Ponty (who appears both as Pradelle and Merleau-Ponty in *Mémoires d'une jeune fille rangée*), see *MJFR*, p. 411 and p. 425 and Bair, *Simone de Beauvoir, A Biography*, p. 136–7.
42 *FA*, p. 157.
43 *Ibid.*, p. 231.
44 *Ibid.*, p. 220.
45 Beauvoir's reading of Heidegger is mentioned in *FA*, p. 93, p. 404 and p. 538.
46 Heidegger's theory of time can be found in Sections 65, 68 and 80–1, and more generally throughout his account of 'Dasein' in *Being and Time*, trans. J. Macquarrie and Edward Robinson (New York: Harper and Row, 1962).
47 Beauvoir's interest in temporality has been largely interpreted by critics as constituting evidence of her personal inability to cope with the process of ageing and death. While this preoccupation occurs in her writing, here I argue that Beauvoir had a philosophical interest in temporality which is evident in both her literary and philosophical writing. To reduce this interest uniquely to what is claimed to be Beauvoir's personal obsession with mortality seems to me to be another instance of the topos of 'reducing the book to the woman' identified by Toril Moi in her survey of clichés in the reception of Beauvoir's writing, although in this particular case, it is a question of 'reducing the philosophy' to a personal obsession with ageing and mortality, see Moi, 'Politics and the Intellectual Woman: Clichés in the Reception of Simone de Beauvoir' in *Feminist Theory and Simone de Beauvoir*, pp. 21–60 (pp. 27–33). In Sartre's fiction, plays and philosophy of the late 1930s and of the 1940s we find a similar interest in temporally-situated subjectivity, yet this interest is not deemed as constituting evidence of Sartre's personal inability to cope with the ageing process.
48 Kate and Edward Fullbrook, *Simone de Beauvoir and Jean-Paul Sartre: The Remaking of a Twentieth Century Legend*, pp. 118–20; I have also discussed the role of time in Beauvoir's writing in 'For the Time Being: Simone de Beauvoir's Representation of Temporality' in *The Existential Phenomenology of Simone de Beauvoir* (Norwell, MA and Dordrecht, The Netherlands: Kluwer Academic Publishers) (forthcoming).

49 *L'Invitée*, p. 70, cited also by Fullbrooks, *Beauvoir and Sartre*, p. 118.
50 *PC*, p. 317.
51 Chantal Moubachir, *Simone de Beauvoir* (Paris: Seghers, 1971), pp. 42–7.
52 Edmund Husserl, *The Phenomenology of Internal Time-Consciousness*, ed. by Martin Heidegger (Bloomington and London: Indiana University Press, 1964).
53 Husserl, *PIT-C*, 14, p. 57.
54 Husserl, *PIT-C*, 14, p. 58.
55 *Ibid.*
56 Merleau-Ponty, *Phenomenology of Perception*, pp. 139–40.
57 *Ibid.*, p. 82.
58 In Kafka's short story 'In the Penal Colony', the condemned prisoner is executed by having the commandment which he has transgressed inscribed on his body and which, during a twelve-hour period, he deciphers through the wounds sustained. Franz Kafka, 'In the Penal Colony' in *The Transformation and Other Stories*, trans. Malcolm Pasley, (Harmondsworth: Penguin, 1992) pp. 127–53.
59 *FCII*, pp. 505–6.
60 See especially the sections concerning 'le contrôle de l'activité' and 'l'organisation des genèses' in 'Les Corps dociles' in the third part of Foucault's *Surveiller et Punir* (Paris: Gallimard 'tel', 1995), pp. 175–90.
61 *MJFR*, pp. 91–2.
62 *MJFR*, p. 93.
63 *La Vieillesse*, p. 383.
64 Moubachir, *Simone de Beauvoir*, pp. 50–1.
65 'Curator' and 'conservative' are expressed by the same word 'conservateur' in French; PMA, p. 128.
66 *PC*, p. 134.
67 This is a central dilemma in both *Le Sang des autres* and Sartre's *Les Mains sales*.
68 Marks, 'I am My Own Heroine', p. 5.
69 Idt, 'Simone de Beauvoir's *Adieux*: A Funeral Rite and a Literary Challenge' in Ronald Aronson and Adrian Van den Hoven (eds.) *Sartre Alive* (Detroit: Wayne State University Press, 1991), pp. 363–84 (p. 368).
70 *FCI*, p. 367.
71 Søren Kierkegaard, *The Diary of Søren Kierkegaard*, ed. Peter Rohde (New York: Philosophical Library, 1960), p. 111.
72 Jacques Derrida, 'La Structure, le signe et le jeu dans le discours des sciences humaines' in *L'Ecriture et la différence* (Paris: Seuil, 1967), pp. 409–28 (p. 423–4). Mark Freeman discusses Derrida's notion of totalisation in relation to the production of narrative in *Rewriting the Self, History, Memory and Narrative* (London: Routledge, 1993), pp. 10–11.
73 Sartre, *La Nausée*, p. 62.
74 This dilemma is at the heart of the disagreement between Sartre and

Beauvoir at Saint-Cloud over the relationship between language and experience, which is examined in Chapter Six.

75 Mannoni, 'Relation d'un sujet à sa propre vie', p. 60.

76 Beauvoir comments on the charges of narcissism in relation to her autobiography on several occasions, for example, in an interview with Jeanson in 1965, see Jeanson, *Simone de Beauvoir ou l'entreprise de vivre*, p. 294.

77 Moi, *Simone de Beauvoir, The Making of an Intellectual Woman*, pp. 80–1.

78 Domna C. Stanton, 'Autogynography: Is the Subject Different?' in Domna Stanton (ed.) *The Female Autograph* (University of Chicago Press, 1984), pp. 4–5.

79 John Taylor, 'Psychasthenia in *La Nausée*', *Sartre Studies International* 1/2 (1995), 77–93.

80 *Ibid.*, p. 81.

81 There are several references to Janet's *L'Obsession et la psychasthénie* (1903) in the second volume of *Le Deuxième sexe*, for example, p. 65, p. 249, p. 287, p. 423 and p. 551. However, given Beauvoir's lifelong interest in psychology and Sartre's engagement with Janet's work, it is very likely that she had read Janet's *L'Evolution de la mémoire et de la notion du temps* (1928).

82 Sheringham, *French Autobiography*, pp. 23–7; this account of 'identité narrative' is taken from Paul Ricoeur, *Temps et récit III: Le Temps raconté* (Paris: Seuil, 1985), and 'Life in Quest of Narrative' and 'Narrative Identity' in David Wood (ed.) *On Paul Ricoeur: Narrative and Interpretation* (London: Routledge, 1991), pp. 20–33 and pp. 188–99.

83 In their recent *Simone de Beauvoir: A Critical Introduction*, Kate and Edward Fullbrook similarly suggest the notion of a 'narrative self', recognising it as a key concept in Beauvoir's writing, although they refer to it only in the context of *Quand prime le spirituel* and the two originally unpublished chapters from *L'Invitée* (later published in Francis and Gontier's *Les Ecrits de Simone de Beauvoir*); in this chapter, I argue that not only was narrative crucial to the construction of identity for Beauvoir, but that it was a linchpin in her testimonial autobiographical project, and am thereby developing this notion (at which the Fullbrooks and I arrived quite separately) in a different direction, see Fullbrooks, *Simone de Beauvoir: A Critical Introduction*, pp. 63–7.

84 Paul Ricoeur, from an unpublished text on 'la souffrance', cited in Olivier Mongin, *Paul Ricoeur* (Paris: Seuil, 1994), p. 130.

85 Paul Ricoeur, *Soi-même comme un autre* (Paris: Seuil, 1990), p. 195.

86 *MJFR*, p. 195.

87 *FA*, p. 418.

88 Ricoeur, 'Discussion: Ricoeur on Narrative' in *On Paul Ricoeur*, p. 186; see also, *Testimony*, p. 201; Beauvoir refers briefly to discussions in the Sartre-Beauvoir entourage concerning Faurisson's revisionist views on the Holocaust in *CDA*, p.153n.

89  Ricoeur, 'Life in Quest of Narrative' in *On Paul Ricoeur*, p. 32.
90  See Butler, *Excitable Speech*, pp. 24–38.

4 NEGOTIATING AUTOBIOGRAPHY

  1  Jane Heath has discussed certain passages in Beauvoir's autobiography
     which function as meta-narratives to the main narrative and her
     reading has been helpful in developing this analysis. However, her
     gendering of Beauvoir's narrative and meta-narrative voices seems
     reductively essentialist and in her reading, there also appears to be a
     veiled antipathy to Beauvoir's project of testimonial autobiography and
     a lack of engagement with its political and philosophical dimensions,
     see Heath, *Simone de Beauvoir*, pp. 47–86.
  2  For example, Heath, *Simone de Beauvoir* and Hewitt, *Autobiographical
     Tightropes* among others.
  3  *LNA*, p. 575.
  4  For an account of the reception of *Le Deuxième Sexe*, see Beauvoir's own
     account in *FCI*, pp. 257–68; Moi, *Simone de Beauvoir, The Making of an
     Intellectual Woman*, pp. 179–85; Lundgren-Gothlin, *Sex and Existence*,
     pp. 244–46 and Joy Bennett and Gabriella Hochmann's useful *Simone de
     Beauvoir: An Annotated Bibliography* (New York and London: Garland
     Publishing, 1988), pp. 348–80.
  5  Lejeune, *L'Autobiographie en France*, pp. 79–80.
  6  Hewitt, *Autobiographical Tightropes*, p. 28.
  7  *MJFR*, p. 195.
  8  Marylea MacDonald, 'Le Pacte autobiographique dans les *Mémoires* de
     Simone de Beauvoir', *Simone de Beauvoir Studies* 9 (1992), 75–9 (p. 76).
  9  *Ibid.*, p. 76.
 10  Marylea MacDonald, '"For Example": Simone de Beauvoir's Par-
     enthetical Presence in Philippe Lejeune's Theory of Autobiography',
     *Simone de Beauvoir Studies* 10 (1993), 237–40.
 11  *FA*, p. 11.
 12  Idt, 'Simone de Beauvoir's *Adieux*', p. 365.
 13  *FA*, p. 13.
 14  Beauvoir's remarks here recall Rousseau's complex view of truth in the
     *Confessions*, which he developed further in the fourth promenade of *Les
     Rêveries du Promeneur solitaire* (1782), where he distinguishes between 'la
     vérité générale et abstraite' (the most valuable),'la vérité particulière et
     individuelle' (of variable value) and 'les vérités qui n'ont aucune sorte
     d'utilité ni pour l'instruction ni dans la pratique'; see Jean-Jacques
     Rousseau, *Les Rêveries du Promeneur solitaire* in *Oeuvres complètes*, tome I
     (Paris: Gallimard Pléiade, 1959), pp. 1026–27.
 15  *FA*, p. 413.
 16  Sartre explained this in *La Transcendance de l'Ego*, (Paris: Librairie
     philosophique J.Vrin, 1988), originally published in *Recherches philoso-*

*phiques* in 1936. He argues against the view that the ego is an inhabitant of consciousness and attempts to explain the relationship between the ego, the psyche and consciousness. Consciousness is an immediately apprehensible entity, whereas the psyche is a collection of phenomena which are not readily accessible to us. My ego, however, exists as a recognisable phenomenon for me in the same way it exists for anyone else. My ego is not within me, but in the world. See *FA*, pp. 210–11 and Peter Caws, *Sartre* (London: Routledge, 1979), especially the chapter on 'Consciousness and Subjectivity', pp. 50–61.

17  *FA*, p. 419.

18  See *EN*, pp. 18–19 and pp. 112–13.

19  *FA*, p. 694.

20  *Ibid.*, p. 33.

21  Heath, *Simone de Beauvoir*, p. 62; *FCI*, p. 8; Montaigne, 'Au lecteur', *Essais* in *Oeuvres complètes*, (Paris: Gallimard Pléiade, 1962).

22  Josyane Savigneau, 'Beauvoir dans la force de l'âge', *Le Monde des Livres*, 13 August 1993, p. 9.

23  Lejeune, *Le Pacte autobiographique*, pp. 235–6.

24  Sartre explains his notion of the past in 'Mon passé' in *EN*, pp. 541–49.

25  Lejeune, *Le Pacte autobiographique*, p. 236.

26  Hewitt, *Autobiographical Tightropes*, p. 47.

27  Lejeune, *Le Pacte autobiographique*, p. 198.

28  *FCI*, pp. 374–75.

29  *Ibid.*, p. 375.

30  Elizabeth Fallaize has argued in her discussion of *Les Belles Images* (which Beauvoir began writing in 1965) that it is 'the most writerly . . . and the most ambitious in literary terms' of her novels because of her use of new literary techniques, inspired in part by some of the developments associated with the Nouveau Roman, see Fallaize, *The Novels of Simone de Beauvoir*, pp. 118–19.

31  For a detailed discussion of the positions taken by the nouveaux romanciers in relation to Sartre, see 'The Reaction Against Sartre' in Celia Britton, *The Nouveau Roman, Fiction, Theory and Politics* (Basingstoke: Macmillan, 1992), pp. 12–47.

32  Beauvoir took an active public stance against the nouveaux romanciers, for example, by participating in the public debate entitled 'Que peut la littérature?' organised by *Clarté* in December 1964, of which she gives an account in *TCF*, pp. 170–71, as well as signalling her rejection of some of their methods in her memoirs. However, as Elizabeth Fallaize has noted (*The Novels of Simone de Beauvoir*, p. 119), it would be erroneous to view Beauvoir as wholeheartedly opposed to the criticisms made of the traditional novel by the 'nouveaux romanciers'. In *Les Belles Images* and *La Femme Rompue*, as well as in her memoirs, she attempts to engage with these new literary developments.

33  *FCI*, pp. 375–6.

34 The reference here to 'totalisation' refers to what Andrew Leak has described as 'the process whereby the For-Itself temporalises itself through its projective movement: each act is like a figure in a column, but the process cannot be stopped and added up (totalisé) until the moment of death', see Andrew N. Leak, *The Perverted Consciousness: Sexuality and Sartre* (Basingstoke: Macmillan, 1989), p. 158. The term 'totalisation' is used regularly by Sartre in his philosophical works, although it assumes a different meaning throughout the development of his philosophy. Beauvoir uses it here in the sense in which Sartre uses it in his later philosophy (*Questions de méthode* and *Critique de la raison dialectique* (1960)) in which, as Peter Caws has noted, 'totalisation' takes place within a social context as the outcome of a historical process, see Caws, *Sartre*, pp. 144–46.

35 *FCII*, p. 491.

36 *Ibid.*

37 'La Passion du "je"', entretien avec Philippe Lejeune par Anne Brunswic, in Catherine Chauchat (ed.) *L'Autobiographie: Les Mots de Sartre* (Paris: Gallimard, 1993), pp. 6–18 (p. 11).

38 *FCII*, p. 497.

39 Beauvoir substantially underplays the public hostility towards her and Sartre at this time. During the writing of *La Force des choses* (1960–63), they both received hate mail from Conservative supporters of French government policy in Algeria, Sartre's appartment was bombed twice by the OAS in July 1961 and 1962, and Beauvoir received personal telephone threats that she would be blown up in her own apartment. This apparently had a lasting effect on her and she became even more reluctant to appear in public (Bair, *Simone de Beauvoir*, pp. 482–488).

40 This increased feminine readership is also noted by Elizabeth Fallaize in 'Reception Problems for Women Writers: the Case of Simone de Beauvoir' in Diana Knight and Judith Still (eds.) *Women and Representation* (Nottingham: WIF Publications at University of Nottingham, 1995), pp. 43–56, see especially pp. 53–5, and Catherine Savage Brosman, *Simone de Beauvoir Revisited* (Boston: Twayne, 1991), p. 37. I am grateful to Elizabeth Fallaize for alerting me to the existence of Brosman's work.

41 *MJFR*, p. 195.

42 *FCII*, p. 497.

43 Hewitt, *Autobiographical Tightropes*, p. 42.

44 *FCII*, p. 498.

45 'Une interview de Simone de Beauvoir par Madeleine Chapsal' in Francis and Gontier (eds.) *Les Ecrits de Simone de Beauvoir*, pp. 381–96 (p. 383).

46 *FCII*, p. 498.

47 Heath, *Simone de Beauvoir*, p. 63.

48 *FCII*, p. 504.

49 See Rousseau, *Les Confessions* in *Oeuvres complètes*, tome I (Paris: Gallimard Pléaide, 1959), pp. 277–78.

50 Jeanson, *Simone de Beauvoir ou l'entreprise de vivre*, p. 270.

51 *FA*, p. 11.

52 *TCF*, p. 9.

53 I am grateful to Claudine Monteil for her suggestion of this reading of the methodology in *Tout compte fait*, during our discussion of Beauvoir's view of psychoanalysis during the later years of her life.

54 Jeanson, *Simone de Beauvoir ou l'entreprise de vivre*, p. 295.

55 'Mon expérience d'écrivain' in Francis and Gontier (eds.) *Les Ecrits de Simone de Beauvoir*, pp. 439–57.

56 Deirdre Bair. ' "My Life . . .This Curious Object" ': Simone de Beauvoir on Autobiography', in Domna C. Stanton and Jeanine Parisier Plottel (eds.) *The Female Autograph* (New York: New York Literary Forum, vols. 12–13, 1984), 237–45. This interesting article is regrettably composed of (amalgamated) answers given by Beauvoir to (unidentified) questions about her memoirs from a series of interviews held in January 1982. The interviews were conducted in English and French and the text is unfortunately published only in English. Nevertheless, Beauvoir makes a number of significant observations which are valuable for this discussion.

57 Sidonie Smith and Julia Watson (eds.) *De/colonising the Subject: The Politics of Gender in Women's Autobiography* (Minneapolis: University of Minnesota Press, 1992), p. xvii.

58 'Mon expérience d'écrivain', in Francis and Gontier (eds.) *Les Ecrits de Simone de Beauvoir*, p. 450.

59 Simone de Beauvoir, Préface de *La Bâtarde* de Violette Leduc (Paris: Gallimard, 1964), p. 7.

60 Leduc, *La Bâtarde*, p. 19.

61 'Mon expérience d'écrivain' in Francis and Gontier (eds.) *Les Ecrits de Simone de Beauvoir*, p. 452.

62 *La Vieillesse*, p. 386.

63 In *La Vieillesse* (p. 385), Beauvoir cites Jean-Paul Delay's work on memory, *Les Dissolutions de la mémoire* (Paris: Presses Universitaires, 1942), which distinguishes between sensor-motor memory, autistic memory (which is governed by the unconscious and is the focus of psychoanalysis), and social memory, which reconstructs past events and facts. Beauvoir asserts that social memory is the only form of memory which 'nous permet dans une certaine mesure de nous raconter notre propre histoire' – a logical position given that her notion of selfhood implies always already being in the world with others.

64 *La Vieillesse*, p. 387.

65 For example, *La Vieillesse*, pp. 385–86.

66 *Ibid.*, p. 226.

67 Bianca Lamblin relates this in *Mémoires d'une jeune fille dérangée* (Paris:

Balland, 1993), pp. 161–62; Nelson Algren expressed his anger on many occasions over appearing in Beauvoir's writing, although he did allow her reluctantly to quote from his letters in *La Force des choses*, see Bettina Drew, *Nelson Algren: A Life on the Wild Side* (Austin: University of Texas Press, 1991), p. 322.

68 Bair, ' "My Life . . . This Curious Object": Simone de Beauvoir on Autobiography', in Stanton and Plottel (eds.) *The Female Autograph*, p. 242.

69 In a letter to Algren, however, Beauvoir comments at length on her admiration for Colette, saying, 'c'est en France le seul grand écrivain femme', see *LNA*, 7 March 1948, p. 189.

70 Bair, ' "My Life . . . This Curious Object": Simone de Beauvoir on Autobiography', in Stanton and Plottel (eds.) *The Female Autograph*, p. 242.

71 *Le DSII*, p. 553; Beauvoir makes the same point in 'Mon expérience d'écrivain', in Francis and Gontier (eds.) *Les Ecrits de Simone de Beauvoir*, pp. 449–50.

72 Bair, ' "My Life . . . This Curious Object" ', p. 242.

5 WRITING THE SELF – *MEMOIRES D'UNE JEUNE FILLE RANGÉE*

1 *MJFR*, p. 195.

2 *FCI*, pp. 135–36.

3 For example, Michel Leiris began publishing his autobiography from 1939, André Gorz's *Le Traître* was published in 1958, Jean Genet's *Journal du voleur* in 1949, and Sartre drafted *Les Mots* in 1953 and rewrote it for publication in 1964. Violette Leduc's *La Bâtarde* was integrally published in 1964, although episodes had appeared in her earlier fiction.

4 Bair, *Simone de Beauvoir*, p. 284.

5 *FCI*, p. 135.

6 'La Passion du "je" ', entretien avec Philippe Lejeune par Anne Brunswic in Chauchat (ed.) *L'Autobiographie, Les Mots de Sartre*, pp. 6–18, (p. 15).

7 Michel Leiris, 'De la littérature considérée comme une tauromachie' in *L'Age d'homme* (Paris: Gallimard, 1946), Folio, 1991, pp. 10–11.

8 In an interview with Asabuki Tomiko in 1966, Beauvoir expressed her views on homosexuality, saying that:

'[l'homosexualité] progresse certainement aussi en France. Le problème se complique du fait que, dans le catholicisme, l'homosexualité est considérée comme un péché mortel . . . Il est sûr que l'homosexualité est une perversion de la nature humaine, mais sa progression résulte sans doute de causes plus profondes',

see Asabuki Tomiko, *Vingt-huit jours au Japon avec Jean-Paul Sartre et Simone de Beauvoir* (Paris: Langues et mondes-L'Asiathèque, 1996), p. 43.

9 Barbara Klaw, '*L'Invitée* Castrated: Sex, Simone de Beauvoir and Getting Published or Why Must a Women Hide Her Sexuality?' in *Simone de Beauvoir Studies* 12 (1995), 126–38.

10 Violette Leduc suffered a similar experience with Gallimard who refused to publish her third novel, *Ravages* (1955), until its first section dealing with a lesbian relationship was removed. In 1966, the censored section was published by Gallimard as *Thérèse et Isabelle*. See Alex Hughes, *Violette Leduc: Mothers, Lovers and Language* (Leeds: W.S. Maney and Son for MHRA, 1994), pp. 3–4. Beauvoir thought highly of Leduc's writing, and her support for Leduc was perhaps also partially motivated by her own experiences of censorship by Gallimard.

11 It is worth noting here that both *Le Deuxième Sexe* and *Les Mandarins* were placed on the Papal Index in July 1956.

12 The US translation of *Les Mandarins* was nevertheless slightly censored because of the portrayal of sexuality in the text, see *FCII*, p. 99.

13 Hewitt, *Autobiographical Tightropes*, pp. 33–4.

14 *FCII*, p. 125.

15 Julien Murphy, 'Beauvoir and the Algerian War: Toward a Postcolonial Ethics', in Simons (ed.) *Feminist Interpretations of Simone de Beauvoir*, pp. 263–97 (p. 282).

16 The look of the Other, according to Sartre, limits our possibilities: 'dans la brusque secousse qui m'agite lorsque je saisis le regard d'autrui, il y a ceci que, soudain, je vis une aliénation subtile de toutes mes possibilités qui sont agencées loin de moi' (Sartre, *EN*, p. 304).

17 *FCII*, pp. 126–7.

18 *Ibid.*, p. 40.

19 *Ibid.*, pp. 126–7.

20 *Ibid.*, p. 143.

21 The defence of Djamila Boupacha was the most important of Beauvoir's actions during the Algerian War. Boupacha was an Algerian Muslim and member of the FLN, who was accused of planting a bomb in Algiers in 1959. The bomb was defused; however, Boupacha was arrested, tortured and raped by French soldiers. Beauvoir was invited by Gisèle Halimi, Boupacha's lawyer, to help her publicise the case so that an official enquiry would be held and the perpetrators brought to justice. In June 1960, Beauvoir wrote a controversial essay defending Boupacha in *Le Monde*. The French government ordered all copies of the newspaper to be seized in Algeria on the day that her article appeared. She also formed an action committee, lobbied officials and wrote a preface to the book describing Boupacha's case and the trial, see Simone de Beauvoir and Gisèle Halimi, *Djamila Boupacha* (Paris: Gallimard, 1962).

22 Murphy, 'Beauvoir and the Algerian War', in Simons (ed.) *Feminist Interpretations of Simone de Beauvoir*, pp. 266–7.

23 Carol Ascher, *Simone de Beauvoir, A Life of Freedom* (Brighton: Harvester, 1981), p. 40.

24 Sartre, *Plaidoyer pour les intellectuels* (Paris: Gallimard 'idées', 1972), pp. 48–9.
25 Beauvoir notes in *La Force de l'âge* (p. 416) for example that 'la littérature apparaît lorsque quelque chose dans la vie se dérègle; pour écrire . . . la première condition c'est que la réalité cesse d'aller de soi; alors seulement on est capable de la voir et de la donner à voir.' In 1957, in an interview with Olivier Todd about writing his own autobiography, Sartre said:

> Il y a des moments où l'on peut le faire. Ce sont les moments où l'on est soit à un point de crise ou à un point de rupture ou à un point d'arrivée, ce qui est plus rare. Ou à un nouveau point de départ. C'est le moment où le changement d'une situation amène la brusque découverte de sa vie sous un nouvel aspect

cited by Olivier Todd, *Un fils rebelle* (Paris: Grasset, 1981), p. 170.
26 This term is borrowed from Sheringham's *French Autobiography*, p. ix. Sheringham explains his use of the term 'device' as

> 'a stratagem, a plan devised to fulfil a certain aim, and an emblematic figure . . . Such features, which give . . . autobiographies their particular flavour, reflect the vicissitudes of autobiographical desire. They betray the writer's awareness of the problems and contradictions which beset his or her undertaking, manifesting the critical insight and self-conscious lucidity which has been a hallmark of French autobiography'.

27 Jeanson, *Simone de Beauvoir ou l'entreprise de vivre*, p. 286.
28 Beauvoir reiterated this point twelve years later in an interview with Alice Jardine when she acknowledged that there is no difference between the narrative style and content of autobiographies, see Alice Jardine, 'Interview with Simone de Beauvoir', *Signs: Journal of Women in Culture and Society* 5 (1979), 224–36 (p. 234).
29 Elaine Marks, 'The Dream of Love: A Study of Three Autobiographies' in George Stambolian (ed.) *Twentieth Century French Fiction: Essays for Germaine Brée* (New Brunswick: Rutgers University Press, 1975), pp. 72–88 (p. 79).
30 There are other episodes which Beauvoir relates in great detail in her auto/biographical writings, for example her mother's death in *Une mort très douce* and in *La Force des choses*, her two-month trip to Brazil with Sartre in 1960.
31 Jeanson, *Simone de Beauvoir ou l'entreprise de vivre*, p. 108.
32 *Ibid.*, p. 110.
33 *MJFR*, p. 9 and p. 39; Sheringham, *French Autobiography*, p. 220.
34 Jonathan Culler, *Flaubert: The Uses of Uncertainty* (London: Elek, 1974), p. 186; for an interesting discussion of patriarchal irony evident in the reception of Beauvoir's writing, see Moi, *Simone de Beauvoir: The Making of an Intellectual Woman*, pp. 91–2.
35 Sigmund Freud, *Jokes and their Relation to the Unconscious*, Standard Edition, Vol. VIII (London: Hogarth Press, 1960), p. 174.
36 Culler, *Flaubert*, p. 190.

37  *Ibid.*, pp. 190–1.
38  *FCII*, p. 497.
39  Claude Roy, on the other hand, describes the *Mémoires* as 'the work of a moralist' and says

> Memoirs is one of those books of which one has the feeling that it did its author good to write and that many others will find it good to read . . . Rather than telling us her story, Simone de Beauvoir is calling herself to account. Her enterprise will thus serve everyone,

'Simone de Beauvoir' in Elaine Marks (ed.) *Critical Essays on Simone de Beauvoir* (Boston: G. K. Hall, 1987), pp. 81–2.
40  *FA*, p. 13.
41  Robert Cottrell, *Simone de Beauvoir* (New York: Frederick Ungar, 1975), p. 8.
42  Marks, 'The Dream of Love: A Study of Three Autobiographies', p. 78.
43  Catherine Savage Brosman notes that Beauvoir's texts should be viewed as memoirs, according to definitions of autobiography as an exercise in self-understanding and memoirs as an interpretation of the experiences and events which happened to the self, rather than an analysis of the self. She observes, however, that the *Mémoires* 'comes closer than the others to being a true autobiography', see Brosman, pp. 134–42 (p. 135).
44  Lee Quinby, 'The Subject of Memoirs: *The Woman Warrior*'s Technology of Ideographic Selfhood' in Smith and Watson (eds.) *De/colonising the Subject*, pp. 297–320 (p. 299).
45  Cottrell, *Simone de Beauvoir*, p. 8.
46  Søren Kierkegaard, *The Concept of Irony*, trans. Lee M.Capel (London: Collins, 1966), p. 273.
47  Hewitt, *Autobiographical Tightropes*, p. 41.
48  Susan Sontag, *On Photography* (Harmondsworth: Penguin, 1979), p. 5.
49  Sontag, *On Photography*, p. 8.
50  *Ibid.*
51  Sontag, *On Photography*, pp. 23–4.
52  In this sense, these photographs represent a former, dead self, from which Beauvoir distances herself and which she also seeks to recover. In *La Chambre claire* (1980) Barthes says that the observer seeks death in a photograph of him or herself, and that every photograph contains a sign of that death:

> 'Ce que je vise dans la photo qu'on prend de moi ("l'intention" selon laquelle je la regarde), c'est la Mort: la Mort est l'eïdos de cette Photo-là' and 'C'est parce qu'il y a toujours en elle ce signe impérieux de ma mort future, que chaque photo, fût-elle apparemment la mieux accrochée au monde excité des vivants, vient interpeller chacun de nous'

Roland Barthes, *La Chambre claire*, (Paris: Seuil, 1980), p. 32 and pp. 151–2.
53  *La Vieillesse*, p. 386.

54  *Ibid.*, p. 387.
55  In *Les Belles Images*, as the title suggests, Beauvoir explores the theme of images and photographs in particular as a means of escape from 'the real'. For example, when Laurence goes to Greece with her father, he condemns American tourists for seeing the country through a camera lens; however, Laurence realises that her father is similarly taking refuge in a narrative production of an alien past, *BI*, pp. 226–7.
56  *MJFR*, p. 19.
57  *Ibid.*, p. 22.
58  Jacques Lacan, 'Le Stade du miroir comme formateur de la fonction du Je', (1936) in *Ecrits* (Paris: Seuil, 1966), pp. 93–100.
59  *MJFR*, p. 20.
60  *Ibid.*, p. 25.
61  *Ibid.*, p. 26.
62  A.M. Henry, *Simone de Beauvoir ou l'échec d'une chrétienté* (Paris: Fayard, 1961).
63  *MJFR*, p. 101.
64  Hélène de Beauvoir, *Souvenirs*, recueillis par Marcelle Routier (Paris: Séguier, 1987), p. 35.
65  *MJFR*, pp. 79–82 (p. 81).
66  Dorothy Kaufmann, 'Autobiographical Intersexts: les mots de deux enfants rangés', *L'Esprit créateur* 29 (1989), 21–32 (p. 22).
67  At the end of *Les Mots* for example, Sartre draws an analogy between literature and religion and notes 'le sacré se déposa dans les Belles-Lettres et l'homme de plume apparut, *ersatz* du chrétien que je ne pouvais être', Sartre, *Les Mots* (Paris: Gallimard, 1964), Folio 1990, pp. 201–2.
68  This terminology is from Michel Foucault's *Surveiller et punir*, p. 160. The term 'Un corps docile' is taken to mean here the body as object and focus of power: 'Est docile un corps qui peut être soumis, qui peut être utilisé, qui peut être transformé et perfectionné'.
69  Foucault defines this as 'un "savoir" du corps qui n'est pas exactement la science de son fonctionnement, et une maîtrise de ses forces qui est plus que la capacité de les vaincre' in *Surveiller et punir*, p. 34.
70  Moi, *Simone de Beauvoir, The Making of an Intellectual Woman*, pp. 24–5.
71  Elizabeth Grosz, *Volatile Bodies: Towards a Corporeal Feminism* (Bloomington and Indianapolis: Indiana University Press, 1994), p. 45.
72  Alex Hughes, 'Murdering the Mother: Simone de Beauvoir's *Mémoires d'une jeune fille rangée*', *French Studies* 48 (1994), pp. 174–83; (also appears in Fallaize, *Simone de Beauvoir: A Critical Reader*, pp. 120–31).
73  Julia Kristeva, *Pouvoirs de l'horreur* (Paris: Seuil, 1980).
74  *MJFR*, pp. 18–19.
75  Hélène de Beauvoir, *Souvenirs*, p. 29.
76  Guillemine de Lacoste (who is related to Zaza's family by marriage) offers a different view of Zaza's life and relationships with her mother

and Beauvoir which challenges the version given in the *Mémoires*. Lacoste describes how the hatred between Beauvoir and Mme Lacoin led Beauvoir to present a highly subjective view of Mme Lacoin as a manipulative figure who ruined Zaza's life in the *Mémoires*. According to Lacoste, this view was based on Beauvoir's inability to understand the nurturing relationship between Zaza and her mother. This lack of comprehension was, according to Lacoste, the result of Beauvoir's own experience of mothering, involving repression and lack of nurturing, which caused her to view autonomy and nurturing as mutually exclusive, see Guillemine de Lacoste, 'Elisabeth Lacoin's Influence on Simone de Beauvoir's Life: What Might Have Been' in *Simone de Beauvoir Studies* 11 (1994), 64–75.

77 *UMTD*, p. 65.
78 *Ibid.*, p. 52 and pp. 54–5.
79 Ray Davies has also noted the example of Beauvoir's omission of her father's adultery in the *Mémoires* in his discussion of *Une Mort très douce*, see 'Introduction', *Une Mort très douce* (London: Methuen, 1986), p. 41n.
80 Hughes, 'Murdering the Mother', *French Studies*, pp. 174–83.
81 The phallic, pre-Oedipal or archaic mother is a childhood, heterosexualised fantasy of an all-powerful figure who can satisfy all the child's desires, see Elizabeth Wright (ed.) *Feminism and Psychoanalysis, A Critical Dictionary* (Oxford: Blackwell, 1992), pp. 314–5.
82 Catherine Portuges, 'Attachment and Separation in the *Memoirs of a Dutiful Daughter*', *Yale French Studies*, 72 (1986), 107–18 (p. 117).
83 Judith Butler, 'The Lesbian Phallus and the Morphological Imaginary' in *Bodies that Matter* (London: Routledge, 1993), pp. 57–91 (p. 91).
84 *Ibid.*, p. 89.
85 *Ibid.*, p. 90.
86 Marcia Ian, *Remembering the Phallic Mother: Psychoanalysis, Modernism and the Fetish* (Ithaca and London: Cornell University Press, 1993), p. 7.
87 The use of the term 'lesbian' may seem anachronistic here; however, it is used to denote a primary attachment between Zaza and Simone existing on the 'lesbian continuum' as formulated by Adrienne Rich. As noted in Chapter 2, Rich describes this continuum as 'a range . . . of woman-identified experience, not simply the fact that a woman has had or consciously desired genital sexual experience with another woman', see Adrienne Rich, 'Compulsory Heterosexuality and Lesbian Existence', *Signs* 5 (1980), 631–60 (p. 648).
88 In *Gender Trouble*, heterosexuality is envisaged by Judith Butler as a compulsory, melancholy and repetitive performance which functions hegemonically through its exclusion of homosexuality.
89 Crosland, *Simone de Beauvoir*, p. 10.
90 Butler, *Bodies That Matter*, p. 91.
91 Louisa Alcott, *Little Women* (London: Penguin, 1953), p. 188.
92 *MJFR*, p. 124.

93 *Ibid.*
94 *Ibid.*, p. 126.
95 *Ibid.*, p. 127.
96 In the *Mémoires*, Simone and Zaza's reading of Alain-Fournier's *Le Grand Meaulnes* (1913) and Rosamond Lehmann's *Dusty Answer* (1927) are represented as significant events in their intimacy. As Margaret Crosland has noted, both texts are concerned with a disappointed search for love (see *Simone de Beauvoir*, p. 95). François Seurel's role in relation to Meaulnes in *Le Grand Meaulnes* parallels Beauvoir's in the *Mémoires* in relation to Zaza, for they both perform the role of surviving narrators bearing witness to their love for their friends. In the *Mémoires* (p. 307), an identification is established between the couples of Alain-Fournier/Jacques Rivière and Zaza/Simone. Alain-Fournier, like Zaza, tragically dies young. *Dusty Answer* is, according to Judy Simons, 'probably the first English novel to deal with a girl's experience of university life' (*Rosamond Lehmann* (Basingstoke and London: Macmillan, 1992), p. 47), which is probably why it was important for Beauvoir, because she was an isolated woman student in a predominantly male peer group. In *Dusty Answer*, Lehmann charts Judith Earle's emotional developments between the ages of 18–21, through her attachment to a family of neighbouring cousins and through her erotic relationship with Jennifer Baird at Cambridge. The importance of these texts in the *Mémoires* lies in their representation of same-sex emotional attachments and the fact that they are evoked in relation to the portrayal of Simone's relationship with Zaza.
97 The erotic imagery here recalls the banal descriptions of Anne and Lewis's lovemaking in *Les Mandarins*, and suggests that Beauvoir lacked experience in writing about eroticism (see *Les Mandarins*, p. 319, pp. 327–8, p. 422 and pp. 438–39).
98 *MJFR*, p. 130.
99 For a wide-ranging critique of psychoanalytic accounts of lesbianism, see Noreen O'Connor and Joanna Ryan, *Wild Desires and Mistaken Identities, Lesbianism and Psychoanalysis* (London: Virago, 1993). Luce Irigaray's work constitutes a challenge to the inability of psychoanalysis to theorise the specificity of lesbian desire, see 'Misère de la psychanalyse' in *Parler n'est jamais neutre* (Paris: Minuit, 1985), pp. 253–79, and 'Retour sur la théorie psychanalytique' in *Ce Sexe qui n'en est pas un* (Paris: Minuit, 1977). In 'Quand nos lèvres se parlent' (in *Ce Sexe*) Irigaray presents the specificity of lesbian desire in terms of bodily touching as an affirmative vision of lesbian eroticism.
100 *MJFR*, p. 131.
101 Margaret Simons, 'Lesbian Connections: Simone de Beauvoir and Feminism', *Signs: Journal of Women in Society and Culture* 18 (1992), 136–62 (p. 146).

102 *MJFR*, p. 164 and Hélène de Beauvoir, *Souvenirs*, p. 67.

103 Elisabeth Lacoin, *Zaza: Correspondance et carnets d'Elisabeth Lacoin 1914–1929* (Paris: Seuil, 1991), p. 77.

104 In his analysis of the rhetoric of bourgeois mythology, Roland Barthes describes tautology as 'un double meurtre: on tue le rationnel parce qu'il vous résiste; on tue le langage parce qu'il vous trahit . . . la tautologie fonde un monde mort, un monde immobile' (Roland Barthes, *Mythologies* (Paris: Seuil, 1957), p. 262).

105 *MJFR*, p. 121.

106 For example, that Simone's first male lover was not Sartre but René Maheu, and that when she met Sartre, Beauvoir was in love with Maheu. This information is endorsed by both Beauvoir's diaries of the time, and by Sartre in an interview with John Gerassi noted in Gerassi's *Jean-Paul Sartre, Hated Conscience of his Century, Volume 1: Protestant or Protester* (University of Chicago Press, 1989), p. 90.

107 Christine Battersby, *Gender and Genius: Towards a Feminist Aesthetics*, (London: The Women's Press, 1989), pp. 150–4.

108 *MJFR*, p. 503.

109 Battersby, *Gender and Genius*, pp. 150–4. Beauvoir's lecture on 'La Femme et la création' is in Francis and Gontier (eds.) *Les Ecrits de Simone de Beauvoir*, pp. 458–74. In an assessment of Battersby's argument, it is important to note that Beauvoir is not claiming in *Le Deuxième Sexe* or in her lecture on 'La Femme et la création' that women cannot be original or be geniuses, but rather that gendered roles and spheres of activity constrain most women from achieving highly original work.

110 In Beauvoir's fiction, the motif of women couples and the murder of the lesbian Other can be traced in *L'Invitée* (Françoise kills Xavière, who is based on Olga Kosakievicz with whom Beauvoir had a relationship) and in *Le Sang des autres* (Hélène dies – a character based on Nathalie Sorokine with whom Beauvoir had a relationship). For a discussion of the theme in *Le Sang des autres*, see Alex Hughes, *Le Sang des autres* (Glasgow French and German Publications, 1995), pp. 48–50. By the time of *Les Belles Images*, the female couple constituted by Catherine and Brigitte is 'allowed' to survive, perhaps because the psychologist diagnoses that Catherine's feelings for Brigitte 'n'ont rien d'excessif'. This last couple is probably based mainly on Beauvoir and Zaza, and interestingly, as Brigitte has no mother, one may conclude that this time, Beauvoir has 'murdered' Zaza's mother, who is blamed in the *Mémoires* for contributing to Zaza's demise.

111 See especially Beauvoir's *Lettres à Sartre* and *Journal de guerre*, in which she mentions certain of her sexual relationships with women, for example, *LSI*, p. 178 and *LSII*, pp. 41–2 and pp. 70–1 which refer to her relationships with Olga Kosakievicz and Nathalie Sorokine.

6 BEARING WITNESS WITH THE OTHER, BEARING WITNESS FOR
                              THE OTHER

1 Carol Ascher has noted similarly, in a discussion of Beauvoir's fiction,
  that the memoirs 'illuminate the tensions of the I and the We', see
  Ascher, *Simone de Beauvoir*, p. 49.
2 Ascher argues that this 'we' is represented in various couples and
  identifications in the memoirs, for example, in Beauvoir's relationships
  with Sartre, Algren, Lanzmann, Sylvie Le Bon and her identification
  with the French people (Ascher, *Simone de Beauvoir*, p. 22, pp. 37–40, and
  p. 47).
3 Moi, *Simone de Beauvoir, The Making of an Intellectual Woman*, pp. 15–19.
4 I am grateful to Sylvie Le Bon de Beauvoir for her comments on this
  section.
5 *MJFR*, p. 482.
6 Beauvoir almost always dedicated her works to members of 'the
  Family'. The only other work to be dedicated to Sartre is *Tous les hommes
  sont mortels*.
7 See also Simons, *Rosamond Lehmann*.
8 Fullbrooks, *Simone de Beauvoir and Jean-Paul Sartre*, see especially,
  pp. 53–9.
9 Bernard Cullen, 'Merleau-Ponty' in Richard Kearney (ed.) *Routledge
  History of Philosophy, Vol. VIII: Continental Philosophy in the Twentieth Century*
  (London: Routledge, 1994), p. 105.
10 *FA*, p. 551; *FCI*, p. 28, p. 91; Cohen-Solal, *Sartre*, p. 305, p. 307.
11 Bair, *Simone de Beauvoir*, p. 629n.
12 The Fullbrooks' account of Sartre's and Maheu's visits to Beauvoir in
   the Limousin dates Maheu's visit as prior to Sartre's (Fullbrooks, *Simone
   de Beauvoir and Jean-Paul Sartre*, p. 61). This account is based on Francis
   and Gontier's biography, *Simone de Beauvoir*, rather than on Beauvoir's
   diaries of this period. Beauvoir engaged in a lengthy rebuttal of this
   biography in *Le Matin* in 1985. Among her scathing comments, she
   noted 'cette biographie, il ne s'agit pas d'un portrait. C'est en fait un
   tissu d'erreurs . . . Je n'aimerais pas que les lecteurs lisent ça en croyant
   que c'est la vérité. Vraiment tout est faux, les plus petites choses comme
   les plus grandes.' In their reply, Francis and Gontier argued that 'nous
   n'avons pas suivi Simone de Beauvoir quand elle était en contradiction
   avec ses propres écrits', 'Simone de Beauvoir: le désaveu', *Le Matin*, 5
   December 1985, pp. 26–7; Francis and Gontier's reply was also published in *Le Matin*, 16 December 1985, p. 30. However, as is evident
   from the discussion here, it is not possible to accept Beauvoir's memoirs
   or a biography for that matter as 'unique' sources of 'truth'.
13 Beauvoir refers to the emotional complications of her involvement with
   both Sartre and Maheu in a letter to Sartre, in which she cites verbatim
   a letter from Maheu, expressing his distress and arranging to meet her

(*LSI*, pp. 15–19). Beauvoir's letter is also cited by the Fullbrooks in *Simone de Beauvoir and Jean-Paul Sartre*, pp. 69–71. They note that in *FA*, p. 68–69, she relates this incident as part of the events of February 1931, that is, a year and one month after it actually happened. As they note, this is a further instance of Beauvoir's creative autobiographical construction.

14 Beauvoir refers to the tenth anniversary of their 'mariage' in *LSI*, 10 October 1939, p. 175.

15 I differentiate here implicitly between women's active presence in the intellectual field and public consciousness of their presence, a distinction which is highlighted in Jean-François Sirinelli's observation that female intellectuals such as Beauvoir, Marguerite Duras, Christiane Rochefort and Elsa Triolet who signed political manifestos frequently were 'avant tout, aux yeux de l'opinion, des épouses, des compagnes, ou des veuves de célébrités masculines vivantes ou décédées', see Sirinelli, *Intellectuels et passions françaises: manifestes et pétitions au vingtième siécle* (Paris: Fayard, 1990), p. 266.

16 Béatrice Didier, *Le Journal intime* (Vendôme: Presses Universitaires de France, 1976), p. 8 and p. 18.

17 Deirdre Bair, '"My Life . . . This Curious Object": Simone de Beauvoir on Autobiography', pp. 243–44.

18 *Ibid.*, p. 243.

19 The latest diary from these earlier diaries was four pages written during the academic year 1930–31, which finishes at the end of 1930. The next period during which it has been established that Beauvoir kept an intermittent diary is from 1 September 1939 until 29 January 1941. This diary has been published by Sylvie Le Bon as the *Journal de guerre*.

20 Bair, '"My Life . . . This Curious Object"', p. 243; this feature of the later diaries is substantiated by Sylvie Le Bon's note at the end of the *Journal de guerre*, which says that the war diary also includes 'exposés philosophiques' for Beauvoir's philosophy classes, notes on philosophical readings, reading lists (especially of philosophical and musical books), reading lists for other people, notes on Beethoven's quartets, records of games of chess played, personal budget details, teaching timetables and notes about trade unions in France between 1922–36 (the latter being presumably research for *Le Sang des autres*).

21 *FCII*, p. 153–233. These intermittent diary entries cover the period from 26 May to 28 October 1958.

22 Bair, 'My Life . . . This Curious Object', p. 244.

23 Keefe has discussed the different versions of this period in *La Force de l'âge*, *Journal de guerre* and the *Lettres à Sartre* in 'Autobiography and Biography: Simone de Beauvoir's Memoirs, Diary and Letters', in Keefe and Smyth (ed.) *Autobiography and the Existential Self*, pp. 61–81.

24 Bair, 'My Life . . . This Curious Object', p. 244.

25 Keefe, 'Autobiography and Biography', p. 78.

26 When Beauvoir wrote her memoirs, she consulted newspaper accounts of the period, which suggests that she did not view her own diaries as a primarily factual record.

27 The use of the term 'événementiel' here refers to Foucault's critique of the view of history as a narrative of continuously unfolding events. He proposes instead a genealogical approach to history which analyses and recovers discourses, see 'Introduction', *L'Archéologie du savoir* (Paris: Gallimard, 1969) and 'Vérité et pouvoir', p. 19.

28 This is a further example of Beauvoir making a connection between spatiality and gendered identity. As noted in Chapter 2, in Beauvoir's writing, a female protagonist often experiences a threat to her autonomy and sense of self when she is in an elevated position looking down over a land or cityscape.

29 *FA*, p. 49.

30 *FA*, pp. 49–50.

31 *FA*, p. 50.

32 Beauvoir joined Shakespeare and Company on 4 September 1935 and remained a member until 1941 when it closed down, although Beach continued to lend English and American books to Beauvoir as a personal friend, see Noel Riley Fitch, *Sylvia Beach and the Lost Generation* (Harmondsworth: Penguin, 1985), pp. 354–5 and p. 408, and *FA*, p. 62.

33 In *Temps et récit II*, Virginia Woolf's *Mrs Dalloway* is one of three texts discussed by Paul Ricoeur because it seeks to represent a range of temporal experience in narrative, see *Temps et récit II* (Paris: Seuil, 1984). Although Beauvoir does not mention this aspect of *Mrs Dalloway* in *La Force de l'âge*, the theme of temporality in Woolf's text is likely to have been a further reason for Beauvoir's interest in Woolf's writing, given the importance of temporality in her own philosophy.

34 *FA*, p. 50.

35 A version of 'Modern Fiction' was published as early as 1919 under the title 'Modern Novels' in the *Times Literary Supplement*, however, Woolf revised this slightly and it appeared later in the first series of *The Common Reader* in 1925, which is probably the version Beauvoir read, see Virginia Woolf, 'Modern Fiction' in *The Common Reader, First Series* (London: The Hogarth Press, 1948), pp. 184–95. I would like to thank Avril Horner for providing information on Woolf's literary project.

36 Woolf, 'Modern Fiction', *The Common Reader First Series*, p. 189.

37 *Jacob's Room* is widely acknowledged by critics to be the first novel in which Woolf experimented with narrative form, building on the success of three earlier experimental short stories, 'Kew Gardens' (1917), 'The Mark on the Wall (1919) and 'An Unwritten Novel' (1920), see Woolf, *The Complete Shorter Fiction*, ed. Susan Dick (London: Hogarth Press, 1985).

38 Roger Fry (1866–1934) was an influential art critic and painter, who edited the *Burlington Magazine* and was involved in various important art and design groups, such as the Omega Workshops and the London

Group. He was also responsible for launching Cézanne on the British art scene and organised the first two exhibitions of Post-Impressionist art in 1910 and 1912. He was a lifelong friend of Woolf's, being also closely associated with the Bloomsbury Group. *Vision and Design* was his first collection of essays on art, see Roger Fry, *Vision and Design* (Harmondsworth: Penguin, 1940).

39 Fry, 'An Essay in Aesthetics' in *Vision and Design*, pp. 31–2.

40 In *Qu'est-ce que la littérature?*, in his condemnation of realist literature – 'on nous livrait du vécu déjà repensé' – Sartre comes close to advocating the literary experimentalism which Beauvoir was defending at the beginning of her writing career, see *Qu'est-ce que la littérature?* (Paris: Gallimard, 1948), Folio 1985, pp. 225–26.

41 Beauvoir comments further on her rejection of literary realism in Yves Buin (ed.) *Que peut la littérature?* (Paris: Union générale d'éditions, 1965), especially pp. 80–1.

42 Sartre, *L'Imaginaire* (Paris: Gallimard, 1940).

43 Sartre, *L'Imaginaire*, p. 170.

44 Sartre, *L'Imaginaire*, p. 161.

45 Sartre, *L'Imaginaire*, p. 246.

46 *FA*, p. 51.

47 *Ibid.*, pp. 167–8.

48 Alice Jardine, 'Interview with Simone de Beauvoir', *Signs: Journal of Women in Culture and Society* 5 (1979), 224–36 (p. 230).

49 Jane Heath uses the phrase 'discourse of mastery' in her discussion of Beauvoir's autobiography (Heath, *Simone de Beauvoir*, p. 50), a concept which is examined by Hélène Cixous and Catherine Clément, *La Jeune née* (Paris: Union générale d'édition, 1975); see especially 'Une maîtresse femme', pp. 251–69.

50 Mary Evans, *Simone de Beauvoir* (London: Sage, 1996), p. 32.

51 Shoshana Felman, 'Education and Crisis or the Vicissitudes of Teaching', in Shoshana Felman and Dori Laub, *Testimony, Crises of Witnessing in Literature, Psychoanalysis, and History* (New York and London: Routledge, 1992), pp. 1–56 (p. 5).

52 Heath, *Simone de Beauvoir*, p. 48.

53 Marianne Alphant, 'L'Album de la mère Castor', *Libération*, 22 February 1990, pp. 19–21.

54 Evans, *Simone de Beauvoir*, p. 29.

55 Charles Hanly, *The Problem of Truth in Applied Psychoanalysis* (New York: Guilford Press, 1992), p. 2.

56 Hanly, *The Problem of Truth*, p. 4.

57 *Les Mandarins*, p. 68.

58 Beauvoir contributed financially to *Shoah* and wrote the preface to the filmscript published in 1985 by Fayard.

59 Felman, 'The Return of the Voice: Claude Lanzmann's *Shoah*', in Felman and Laub, *Testimony*, p. 206.

60 Felman, 'Education and Crisis, or the Vicissitudes of Teaching' in Felman and Laub, *Testimony*, p. 5; for a philosophical discussion of the variety of testimonies which exist, see C.A.J. Coady, *Testimony: A Philosophical Study* (Oxford, Clarendon Press, 1992), especially Chapter 2, 'What is Testimony'; in Beauvoir's case, I am particularly interested in ideological and ethical investments in the production and reception of autobiographical truth, which Coady understandably does not explore.

61 J. L. Austin, *How To Do Things with Words* (Oxford University Press, 1962), p. 6.

62 *Ibid.*, pp. 150–7.

63 Felman, 'Education and Crisis, or the Vicissitudes of Teaching' in Felman and Laub, *Testimony*, p. 6.

64 Foucault, *Surveiller et punir*, pp. 25–7.

65 Felman, 'The Betrayal of the Witness: Camus's *La Chute*' in Felman and Laub, *Testimony*, pp. 187–9.

66 See Chapters 1 and 2 in Moi, *Simone de Beauvoir, The Making of an Intellectual Woman*, especially pp. 62–8.

67 For example, her dismissive attitude to the significance of gender is related in *FC*, pp. 135–6. In *FA*, pp. 75–7, Beauvoir discusses her experiences of physicality and sexuality, although these areas are undeveloped in her memoirs.

68 Kruks, 'Gender and Subjectivity: Simone de Beauvoir and Contemporary Feminism', pp. 104–7.

69 Sirinelli, *Intellectuels et passions françaises*, pp. 265–6.

70 Jean-Paul Sartre, *Qu'est-ce que la littérature?*, p. 27.

71 *Ibid.*, p. 288.

72 *FR*, p. 89.

73 Fallaize, *The Novels of Simone de Beauvoir*, p. 154.

74 *FR*, p. 90.

75 *TCF*, p. 634.

76 I am grateful to Elizabeth Fallaize for raising this question.

77 Foucault, *La Volonté de savoir. Histoire de la sexualité I*, p. 133.

78 Samuel Beckett, *En attendant Godot* (Paris: Minuit, 1952), p. 112.

79 Simone de Beauvoir, 'Mon expérience d'écrivain', in Francis and Gontier (eds.) *Les Ecrits de Simone de Beauvoir*, pp. 456–7.

80 Jean Baudrillard sets out his concept of the loss of the real and its replacement by 'hyperreality' in *Simulacres et Simulations* (Paris: Galilée, 1981).

### 7 WRITING THE OTHER

1 The first part of *La Cérémonie des adieux* will hereafter be referred to as *Adieux* in the main text of this chapter.

2 Several critics have noted the autobiographical dimensions of these texts; Ray Davies says for example that '*Une Mort très douce* tells us more

about Beauvoir than about her mother', Introduction, *Une Mort très douce* (London: Methuen, 1986), p. 29.

3 For example, the lengthy episode concerning 'Louise Perron' in *FA* (pp. 193–206), and various portraits offered in *TCF*, especially pp. 51–112.

4 I draw here on Liz Stanley's reference to 'auto/biography' as 'a term which refuses any easy distinction between biography and auto-biography, instead recognising their symbiosis', see Liz Stanley, *The Auto/Biographical I* (Manchester University Press, 1992), p. 127; more-over, in *Tout compte fait*, Beauvoir notes the frequent slippage between autobiography and biography, commenting: 'il y a des autobiographies qui ne se distinguent guère des biographies écrites par un tiers', *TCF*, p. 165.

5 Geneviève Idt, 'Simone de Beauvoir's *Adieux*: A Funerary Rite and a Literary Challenge' in Ronald Aronson and Adrian van den Hoven (eds.) *Sartre Alive* (Detroit: Wayne State University Press, 1991), pp. 363–84 (p. 380).

6 Sidonie Smith, *Subjectivity, Identity and the Body* (Bloomington and India-napolis: Indiana University Press, 1993), pp. 22–3.

7 Julia Kristeva, *Pouvoirs de l'horreur* (Paris: Seuil, 1980), p. 11.

8 *Ibid.*, p. 12.

9 *Ibid.* pp. 12–13.

10 See Kafka's essay, 'In the Penal Colony' in *The Transformation ('Metamor-phosis') and Other Stories*, pp. 127–53.

11 Foucault, 'Nietzsche, Genealogy, History' in *The Foucault Reader*, pp. 76–100 (p. 83).

12 Foucault, 'N,G,H', p. 87.

13 Foucault, 'N,G,H', p. 88.

14 See Idt, 'Simone de Beauvoir's *Adieux*', pp. 364–65.

15 Elaine Marks, 'Transgressing the (In)cont(in)ent Boundaries: The Body in Decline' in 'Simone de Beauvoir: Witness to a Century', *Yale French Studies* 72 (1986), 181–200 (p. 200).

16 *UMTD* (Paris: Gallimard, 1964), p. 28.

17 *UMTD*, p. 28–9.

18 *UMTD*, p. 29.

19 *CDA*, p. 159.

20 Nancy K. Miller, 'Autobiographical Deaths' in *Massachusetts Review: A Quarterly Review of Literature, the Arts and Public Affairs* 33 (1992), 19–47.

21 *UMTD*, p. 47.

22 Jardine, 'Death Sentences: Writing Couples and Ideology' in Susan R. Suleiman (ed.) *The Female Body in Western Culture* (Cambridge, MA.: Harvard University Press, 1985), pp. 84–96; Hughes, 'Murdering the Mother', *French Studies*, pp. 174–83.

23 Marks, 'Transgressing the (In)cont(in)ent Boundaries', p. 189.

24 *CDA*, p. 21.

25 Sandra Beyer, 'A Dieu X: The Fragmentation of the Self in Simone de

Beauvoir's *Cérémonie des adieux*' in Ginette Adamson and Eunice Myers (eds.) *Continental, Latin-American and Francophone Women Writers, Vol. II, Selected Papers from the Wichita State Conference on Foreign Literature, 1986–87* (Lanham, MD: University Press of America, 1987), pp. 131–6 (pp. 132–3).

26 *UMTD*, pp. 28–9.

27 The concept of 'double-bind' was formulated by Gregory Bateson, an anthropologist who worked with schizophrenics and their families, in a 1956 paper, 'Towards a Theory of Schizophrenia'. It was developed by R.D.Laing, a key figure in the British anti-psychiatry movement, who was influenced by Sartre's *Critique de la raison dialectique*. According to John Clay, this influence was mediated by Beauvoir who had read *The Divided Self* and encouraged Sartre to read Laing's work. The double-bind involves two people who are involved with each other in a primary way, e.g., as lover or parent, confusing and binding each other by expressing different orders of message – effectively operating as an ironical, psychological control strategy – so that one of them cannot identify the meaning accurately. It involves mystification by converting (in Sartre's and Laing's terms) praxis (what a person does in a social context) into process (an impersonal series of events with no apparent agent). The sufferer of the double-bind is mystified by the contradictory demands made upon him/her, yet is held back from responding by forces of convention and anxiety, see R.D.Laing, *Self and Others* (London: Tavistock Publications, 1961), Penguin, 1990, pp. 144–8; John Clay, *R.D.Laing, A Divided Self* (London: Hodder and Stoughton, 1996), pp. 87–9 and pp. 104–8.

28 See, for example, Françoise de Beauvoir's phobic attitude towards physicality and sexuality, *MJFR*, p. 54, p. 56, p. 58.

29 Bateson et al, 1956, cited by Laing in *Self and Others*, p. 144.

30 In the late 1970s, Sartre and Beauvoir led somewhat separate intellectual lives, partly because of Sartre's infirmity and blindness, and because of the role of Benny Lévy (alias Pierre Victor, a young Maoist intellectual) in Sartre's life. Sartre's daily life was also divided between various younger female companions, such as his adopted daughter, Arlette Elkaïm. Beauvoir had, in turn, partly substituted for Sartre's companionship that of Sylvie Le Bon. Beauvoir and Lévy's mutual antipathy came to a head over an Israeli-Palestinian conference, organised mainly by Lévy, under the aegis of *Les Temps modernes* (see Beauvoir's account in *CDA*, pp. 139–45). This disastrous conference was the minor sequel to a major quarrel between Beauvoir, the *Temps modernes* team and Lévy in 1978 concerning Lévy's attempt to publish an article in *Le Nouvel Observateur*, based on a tape-recorded conversation with Sartre on the Arab-Israeli conflict. The rift between Sartre, Lévy and Beauvoir was not resolved after the quarrel in 1978, and came to signify an intellectual breach between Sartre and Beauvoir at the end of

Sartre's life. Sartre has commented on his relationship with Lévy and the role of 'l'intellectuel nouveau' in 'Autoportrait à soixante-dix ans' in *Situations X*, pp. 210–13.

31 *CDA*, p. 157.
32 In his essay on 'The Uncanny', Freud notes that 'an uncanny effect is often and easily produced when the distinction between imagination and reality is effaced', see Freud, *An Infantile Neurosis and Other Works*, Standard Edition Vol. XVII (London: Hogarth Press, 1955), p. 244.
33 Sartre, *Le Diable et le bon dieu* (Paris: Gallimard, 1951), p. 253.
34 *FA*, p. 691.
35 *MJFR*, pp. 130–31.
36 *UMTD*, p. 154.
37 I refer here to Freud's notion that the uncanny constitutes something familiar yet frightening which is repressed but nevertheless recurs, see Freud, 'The Uncanny', p. 241.
38 For example, Beauvoir discusses in *La Vieillesse* the relationship between the body and intellectual faculties (pp. 334–6) and later, she describes old age as 'une délivrance' for women, (pp. 513–14).
39 Michel Contat, 'Sartre/Beauvoir, légende et réalité d'un couple' in Peter Davidházi and Judit Karafiáth (eds.) *Literature and its Cults, an Anthropological Approach*, (Budapest, Argumentum, 1994), pp. 123–56 (p. 131).
40 *UMTD*, pp. 168–9.
41 In *CDA*, Beauvoir also refers inter alia to Vol. VI of Claude Mauriac's *Le Temps immobile*, Olivier Todd's *Un Fils rebelle*, her own volumes of memoirs and Sartre's interview with Michel Contat, 'Autoportrait à soixante-dix ans' in *Situations X* (Paris: Gallimard, 1976) pp. 133–226.
42 'Préface', *CDA*.
43 *CDA*, p. 95.
44 Jean-Paul Sartre, 'Autoportrait à soixante-dix ans', *Situations X*; *Sartre par lui-même*, dir. Alexandre Astruc and Michel Contat, Institut National de l'audiovisuel, 1976.
45 'Simone de Beauvoir interroge Jean-Paul Sartre', *L'Arc* 61 (1975), special issue, *Simone de Beauvoir et la lutte des femmes*, 3–12, reprinted in Jean-Paul Sartre, *Situations X*, pp. 116–32 and *Les Ecrits de Simone de Beauvoir*, pp. 533–46; Terry Keefe and Jean-Pierre Boulé, 'Simone de Beauvoir as Interviewer of Sartre: Convergence and Divergence', *Simone de Beauvoir Studies* 10 (1993), 247–55. Moreover, there are several joint interviews of Beauvoir and Sartre, such as Alice Schwarzer's interview in *Simone de Beauvoir Today*, pp. 49–64, conducted in 1973 and an interview with Michel Sicard in *Obliques* 18–19 (1979), 325–9, conducted in July 1978.
46 'Préface aux entretiens', *CDA*.
47 Lévy's interviews were published first in issues 800–802 of *Le Nouvel Observateur* in March 1980 and then as *L'Espoir maintenant* (Lagrasse: Verdier, 1991).

48 Keefe and Boulé have also analysed these interviews, arguing that they present a 'convergent' picture of Sartre's and Beauvoir's views; my purpose here, however, is to analyse Beauvoir's self-representation in biography.

49 *CDA*, p. 190.

50 *CDA*, p. 320 and p. 310.

51 *CDA*, p. 402.

52 *CDA*, p. 365.

53 *CDA*, p. 366.

54 *CDA*, pp. 396–402.

55 *CDA*, p. 408.

56 *CDA*, p. 494.

57 *CDA*, p. 502.

58 Keefe and Boulé emphasise Beauvoir's comment here as 'remarkable', see Keefe and Boulé, 'Simone de Beauvoir as Interviewer of Sartre', p. 249.

59 *FA*, 'Prologue'.

60 *TCF*, p. 202.

61 Beauvoir explains her view of the singular/universal perspective and literature as 'le lieu privilégié de l'intersubjectivité' in 'Mon expérience d'écrivain' in Francis and Gontier (eds.), *Les Ecrits de Simone de Beauvoir*, pp. 439–57.

62 *Ibid.*, pp. 456–7.

63 A notable exception is Michel Contat's interview of Sartre, 'Autoportrait à soixante-dix ans' in *Situations X*.

64 Sartre, *Le Diable et le bon dieu*, p. 213.

### EPILOGUE

1 *TCF*, p.162.

2 'Mon expérience d'écrivain', in Francis and Gontier (eds.) *Les Ecrits de Simone de Beauvoir*, p. 456.

3 *FCI*, p.23.

4 This is particularly evident in her fiction, and is discussed by Elizabeth Fallaize in *The Novels of Simone de Beauvoir*, see especially, pp. 179–81.

5 Dori Laub, 'Bearing Witness or the Vicissitudes of Listening' in Felman and Laub, *Testimony*, pp. 73–4.

6 Albert Camus, 'Jonas ou l'artiste au travail' in *L'Exil et le royaume* (Paris: Gallimard, 1957), Folio 1991, p.139.

# Bibliography

## WORKS BY SIMONE DE BEAUVOIR

Carnet I: 24 September, 1928 to 12 September, 1929; Carnet II: 1929–30, 1930–31 (unpublished diaries), Salle des manuscrits, Bibliothèque nationale de France, Paris.

*L'Invitée*. Paris: Gallimard, 1943, Folio, 1977.

*Le Sang des autres*. Paris: Gallimard, 1945, 1984.

*Les Bouches inutiles*. Paris: Gallimard, 1945, 1948.

'La Phénoménologie de la perception', *Les Temps modernes*, 2, 1945, 363–67.

*Tous les hommes sont mortels*. Paris: Gallimard, 1946, 1967.

*Pour une morale de l'ambiguïté*, suivi de *Pyrrhus et Cinéas*. Paris: Gallimard, 1947, 1944, Collection 'Idées' 1983.

*L'Existentialisme et la sagesse des nations*. Paris: Nagel, 1948, 1986 edn.

*Le Deuxième Sexe*. Paris: Gallimard, 1949, Vol. I, Gallimard 1966, Vol. II Gallimard, 1958.

*L'Amérique au jour le jour*. Paris: Gallimard, 1954.

*Les Mandarins*. Paris: Gallimard, 1954.

*Privilèges*. Paris: Gallimard, 1955, 1977.

*Mémoires d'une jeune fille rangée*. Paris: Gallimard, 1958, Folio, 1988.

*La Force de l'âge*. Paris: Gallimard, 1960, Folio, 1989.

*Djamila Boupacha*, avec Gisèle Halimi Paris: Gallimard, 1962, 1991 edn.

*La Force des choses I*. Paris: Gallimard, 1963, Folio, 1988.

*La Force des choses II*. Paris: Gallimard, 1963, Folio, 1983.

*Une Mort très douce*. Paris: Gallimard, 1964, Folio, 1972.

Contribution to 'Que peut la littérature?' debate published as Yves Buin (ed.) *Que peut la littérature?* Paris: Union générale d'éditions, 1965, pp. 73–92.

*Les Belles Images*. Paris: Gallimard, 1966, 1967.

*La Femme rompue*. Paris: Gallimard, 1967, Folio, 1989.

*La Vieillesse*. Paris: Gallimard, 1970.

*Tout compte fait*. Paris: Gallimard, 1972, Folio, 1989.

'Simone de Beauvoir interroge Jean-Paul Sartre', *L'Arc* 61 (1975), 3–12.

*Quand prime le spirituel*. Paris: Gallimard, 1979.

'Deux chapitres inédits de *L'Invitée*' in (eds.) Claude Francis and Fernande Gontier, *Les Ecrits de Simone de Beauvoir*, Paris: Gallimard, 1979, pp. 275–316.

'Jean-Paul Sartre: strictement personnel' in Francis and Gontier (eds.), *Les Ecrits de Simone de Beauvoir*, pp. 332–6.

'Introduction à une morale de l'ambiguïté' in Francis and Gontier (eds.), *Les Ecrits de Simone de Beauvoir*, pp. 337–43.

'Brigitte Bardot et le syndrome de Lolita' in Francis and Gontier (eds.) *Les Ecrits de Simone de Beauvoir*, pp. 363–76.

'Situation de la femme aujourd'hui' in Francis and Gontier (eds.) *Les Ecrits de Simone de Beauvoir*, pp. 422–38.

'Mon expérience d'écrivain' in Francis and Gontier (eds.) *Les Ecrits de Simone de Beauvoir*, pp. 439–57.

'La Femme et la création' in Francis and Gontier (eds.) *Les Ecrits de Simone de Beauvoir*, pp. 458–74.

'En France aujourd'hui on peut tuer impunément' in Francis and Gontier (eds.) *Les Ecrits de Simone de Beauvoir*, pp. 475–81.

'Le sexisme ordinaire' in Francis and Gontier (eds.) *Les Ecrits de Simone de Beauvoir*, p. 514.

'Solidaire d'Israël: un soutien critique' in Francis and Gontier (eds.) *Les Ecrits de Simone de Beauvoir*, pp. 522–32.

'*Le Deuxième Sexe*, vingt-cinq ans après' in Francis and Gontier (eds.) *Les Ecrits de Simone de Beauvoir*, pp. 547–65.

*La Cérémonie des adieux*, suivi de *Entretiens avec Jean-Paul Sartre*, Paris: Gallimard, 1981.

'La Mémoire de l'horreur', preface to transcript of *Shoah*, Paris: Fayard, 1985.

*Journal de guerre*. Paris: Gallimard, 1990.

*Lettres à Sartre, I, 1930–1939*. Paris: Gallimard, 1990.

*Lettres à Sartre, II, 1940–1963*. Paris: Gallimard, 1990.

'Malentendu à Moscou' in *Roman 20–50 'Simone de Beauvoir'* 13 (1992), 137–88

*Lettres à Nelson Algren, un amour transatlantique 1947–64*. Paris: Gallimard, 1997.

INTERVIEWS WITH SIMONE DE BEAUVOIR

'Interview de Simone de Beauvoir par J.-F. Rolland' in Francis and Gontier (eds.) *Les Ecrits de Simone de Beauvoir*, pp. 358–62.

'Une interview de Simone de Beauvoir par Madeleine Chapsal', in Francis and Gontier (eds.) *Les Ecrits de Simone de Beauvoir*, pp. 381–396.

'Entretien avec Claude Francis' in Francis and Gontier (eds.) *Les Ecrits de Simone de Beauvoir*, pp. 568–76.

'Entretien avec Simone de Beauvoir' in Francis and Gontier (eds.) *Les Ecrits de Simone de Beauvoir*, pp. 583–92.

Jardine, Alice. 'Interview with Simone de Beauvoir', *Signs: Journal of Women in Culture and Society* 5, (1979), 224–36.

Bair, Deirdre. ' "My Life . . . This Curious Object": Simone de Beauvoir on Autobiography' in Domna Stanton and Jeanine Parisier Plottel (eds.) *The Female Autograph*, New York: New York Literary Forum 12–13 (1984), 237–45.

Lazar, Liliane. 'Conversation avec Simone de Beauvoir', *Simone de Beauvoir Studies* 2 (1984), 4–11.

Patterson, Yolanda. 'Entretien avec Simone de Beauvoir', *The French Review* 52 (1979), 745–54.

Pedneault, Hélène and Marie Sabourin. 'Simone de Beauvoir, féministe', *La Vie en rose* (March 1984), 25–37.

Schwarzer, Alice. *Simone de Beauvoir Today: Conversations 1972–82*, London: Chatto and Windus, The Hogarth Press, 1984.

Simons, Margaret A. 'Two Interviews with Simone de Beauvoir' in Nancy Fraser and Sandra Lee Bartky (eds.) *Revaluing French Feminism: Critical Essays on Difference, Agency and Culture*, Bloomington and Indianapolis: Indiana University Press, 1992, pp. 25–41.

Wenzel, Hélène V. 'Interview with Simone de Beauvoir', *Yale French Studies* 72 (1986), 5–32.

### WORKS ON SIMONE DE BEAUVOIR

Alphant, Marianne, 'L'Album de la mère Castor', *Libération*, 22 February 1990, pp. 19–21.

Appignanesi, Lisa, *Simone de Beauvoir*, London: Penguin, 1988.

Arnaud Hibbs, Françoise, *L'Espace dans les romans de Simone de Beauvoir*, Saratoga: ANMA Libri, 1988.

Ascher, Carol, *Simone de Beauvoir, A Life of Freedom*, Brighton: Harvester, 1981.

Atack, Margaret, 'Writing from the Centre: Ironies of Otherness and Marginality' in Ruth Evans (ed.) *Simone de Beauvoir's The Second Sex, New Interdisciplinary Essays*, Manchester University Press, 1998, pp. 31–58.

Audet, Jean-Raymond, *Simone de Beauvoir face à la mort*, Lausanne: L'âge d'homme, 1979.

Audry, Colette, 'Simone de Beauvoir, vue par Colette Audry', *F. Magazine* 12 (1979), 52–55.

Bair, Deirdre, 'Simone de Beauvoir: Politics, Language and Feminist Identity', *Yale French Studies* 72 (1986), 149–62.

  'Madly Sensible and Brilliantly Confused: From *Le Deuxième Sexe* to *The Second Sex*', *Dalhousie French Studies*, 13 (1987), 23–35.

  'Simone de Beauvoir: Reflections on a Work in Progress', *L'Esprit créateur*, Vol. 29, No.4 1989, 75–85.

  *Simone de Beauvoir*, London: Jonathan Cape, 1990.

Baisnée, Valérie, *Gendered Resistance, The Autobiographies of Simone de Beauvoir, Maya Angelou, Janet Frame and Marguerite Duras*, Amsterdam and Atlanta, GA: Rodopi, 1997.

Beauvoir, Hélène de, *Souvenirs*, recueillis par Marcelle Routier, Paris: Séguier, 1987.

'Simone ma soeur', *Marie-Claire*, August 1986, pp. 61–8.

'Simone et moi', 'Histoire des deux petites Russes et la naissance de *L'Invitée*' and 'Simone et Lionel', unpublished papers.

Bennett, Joy and Hochmann, Gabriella, *Simone de Beauvoir, An Annotated Bibliography*, New York and London: Garland Publishing, 1988.

Bergoffen, Deborah, 'Simone de Beauvoir: Cartesian Legacies', *Simone de Beauvoir Studies* 7 (1990), 15–28.

*The Philosophy of Simone de Beauvoir, Gendered Phenomenologies, Erotic Generosities*, New York: SUNY, 1997.

Beyer, Sandra, 'A Dieu X: The Fragmentation of the Self in Simone de Beauvoir's *Cérémonie des adieux*' in Ginette Adamson and Eunice Myers (eds.) *Continental, Latin-American and Francophone Women Writers, Vol. II, Selected Papers from the Wichita State Conference on Foreign Literature, 1986–87*, Lanham, MD: University Press of America, 1987, pp. 131–6.

Bieber, Konrad, *Simone de Beauvoir*, Boston: Twayne, 1979.

Brochier, Jean-Jacques, 'La littérature engagée: cette évidence', *Magazine littéraire*, 145, 1979, 24–25.

Brosman, Catherine Savage, *Simone de Beauvoir Revisited*, Boston: Twayne, 1991.

Butler, Judith, 'Sex and Gender in Simone de Beauvoir's *Second Sex*', *Yale French Studies* 72 (1986), 35–49.

Card, Claudia, 'Lesbian Attitudes and *The Second Sex*' in Azizah Y. al-Hibri and Margaret A. Simons (eds.) *Hypatia Reborn: Essay in Feminist Philosophy*, Bloomington and Indianapolis: Indiana University Press, 1990, pp. 290–9.

Carter, Angela, 'The Intellectuals' Darby and Joan', *New Society*, 28 January 1982, 156–7.

Celeux, Anne-Marie, *Jean-Paul Sartre, Simone de Beauvoir: une expérience commune, deux écritures*, Paris: Nizet, 1986.

Christensen, Peter, 'The Faust Theme in *All Men are Mortal*', *Simone de Beauvoir Studies* 5 (1988), 40–54.

Cismaru, Alfred, 'Simone de Beauvoir and the Spanish Civil War: From Apoliticism to Commitment', in Janet Pérez and Wendell Aycock (eds.) *The Spanish Civil War in Literature*, Texas: Texas Tech. Universities Press, 1990, pp. 67–73.

Clément, Catherine, 'Les pelures du réel', *Magazine littéraire*, 145, 1979, 25–7.

Contat, Michel, 'Sartre/Beauvoir, légende et réalité d'un couple' in Peter Dávidházi and Judit Karafiáth (eds.) *Literature and its Cults, an Anthropological Approach*, Budapest: Argumentum, 1994, pp. 123–56.

Cottrell, Robert D., *Simone de Beauvoir*, New York: Frederick Ungar, 1975, 1976 edn.

Courtivron, Isabelle de, 'From Bastard to Pilgrim: Rites and Writing for Madame', *Yale French Studies* 72 (1986), 133–48.

Crosland, Margaret, *Simone de Beauvoir, The Woman and her Work*, London: Heinemann, 1992.

Cumming, Laura, 'Too Soft on this Monster of Egotism', *Literary Review*, No.144, June 1990, 36–7.

Davies, Ray, 'Introduction', Simone de Beauvoir, *Une mort très douce*, London: Methuen, 1986, pp. 1–42.

Dayan, Josée and Ribowska, Malka, *Simone de Beauvoir, un film*, Paris: Gallimard, 1979.

Delavers, Lauren Pringle, 'An Annotated and Indexed Calendar and Abstract of the Ohio State University Collection of Simone de Beauvoir's Letters to Nelson Algren' unpublished doctoral dissertation, Ohio State University, 1985.

Desanti, Dominique, 'De *L'Invitée* au *Deuxième Sexe*, souvenirs d'une emprise', *Dalhousie French Studies* 13 (1987), 8–13.

Ehrmann, Jacques, 'Simone de Beauvoir and the Related Destinies of Woman and Intellectual', *Yale French Studies* 27 (1961), 26–32.

Evans, Martha Noel, 'Murdering *L'Invitée*: Gender and Fictional Narrative', *Yale French Studies* 72 (1986), 67–86.

*Masks of Tradition: Women and the Politics of Writing in Twentieth Century France*, Ithaca: Cornell, 1987.

Evans, Mary, *Simone de Beauvoir, a Feminist Mandarin*, London: Tavistock, 1985.

*Simone de Beauvoir*, London: Sage, 1996.

Evans, Ruth (ed.) *Simone de Beauvoir's The Second Sex, New Interdisciplinary Readings*, Manchester University Press, 1998.

Fallaize, Elizabeth, *The Novels of Simone de Beauvoir*, London: Routledge, 1988.

'Resisting Romance: Simone de Beauvoir, *The Woman Destroyed* and the Romance Script' in Margaret Atack and Phil Powrie (eds.) *Contemporary French Fiction by Women: Feminist Perspectives*, Manchester University Press, 1990.

'Reception Problems for Women Writers: the case of Simone de Beauvoir' in Diana Knight and Judith Still (eds.) *Women and Representation*, Nottingham: WIF Publications at the University of Nottingham, 1995, pp. 43–56.

*Simone de Beauvoir: A Critical Reader*, London and New York: Routledge, 1998.

Fauré, Christine, 'Simone de Beauvoir et Simone Weil: deux trajectoires philosophiques', *Simone de Beauvoir Studies* 2 (1984), 99–116.

Ferguson, Ann, 'Lesbian Identity, Beauvoir and History' in al-Hibri and Simons (eds.) *Hypatia Reborn, Essays in Feminist Philosophy*, pp. 280–9.

Forster, Penny and Imogen Sutton, (eds.) *Daughters of de Beauvoir*, London: The Women's Press, 1989.

Francis, Claude and Fernande Gontier (eds.). *Les Ecrits de Simone de Beauvoir*, Paris: Gallimard, 1979.

*Simone de Beauvoir*, Paris: Perrin, 1985.

'Simone de Beauvoir et ses biographes. Polémique', *Le Matin*, 16 December 1985.

Fullbrook, Kate and Edward, *Simone de Beauvoir and Jean-Paul Sartre: The Remaking of a Twentieth Century Legend*, Hemel Hempstead: Harvester Wheatsheaf, 1993.

'Whose Ethics? Sartre's or Beauvoir's?', *Simone de Beauvoir Studies* 12 (1995), 84–90.

'Beauvoir's Literary-Philosophical Method' in *Simone de Beauvoir Studies* 14 (1997), 29–38.

*Simone de Beauvoir: A Critical Introduction*, Cambridge: Polity, 1998.

Gagnebin, Laurent, *Simone de Beauvoir ou le refus de l'indifférence*, Paris: Fischbacher, 1968.

Girard, René, 'Memoirs of a dutiful existentialist', *Yale French Studies* 27 (1961), 41–6.

Heath, Jane, *Simone de Beauvoir*, Brighton: Harvester Wheatsheaf, 1989.

Henry, A.M., *Simone de Beauvoir ou l'échec d'une chrétienté*, Paris: Fayard, 1961.

Hirschman, Sarah, 'Simone de Beauvoir, Lycée Teacher, *Yale French Studies* 22 (1958–59), 79–82.

Hoffman Baruch, Elaine, 'Simone de Beauvoir: Feminism and Biology', unpublished conference paper given at colloquium on Simone de Beauvoir at Columbia University, New York, 4–6 April, 1985.

Holveck, Elaine, 'Simone de Beauvoir: Autobiography as Philosophy', *Simone de Beauvoir Studies* 8 (1991), 103–10.

'Can a Woman be a Philosopher? Reflections of a Beauvoirian Housemaid', in Margaret A. Simons (ed.) *Feminist Interpretations of Simone de Beauvoir*, Pennsylvania, Pennsylvania State University Press, 1995, pp. 67–78.

Houlding, Elizabeth A, 'Simone de Beauvoir: From the Second World War to *The Second Sex*', *L'Esprit créateur* 33 (1993), 39–51.

Houston, Mona Tobin, 'The Sartre of Madame de Beauvoir', *Yale French Studies* 30 (1964), 23–9.

Hughes, Alex. 'Murdering the Mother: Simone de Beauvoir's *Mémoires d'une jeune fille rangée*', *French Studies* 48 (1994), 174–83 and reprinted in Fallaize (ed.) *Simone de Beauvoir: A Critical Reader*.

*Le Sang des autres*, University of Glasgow French and German Publications, 1995.

'The City and the Female Autograph' in Michael Sheringham (ed.) *Parisian Fields*, London: Reaktion Books, 1995, pp. 115–32.

Huston, Nancy. 'Les enfants de Simone de Beauvoir', *La Vie en rose* 16, 1984, 41–4.

'Castor and Poulou: The Trials of Twinship', *L'Esprit créateur* 29 (1989), 8–18.

Idt, Geneviève, 'Simone de Beauvoir's Adieux: A Funerary Rite and a Literary Challenge', in Ronald Aronson and Adrian Van Den Hoven (eds.) *Sartre Alive*, Detroit: Wayne State University Press, 1991, pp. 363–84.

Jaccard, Annie-Claire, *Simone de Beauvoir*, Zurich: Juris Druck and Verlag, 1968.

Jardine, Alice, 'Death Sentences: Writing Couples and Ideology' in Susan R. Suleiman (ed.) *The Female Body in Western Culture*, Cambridge, MA.: Harvard University Press, 1985, pp. 84–96.

Joseph, Gilbert, *Une si douce occupation: Simone de Beauvoir et Jean-Paul Sartre, 1940–44*, Paris: Albin Michel, 1991.

Joyaux, Georges J., 'Le Problème de la gauche intellectuelle et *Les Mandarins* de Simone de Beauvoir', *Kentucky Foreign Language Quarterly* 3 (1956), 120–8.

Julienne-Caffié, Serge, *Simone de Beauvoir*, Paris: Gallimard, 1966.

Kaufmann, Dorothy, 'Simone de Beauvoir: Questions of Difference and Generation', *Yale French Studies* 72 (1986), 121–31.

'Autobiographical Intersexts: Les mots de deux enfants rangés', *L'Esprit créateur 29*, No.4, 1989, 21–32.

Keefe, Terry, 'Psychiatry in the Postwar Fiction of Simone de Beauvoir', *Literature and Psychology* 29 (1979), 123–32.

'Simone de Beauvoir and Sartre on "Mauvaise Foi" ', *French Studies* 34 (1980), 300–14.

*Simone de Beauvoir, A Study of her Writings*, Totowa: New Jersey, Barnes and Noble, 1983.

'Simone de Beauvoir's Second Look at her Life', *Romance Studies* 8 (1986), 41–55.

*Les Belles images, La Femme rompue*, University of Glasgow French and German Publications, 1991.

and Boulé, Jean-Pierre. 'Simone de Beauvoir as Interviewer of Sartre: Convergence and Divergence' in *Simone de Beauvoir Studies* 10 (1993), 247–55.

'Autobiography and Biography: Simone de Beauvoir's Memoirs, Diaries and Letters', in Terry Keefe and Edmund Smyth (eds.) *Autobiography and the Existential Self*, Liverpool University Press, 1995, pp. 61–81.

'Sartre and Beauvoir: Refining rather than "Remaking" the Legend', *Simone de Beauvoir Studies* 12 (1995), 91–9.

Klaw, Barbara, '*L'Invitée* Castrated: Sex, Simone de Beauvoir and Getting Published or Why Must a Woman Hide Her Sexuality?', *Simone de Beauvoir Studies* 12 (1995), 126–38.

Kruks, Sonia. 'Teaching Sartre about Freedom' in Ronald Aronson and Adrian Van Den Hoven (eds.) *Sartre Alive*, Detroit:Wayne State University Press, 1991, pp. 285–300.

'Gender and Subjectivity: Simone de Beauvoir and Contemporary Feminism', *Signs: Journal of Women in Culture and Society* 18, 1992, 89–110.

Lacoste, Guillemine de, 'Elisabeth Lacoin's Influence on Simone de Beauvoir's Life: What Might Have Been', in *Simone de Beauvoir Studies* 11 (1994), 64–75.

Lamblin, Bianca, *Mémoires d'une jeune fille dérangée*, Paris: Balland, 1993.

Larsson, Björn, *La Réception des Mandarins: Le roman de Simone de Beauvoir face à la critique littéraire en France*, Lund University Press, 1988.

Le Doeuff, Michèle, 'Operative Philosophy', *Ideology and Consciousness* 6 (1979), 47–57.

'Cheveux longs, idées courtes', *Recherches sur l'imaginaire philosophique*, Paris: Payot, 1980.

'Sartre, l'unique sujet parlant', *Esprit* (May/June 1984), 181–91.

*L'Etude et le rouet: des femmes, de la philosophie, etc.* Paris: Seuil, 1989.

'Simone de Beauvoir: les ambiguïtés d'un ralliement', *Magazine littéraire* 320 (1994), 58–61.

Leighton, Jean, *Simone de Beauvoir on Woman*, Rutherford: Fairleigh Dickinson, 1975.

Lilar, Suzanne, *Le Malentendu du Deuxième Sexe*, Paris: Presses universitaires de France, 1969.

Lundgren-Gothlin, Eva, *Sex and Existence: Simone de Beauvoir's The Second Sex*, London: Athlone, 1996.

MacDonald, Marylea, 'Le Pacte autobiographique dans les *Mémoires* de Simone de Beauvoir', *Simone de Beauvoir Studies* 9 (1992), 75–9.

' "For Example": Simone de Beauvoir's Parenthetical Presence in Philippe Lejeune's Theory of Autobiography', *Simone de Beauvoir Studies* 10 (1993), 237–40.

Mahon, Joseph, *Existentialism, Feminism and Simone de Beauvoir*, Basingstoke: Macmillan, 1998.

Mannoni, Octave, 'Relation d'un sujet à sa propre vie', *Les Temps modernes* 528, (July 1990), 57–77.

Marinacci, Beth-Ann, 'Fictions, Faits et Faits "Gommés": L'Entreprise autobiographique chez Simone de Beauvoir', unpublished Master's thesis, Carleton University, Ottawa, Canada, 1994.

Marks, Elaine, *Simone de Beauvoir, Encounters with Death*, New Brunswick: Rutgers University Press, 1973.

'The Dream of Love: A Study of Three Autobiographies', in George Stambolian (ed.) *Twentieth Century French Fiction: Essays for Germaine Brée*, New Brunswick: Rutgers University Press, 1975, pp. 72–88.

'Transgressing the Incontinent Boundaries: The Body in Decline', *Yale French Studies* 72 (1986), 181–200.

(ed.), *Critical Essays on Simone de Beauvoir*, Boston, G.K.Hall, 1987.

McPherson, Karen S., 'Simone de Beauvoir: Generic Boundaries Transgressed', *Simone de Beauvoir Studies* 6 (1989), 5–12.

Merleau-Ponty, Maurice, 'Le Roman et la métaphysique' in *Sens et non-sens*, Paris: Nagel, 1965, pp. 45–71.

Messaoudi, Khalida, 'Le Courage du Castor', *Le Monde des livres*, 19 April 1996, p. 7.

Moi, Toril, 'An Intellectual Woman in Postwar France' in Denis Hollier (ed.) *A New History of French Literature*, London and Cambridge, MA.: Harvard University Press, 1989, pp. 982–8.

*Feminist Theory and Simone de Beauvoir*, Oxford: Blackwell, 1990.

'Simone de Beauvoir's *L'Invitée*: An Existentialist Melodrama' in *Paragraph* 14 (1991), 151–69.

*Simone de Beauvoir: The Making of an Intellectual Woman*, Oxford and Cambridge, USA: Blackwell, 1994.

Monteil, Claudine, *Simone de Beauvoir, Le Mouvement des femmes, Mémoires d'une jeune fille rebelle*, Monaco: du Rocher, 1996.

Moubachir, Chantal, *Simone de Beauvoir*, Paris: Seghers, 1971.

Murphy, Julien, 'Beauvoir and the Algerian War: Toward a Postcolonial Ethics', in Margaret Simons (ed.) *Feminist Interpretations of Simone de Beauvoir*, pp. 263–97.

Okely, Judith, *Simone de Beauvoir: A Re-Reading*, London: Virago, 1986.

Ophir, Anne, *Regards féminins: Beauvoir/Etcherelli/Rochefort. Condition féminine et création littéraire*, Paris: Denoël/Gonthier, 1976.

Patterson, Yolanda, *Simone de Beauvoir and the Demystification of Motherhood*, Ann Arbor/London: UMI Research Press, 1989.

'Who was this H.M.Parshley? The Saga of Translating Simone de Beauvoir's *The Second Sex*', *Simone de Beauvoir Studies* 9 (1992), 41–6.

Pilardi, Jo-Ann, 'Female Eroticism in the Works of Simone de Beauvoir' in Jeffner Allen and Iris Marion Young (eds.) *The Thinking Muse: Feminism and Modern French Philosophy*, Bloomington and Indiana: Indiana University Press, 1989, pp. 18–34.

Portuges, Catherine, 'Attachment and Separation in *Memoirs of a Dutiful Daughter*', *Yale French Studies* 72 (1986), 107–18.

Pringle, Lauren, 'An Annotated and Indexed Calendar and Abstract of the Ohio State University Collection of Simone de Beauvoir's Letters to Nelson Algren', unpublished Doctoral dissertation, Ohio State University, 1985.

Pucciani, Oreste F, 'En déjeunant avec Simone de Beauvoir', *Dalhousie French Studies* 13 (1987), 15–20.

Ravoux-Rallo, Elizabeth, 'Un souvenir d'enfance de Simone de Beauvoir', *Dalhousie French Studies* 13 (1987), 33–7.

Reeves, Margaret, 'Simone de Beauvoir and the Writing of Contemporary Feminist Theory: Rich, Butler and *The Second Sex*' in *Simone de Beauvoir Studies* 10 (1993), 159–64.

Rétif, Françoise, 'Simone de Beauvoir et l'autre', in *Les Temps modernes* 538 (1991), 76–95.

Robert, Georgette, 'Simone de Beauvoir et le féminisme', *Magazine littéraire* 145 (1979), 22–3.

Roberts, Mary Louise, 'Simone de Beauvoir: Coming of Age in the Twenties', *Simone de Beauvoir Studies* 8 (1991), 83–91.

Rochester, Myrna Bell and Mary Lawrence Test, 'From Moscow to Chicago and Back: Simone de Beauvoir, Political Peripatetic', *Simone de Beauvoir Studies* 12 (1995), 59–72.

Roy, Claude, 'Simone de Beauvoir', in Elaine Marks (ed.) *Critical Essays*, pp. 81–2.

Saccani, Jean-Pierre, *Nelson et Simone*, Monaco: Du Rocher, 1994.

Sallenave, Danièle, 'Beauvoir sans relâche', *Le Monde des Livres*, 19 April 1996, p. 6.

Sankovitch, Tilde, 'Simone de Beauvoir's Autobiographical Legacy', *Simone de Beauvoir Studies* 8 (1991), 93–101.

Savigneau, Josyane, 'Beauvoir dans la force de l'âge', *Le Monde des livres*, 13 August 1993, p. 9.

'Pour une morale de lucidité', *Le Monde des livres*, 19 April 1996, p. 7.

Seigfried, Charlene Haddock, '*Second Sex*: Second Thoughts' in al-Hibri and Simons, pp. 305–22.

Serre, Claudine, 'Les Beauvoir', *Le Monde Aujourd'hui*, 20–21 April 1986, p. 11.

Simons, Margaret, 'A Tribute to *The Second Sex* and Simone de Beauvoir', paper given at '*The Second Sex* – Thirty Years Later, A Commemorative Conference on Feminist Theory', September 27–29, 1979, New York University.

'Beauvoir and Sartre: The Philosophical Relationship', *Yale French Studies* 72 (1986), 165–79.

'Lesbian Connections: Simone de Beauvoir and Feminism', *Signs: Journal of Women in Culture and Society* 18, No.1 (1992), 136–62.

(ed.) *Feminist Interpretations of Simone de Beauvoir*, Pennsylvania State University Press, 1995.

Singer, Linda, 'Interpretation and Retrieval: Rereading Beauvoir' in al-Hibri and Simons (eds.), *Hypatia Reborn: Essay in Feminist Philosophy*, Bloomington and Indianapolis: Indiana University Press, 1990, pp. 323–35.

Vinteuil, Frédérique, 'Une grande intellectuelle', *Cahiers du féminisme*, 36 (1986), 30–1.

Vintges, Karen, *Philosophy as Passion, The Thinking of Simone de Beauvoir* Bloomington and Indianapolis: Indiana University Press, 1996.

Ward Jouve, Nicole, 'How *The Second Sex* Stopped my Aunt from Watering the Horse-chestnuts: Simone de Beauvoir and Contemporary Feminism' in *White Woman Speaks with Forked Tongue: Criticism as Autobiography*, London: Routledge, 1991, pp. 101–15.

Warren, Denise, 'Beauvoir on Bardot: The Ambiguity Syndrome', *Dalhousie French Studies* 13 (1987), 39–50.

Whitmarsh, Anne, *Simone de Beauvoir and the Limits of Commitment*, Cambridge University Press, 1981.

Winegarten, Renée, *Simone de Beauvoir*, Oxford: Berg, 1988.

Yalom, Marilyn, 'Sartre, Beauvoir and the Autobiographical Tradition', *Simone de Beauvoir Studies* 8 (1991), 75–81.

Young, Iris Marion, 'Humanism, Gynocentrism and Feminist Politics' in al-Hibri and Simons (eds), *Hypatia Reborn*, pp. 231–48.

Zéphir, Jacques J., *Le Néo-féminisme de Simone de Beauvoir*, Paris: Denoël/Gonthier, 1982.


OTHER WORKS

Alain-Fournier, *Le Grand Meaulnes*, Paris: Librairie générale française, 1983.

Albistur, Maïté et Armogathe, Daniel. *Histoire du féminisme français, tome II*, Paris: des femmes, 1977.

Alcott, Louisa M., *Little Women*, London: Penguin, 1953.

Algren, Nelson, *Never Come Morning*, London: Fourth Estate, 1988.
  *The Man with the Golden Arm*, New York: Four Walls and Eight Windows, 1990.

al-Hibri, Azizab Y. and Simons, Margaret A., (eds.), *Hypatia Reborn: Essays in Feminist Philosophy*, Bloomington and Indianapolis: Indiana University Press, 1990.

Anderson, Bonnie S. and Zinsser, Judith P., *A History of Their Own, Women in Europe from Prehistory to the Present, Vol. II*, Harmondsworth: Penguin, 1990.

Archer, John and Lloyd, Barbara *Sex and Gender*, Harmondsworth: Penguin, 1982.

Aronson, Ronald. 'Sartre and Marxism, A Double Retrospective', *Sartre Studies International* 1/2 (1995), 21–36.

Atack, Margaret, *Literature and the French Resistance: Cultural Politics and Narrative Forms 1940–50*, Manchester University Press, 1989.

Aubin, Claire et Gisserot, Hélène, *Les Femmes en France: 1985–1995*, Paris: La Documentation française, 1994.

Augustine, St., *Confessions*, trans. R.S. Pine-Coffin, Harmondsworth: Penguin, 1961.

Austin, J.L., *How To Do Things With Words*, Oxford University Press, 1962.

Balbus, Isaac D., 'Disciplining Women, Michel Foucault and the Power of Feminist discourse', in Seyla Benhabib and Drucilla Cornell (eds.) *Feminism as Critique*, Cambridge: Polity Press, 1992.

Barthes, Roland, *Mythologies*, Paris: Seuil, 1957.
  *La Chambre claire*, Paris: Seuil, 1980.

Bartky, Sandra Lee, 'Foucault, Femininity and the Modernisation of Patriarchal Power' in Irene Diamond and Lee Quinby (eds.) *Feminism and Foucault: Reflections on Resistance*, Boston: Northeastern University Press, 1988, pp. 61–86.

Battersby, Christine, *Gender and Genius: Towards a Feminist Aesthetic*, London: The Women's Press, 1989.
'Philosophy: The Recalcitrant Discipline' in *Women: A Cultural Review* 3 (1992), 121–32.
Baudrillard, Jean, *Simulacres et simulations*, Paris: Galilée, 1981.
Beckett, Samuel, *En attendant Godot*, Paris: Minuit, 1952.
*Fin de partie*, Paris: Minuit, 1957.
Benstock, Shari, *Women of the Left Bank*, London: Virago, 1987.
(ed.), *The Private Self*, London: Routledge, 1988.
Benveniste, Emile, *Problème de linguistique générale*, Paris: Gallimard, 1966.
Birchall, Ian, 'Prequel to the Heidegger Debate, Audry and Sartre', *Radical Philosophy* 88 (1998), 19–27.
Boak, Denis, *Sartre: Les Mots*, London: Grant and Cutler, 1987.
Brée, Germaine, *Camus and Sartre: Crisis and Commitment*, London: Calder and Boyars, 1974.
'Narcissus Absconditus: The Problematic Art of Autobiography in Contemporary France', Oxford: Clarendon Press, 1978.
Britton, Celia, *The Nouveau Roman, Fiction, Theory and Politics*, Basingstoke: Macmillan, 1992.
Brodzki, Bella and Celeste Schenck (eds.), *Life/Lines: Theorizing Women's Autobiography*, Ithaca: Cornell University Press.
Bruss, Elizabeth, *Autobiographical Acts: The Changing Situation of a Literary Genre*, Baltimore: Johns Hopkins University Press, 1976.
Butler, Judith, 'Variations on Sex and Gender: Beauvoir, Wittig and Foucault' in Seyla Benhabib and Drucilla Cornell (eds.) *Feminism as Critique*, Cambridge: Polity, 1987, pp. 128–42.
'Sexual Ideology and Phenomenological Description: A Feminist Critique of Merleau-Ponty's *Phenomenology of Perception*' in Jeffner Allen and Iris Marion Young (eds.) *The Thinking Muse, Feminism in Modern French Philosophy*, Bloomington and Indianapolis: Indiana University Press, 1989, pp. 85–100.
*Gender Trouble*, London and New York: Routledge, 1990.
*Bodies that Matter*, London: Routledge, 1993.
'Gender as Performance: An Interview with Judith Butler', *Radical Philosophy* 67 (1994), 32–9.
*Excitable Speech, A Politics of the Performative*, London and New York: Routledge, 1997.
Campbell, James, *Paris Interzone*, London: Secker and Warburg, 1994, Minerva 1995.
Camus, Albert, *La Chute*, Paris: Gallimard, 1956; Folio, 1992.
*L'Exil et le royaume* Paris: Gallimard, 1957; Folio, 1991.
*Le Premier Homme*, Paris: Gallimard, 1994.
Cardinal, Marie, *Les Mots pour le dire*, Paris: Grasset, 1975.
*Autrement dit*, Paris: Grasset, 1977.
Caws, Peter, *Sartre*, London: Routledge, 1979.

Charle, Christophe, *Naissance des "intellectuels"*, Paris: Minuit, 1990.

Chauchat, Catherine, *L'Autobiographie: Les Mots de Sartre*, Paris: Gallimard, 1993.

Clay, John, *R.D.Laing, A Divided Self*, London: Hodder and Stoughton, 1996.

Coady, C.A.J. *Testimony, A Philosophical Study*, Oxford: Clarendon Press, 1992.

Cohen-Solal, Annie, *Sartre, a Life*, London: Heinemann, 1988.

Copley, Anthony, *Sexual Moralities in France 1780–1980*, London: Routledge, 1989.

Courtivron, Isabelle de, *Violette Leduc*, Boston: Twayne, 1985.

Cullen, Bernard, 'Merleau-Ponty', in Richard Kearney (ed.) *Routledge History of Philosophy, Vol. VIII: Continental Philosophy in the Twentieth Century*, London: Routledge, 1994, pp. 105–30.

Culler, Jonathan, *Flaubert: The Uses of Uncertainty*, London: Elek, 1974.

Delay, Jean-Paul, *Les Dissolutions de la mémoire*, Paris: Presses universitaires, 1942.

De Lauretis, Teresa, 'Sexual Indifference and Lesbian Representation' in Sue-Ellen Case (ed.) *Performing Feminisms: Feminism, Critical Theory and Theatre*, Baltimore and London: John Hopkins University Press, 1990, pp. 17–39.

Delphy, Christine, 'The Invention of French Feminism: An Essential Move', *Yale French Studies* 87, (1995), 190–221.

De Man, Paul, 'Autobiography as De-Facement', *Modern Language Notes* 94 (1979), 919–30.

Derrida, Jacques, 'La Structure, le signe et le jeu dans le discours des sciences humaines' in *L'Ecriture et la différence*, Paris: Seuil, 1967, pp. 409–28.

'Signature, événement, contexte' in *Marges de la philosophie*, Paris: Minuit, 1972, pp. 365–93.

'La Loi du genre' in *Parages*, Paris: Galilée, 1986, pp. 250–87.

Deutsch, Helene, *The Psychology of Women*, New York: Grune and Stratton, 1944.

Didier, Béatrice, *Le Journal intime*, Vendôme: PUF, 1976.

Donohue, H.E.F., *Conversations with Nelson Algren*, New York: Hill and Wang, 1964.

Drew, Bettina, *Nelson Algren: A Life on the Wild Side*, Austin: University of Texas Press, 1989.

Duchen, Claire, *Feminism in France, From May '68 to Mitterand*, London: Routledge, 1986.

(ed.) and trans., *French Connections: Voices from the Women's Movement in France*, London: Hutchinson, 1987.

Duras, Marguerite, *L'Amant*, Paris: Minuit, 1984.

*La Douleur* Paris: P. O. L., 1985.

Eagleton, Terry, *The Ideology of the Aesthetic*, Oxford: Blackwell, 1990.

Elbaz, Robert, *The Changing Nature of the Self*, London: Crook Helm, 1988.

Eliot, George, *The Mill on the Floss*, Glasgow: Collins, 1979.

Ewald, François, Farge, Arlette and Perrot, Michelle, 'Une pratique de la vérité' in *Michel Foucault: une histoire de la vérité*, Paris: Syros, 1985, pp. 9–18.

Fabre, Michel, *The World of Richard Wright*, Jackson: University Press of Mississippi, 1985.

Faderman, Liliane, *Surpassing the Love of Men*, London: The Women's Press, 1985.

Fallaize, Elizabeth, *French Women's Writing*, Basingstoke and London: Macmillan, 1993.

Fanon, Frantz, *Peau noire, masques blancs*, Paris: Seuil, 1952.

Felman, Shoshana and Laub, Dori, *Testimony: Crises of Witnessing in Literature, Psychoanalysis and History*, London: Routledge, 1992.

Felski, Rita, *Beyond Feminist Aesthetics*, London: Hutchinson Radius, 1989.

Flieger, Jerry Aline, *Colette and the Fantom Subject of Autobiography*, Ithaca and London: Cornell University Press, 1992.

Foucault, Michel, *L'Archéologie du savoir*, Paris: Gallimard, 1969.

  *Surveiller et punir*, Paris: Gallimard, 1975.

  'Vérité et pouvoir', *L'Arc* 70 (1977), 16–26.

  *La Volonté de savoir. Histoire de la sexualité I*, Paris: Gallimard, 1976.

  *Herculine Barbin, dite Alexina B*, présenté par Michel Foucault, Paris: Gallimard, 1978.

  'Introduction' to *Herculine Barbin, Being the Recently Discovered Memoirs of a Nineteenth Century French Hermaphrodite*, trans. Richard McDougall, New York: Pantheon Books, 1980.

  'The Subject and Power' in Hubert L. Dreyfus and Paul Rabinow (eds.) *Michel Foucault: Beyond Structuralism and Hermeneutics*, Brighton: Harvester Wheatsheaf, 1982, pp. 208–26.

  *L'Usage des plaisirs. Histoire de la sexualité II*, Paris: Gallimard, 1984.

  *Le Souci de soi. Histoire de la sexualité III*, Paris: Gallimard, 1984.

  'The Ethic of Care for the Self as a Practice of Freedom' in J. Bernauer and D. Rasmussen (eds.) *The Final Foucault*, Cambridge, MA.: MIT Press, 1988, pp. 112–31.

  'Technologies of the Self' in Hutton, Patrick, Martin, Luther H. and Gutman, Huck (eds.) *Technologies of the Self: A Seminar with Michel Foucault*, London: Tavistock, 1988, pp. 16–49.

  'L'Herméneutique du sujet' in *Résumé des cours 1970–1982*, Paris: Julliard, 1989, pp. 145–66.

Freeman, Mark, *Rewriting the Self: History, Memory, Narrative*, London and New York: Routledge, 1993.

Fretz, Léo, 'Le Concept de l'individualité', *Obliques*, 'Sartre', numéro spécial 18–19 (1979), 221–34.

Freud, Sigmund, 'The Psychogenesis of a Case of Homosexuality in a Woman' in *Case Histories II*, Harmondsworth: Penguin, 1981.

*Jokes and their Relation to the Unconscious*, Standard Edition Col. VIII, London: Hogarth Press, 1960.

'The Vol. XVII, London: Hogarth Press, 1955.

Friedan, Betty, *The Feminine Mystique*, Harmondsworth: Penguin, 1979.

Fry, Roger, *Vision and Design*, Harmondsworth: Penguin, 1940.

Furman, Nelly, 'The Languages of Pain in *Shoah*' in Lawrence D. Kritzman (ed.) *Auschwitz and After, Race, Culture and the Jewish Question in France*, London: Routledge, 1995, pp. 299–312.

Genet, Jean, *Journal du voleur*, Paris: Gallimard, 1949, 1962.

Gerassi, John, *Jean-Paul Sartre, Hated Conscience of his Century, Vol. I: Protestant or Protester*, Chicago: University of Chicago Press, 1989.

Gilmore, Leigh, *Autobiographics: A Feminist Theory of Women's Self-Representation*, Ithaca and London: Cornell University Press, 1994.

Gramsci, Antonio, *Selections from the Prison Notebooks of Antonio Gramsci*, (ed.) and trans. Quintin Hoare and Geoffrey Nowell Smith, London: Lawrence and Wishart, 1971.

Grimshaw, Jean, 'Practices of Freedom' in Caroline Ramazanoglu (ed.) *Up Against Foucault*, London and New York: Routledge, 1993, pp. 51–72.

Grosz, Elizabeth, *Sexual Subversions*, St Leonards, Australia: Allen and Unwin, 1989.

*Volatile Bodies, Towards a Corporeal Feminism*, Bloomington and Indianapolis: Indiana University Press, 1994.

(ed.) with Probyn, Elspeth, *Sexy Bodies*, London: Routledge, 1995.

Guibert, Hervé, *A l'ami qui ne m'a pas sauvé la vie*, Paris: Gallimard, 1990.

Gusdorf, Georges, 'Conditions and Limits of Autobiography' in James Olney (ed.) *Autobiography: Essays Theoretical and Critical*, Princeton University Press, 1980, pp. 28–48.

Gutman, Huck, 'Rousseau's *Confessions*: A Technology of the Self', in Hutton, Patrick, Martin, Luther H. and Gutman, Huck (eds.) *Technologies of the Self: A Seminar with Michel Foucault*, London: Tavistock, 1988, pp. 99–120.

Hamer, Diane. 'Significant Others: Lesbians and Psychoanalytic Theory, *Feminist Review* 34 (1990), 134–51.

Hanly, Charles, *The Problem of Truth in Applied Psychoanalysis*, New York: Guilford Press, 1992.

Havelock Ellis, Henry, *Studies in the Psychology of Sex*, Philadelphia: F.A. Davis, 1897–1928.

Hegel, G.W.F., *Phenomenology of Spirit*, trans. Miller, A.V., Oxford University Press, 1977.

Heidegger, Martin, *Being and Time*, trans. Macquarrie, J. and Robinson, Edward, New York: Harper and Row, 1962.

Hekman, Susan J., *Gender and Knowledge: Elements of a Postmodern Feminism*, Cambridge: Polity Press, 1990.

Hellman, John, *Simone Weil: An Introduction to her Thought*, Ontario, Canada: Wilfrid Laurier Press, 1982.

Hewitt, Leah D., *Autobiographical Tightropes*, Lincoln: University of Nebraska Press, 1990.

Hooks, Bell, *Talking Back: Thinking Feminist, Thinking Black*, Boston: South End, 1989.

Hughes, Alex, *Violette Leduc: Mothers, Lovers and Language*, Leeds: W.S.Maney and Son for MHRA, 1994.

Hutton, Patrick H. 'Foucault, Freud and the Technologies of the Self' in Hutton, Martin and Gutman (eds.) *Technologies of the Self: A Seminar with Michel Foucault*, pp. 121–44.

Husserl, Edmund, *The Phenomenology of Internal Time-Consciousness*, (ed.) Heidegger, Martin, Bloomington and London: Indiana University Press, 1964.

Ian, Marcia, *Remembering the Phallic Mother: Psychoanalysis, Modernism and the Fetish*, Ithaca and London: Cornell University Press, 1993.

Irigaray, Luce, *Speculum de l'autre femme*, Paris: Minuit, 1974.

*Ce Sexe qui n'en est pas un*, Paris: Minuit, 1977.

'Misère de la psychanalyse' in *Parler n'est jamais neutre*, Paris: Minuit, 1985, pp. 253–79.

Jelinek, Estelle. (ed.), *Women's Autobiography: Essays in Criticism*, Bloomington: Indiana Press, 1980.

Kafka, Franz, *The Transformation 'Metamorphosis' and Other Stories*, Harmondsworth: Penguin, 1992.

*The Castle*, Harmondsworth: Penguin, 1981.

Kaufmann, Dorothy, 'Uncovering a Woman's Life: Edith Thomas, novelist, historian, résistante', *The French Review* 67 (1993), 61–73.

Keefe, Terry, 'The Other in Sartre's Early Concept of "Situation"', *Sartre Studies International* 1–2 (1995), 95–113.

(ed.) with Smyth, Edmund, *Autobiography and the Existential Self*, Liverpool University Press, 1995.

Kelly, Michael, *Hegel in France*, Birmingham Modern Languages Publications, 1992.

Kierkegaard, Søren. *The Diary of Søren Kierkegaard*, (ed.) Rohde, Peter, New York: Philosophical Library, 1960.

*The Concept of Irony*, trans. Capel, Lee M., London: Collins, 1966.

Kleinbord Labovitz, Esther. *The Myth of the Heroine, The Female Bildungsroman in the Twentieth Century*, New York: Peter Lang, 1986.

Kolakowski, Leszek, *Bergson*, Oxford University Press, 1985.

Kristeva, Julia, 'Le Temps des femmes', *33/44: Cahiers de recherche de sciences des textes et documents* 5 (1979), 5–19.

*Pouvoirs de l'horreur*, Paris: Seuil, 1980.

Kritzman, Lawrence D., *Michel Foucault: Politics, Philosophy, Culture: Interviews and Other Writings 1977–84*, London: Routledge, 1988.

Kruks, Sonia, *Situation and Human Existence*, London: Unwin Hyman, 1990.

Lacan, Jacques, 'Le stade du miroir comme formateur de la fonction du Je,' 1936, in *Ecrits*, Paris: Seuil, 1966, pp. 93–100.

*Les Complexes familiaux dans la formation de l'individu: essai d'analyse d'une fonction en psychologie*, Paris: Navarin, 1984, 1938.

Lacoin, Elisabeth, *Zaza: Correspondance et carnets 1914–1929*, Paris: Seuil, 1991.

Laing, R.D., *Self and Others*, London: Tavistock Publications, 1961; Penguin 1990.

Langer, Monika M., *Merleau-Ponty's Phenomenology of Perception: A Guide and Commentary*, Basingstoke and London: Macmillan, 1989.

Lavers, Annette, 'Sartre and Freud', *French Studies* 41 (1987), 298–317.

Leak, Andrew N., *The Perverted Consciousness, Sexuality and Sartre*, Basingstoke: Macmillan, 1989.

Le Bon, Sylvie. 'Un Positiviste Désespéré: Michel Foucault', *Les Temps modernes* 258 (1967), 1299–319.

Leduc, Violette, *L'Affamée*, Paris: Gallimard, 1948.

*La Bâtarde*, préface de Simone de Beauvoir, Paris: Gallimard, 1964.

'Lettres à Simone de Beauvoir', *Les Temps modernes* 495 (1987), 1–41.

Lehmann, Rosamond, *Dusty Answer*, London: Chatto and Windus, 1927; London: Penguin, 1936.

*A Note in Music*, London: Chatto and Windus, 1930; London: Virago, 1985.

*Invitation to the Waltz*, 1932; Harmondsworth: Penguin, 1962.

*The Weather in the Streets*, London: Collins, 1936; London: Virago, 1991.

*Rosamond Lehmann's Album;* London: Chatto and Windus, 1985.

Leiris, Michel, *L'Age d'homme*; Paris: Gallimard, 1939; Folio, 1991.

Lejeune, Philippe, *L'Autobiographie en France*, Paris: Armand Colin, 1971.

*Le Pacte autobiographique*, Paris: Seuil, 1975.

*Moi aussi*, Paris: Seuil, 1986.

'Nouveau Roman et retour à l'autobiographie' in Michel Contat (ed.) *L'Auteur et le manuscrit*, Paris: Presses universitaires de France, 1991, pp. 51–70.

Loftus, Elizabeth F., *Eyewitness Testimony*, Cambridge, MA.: Harvard University Press, 1979.

McLellan, David, *Simone Weil, Utopian Pessimist*, London and Basingstoke: Macmillan 1989, Papermac 1991 edn.

McMahon, Frank, 'Rereading *The Outsider*: Double Consciousness and the Divided Self', unpublished paper.

'Richard Wright's Paris Period: the Black Intellectual as Outsider', unpublished paper.

McMillan, James F., *Twentieth Century France, Politics and Society 1898–1991*, London: Arnold, 1992.

McNay, Lois, *Foucault and Feminism: Power, Gender and the Self*, Cambridge: Polity, 1992.

Macey, David, *The Lives of Michel Foucault*, London: Vintage, 1994.

Malraux, André, *Le Miroir des limbes I, Antimémoires*, Paris: Gallimard, 1972; Folio, 1992.

Marcus, Laura, *Auto/Biographical Discourses, Theory, Criticism, Practice*, Manchester University Press, 1994.

Marks, Elaine, 'I am My Own Heroine: Some Thoughts about Women and Autobiography in France' in Sidonie Cassirer (ed.) *Female Studies IX: Teaching About Women in the Foreign Languages*, New York: Feminine Press, 1975, pp. 1–10.

'The Dream of Love: A Study of Three Autobiographies' in George Stambolian (ed.) *Twentieth Century Fiction: Essays for Germaine Brée*, New Brunswick: Rutgers University Press, 1975, pp. 72–88.

'Lesbian Intertextuality' in George Stambolian and Elaine Marks (eds.) *Homosexualities and French Literature*, Ithaca and London: Cornell University Press, 1979, pp. 353–77.

Martin, Biddy, 'Lesbian Identity and Autobiographical Differences' in Brodzki and Schenck (eds.) *Life/Lines*, pp. 77–103.

Meredith, George, *Diana of the Crossways*, London: Constable, 1902.

Merleau-Ponty, Maurice, *Phénoménologie de la perception*, Paris: Gallimard, 1945 édition 'tel' 1994.

Miller, Nancy, *Subject to Change: Reading Feminist Writing*, New York: Columbia University Press, 1988.

'Writing Fictions: Women's Autobiography in France' in Brodzki and Schenck (eds.), *Life/Lines*, pp. 45–61.

Moi, Toril, 'Jealousy and Sexual Difference', *Feminist Review* 11 (1982), 53–68.

'Power, Sex and Subjectivity: Feminist Reflections on Foucault', *Paragraph* 5 (1985), 95–102.

'Existentialism and Feminism' in *Oxford Literary Review* 8 (1986), 88–95.

(ed.), *French Feminist Thought*, Oxford: Blackwell, 1987.

*Sexual/Textual Politics*, London: Routledge, 1988.

Montaigne, Michel de *Essais* in *Oeuvres complètes*, Paris: Gallimard Pléiade, 1962.

Mootry, Maria K., 'Bitches, Whores and Woman Haters: Archetypes and typologies in the Art of Richard Wright' in Richard Macksey and Frank E.Moorer (eds.) *Richard Wright, A Collection of Critical Essays*, New Jersey: Prentice-Hall, 1984, pp. 117–27.

Myrdal, Alva. 'A Parallel to the Negro Problem' in Myrdal, Gunnar, *An American Dilemma, Vol. II, The Negro Social Structure*, New York: McGraw-Hill, 1964, pp. 1073–78.

Niedzwiecki, Patricia, *Beauvoir peintre*, Paris: Côté-Femmes, 1991.

O'Connor, Noreen and Ryan, Joanna. *Wild Desires and Mistaken Identities, Lesbianism and Psychoanalysis*, London: Virago, 1993.

Olney, James, 'Autobiography and the Cultural Moment' and 'Some Versions of Memory/Some Versions of Bios: The Ontology of Autobiography' in James Olney (ed.), *Autobiography: Essays Theoretical and Critical*, Princeton University Press, 1980, pp. 3–27 and pp. 236–67.

Ory, Pascal and Jean-François Sirinelli, *Les Intellectuels en France: de l'Affaire Dreyfus à nos jours*, Paris: Armand Colin, 1986.

Ozouf, Mona, *Les Mots des femmes, essai sur la singularité française*, Paris: Fayard, 1995.

Pascal, Roy, *Design and Truth in Autobiography*, London: Routledge, 1960.

Pétrement, Simone, *La Vie de Simone Weil*, Paris: Fayard, 1973.

Poster, Mark, *Existential Marxism in Postwar France: From Sartre to Althusser*, Princeton University Press, 1975.

'Foucault and the Tyranny of Greece' in David Couzens Hoy (ed.) *Foucault: A Critical Reader*, Oxford: Blackwell, 1986, pp. 205–20.

Quinby, Lee, 'The Subject of Memoirs: The Woman Warrior's Technology of Ideographic Selfhood', in Sidonie Smith and Julia Watson (eds.) *De/Colonising the Subject*, pp. 297–320.

Rabinow, Paul (ed.) *The Foucault Reader*, Harmondsworth: Penguin, 1991.

Ramazanoglu, Caroline, (ed.) *Up Against Foucault*, London: Routledge, 1993.

Renza, Louis A., 'The Veto of the Imagination: A Theory of Autobiography' in Olney (ed.), *Autobiography: Essays Theoretical and Critical*, pp. 268–95.

Rich, Adrienne, 'Compulsory Heterosexuality and Lesbian Existence', *Signs* 5 (1980), 631–60.

Ricoeur, Paul, *Temps et récit II: La Configuration du temps dans le récit de fiction*, Paris: Seuil, 1984.

*Temps et récit III: Le Temps raconté*, Paris: Seuil, 1985.

'Life in Quest of Narrative' and 'Narrative Identity' in David Wood (ed.) *On Paul Ricoeur: Narrative and Interpretation*, London: Routledge, 1991, pp. 20–33 and pp. 188–99.

*Soi-même comme un autre*, Paris: Seuil, 1990.

Robinson, Christopher, *Scandal in the Ink: Male and Female Homosexuality in Twentieth Century French Literature*, London: Cassell, 1995.

Rosenblatt, Roger, 'Black Autobiography: Life as the Death Weapon' in Olney (ed.), *Autobiography: Essays Theoretical and Critical*, pp. 169–80.

Rousseau, Jean-Jacques, *Les Confessions* in *Oeuvres complètes*, tome I (Paris: Gallimard Pléiade, 1959).

*Les Rêveries du promeneur solitaire* in *Oeuvres complètes*, tome I (Paris: Gallimard Pléiade, 1959).

Sachs, Maurice, *Le Sabbat*, Paris: Gallimard, 1946, 1960.

Said, Edward W., 'Foucault and the Imagination of Power' in David Couzens Hoy (ed.) *Foucault: A Critical Reader*, Oxford: Blackwell, 1986, pp. 149–55.

*Representations of the Intellectual, The 1993 Reith Lectures*, London: Vintage, 1994.

Sarraute, Nathalie, *Enfance*, Paris: Gallimard, 1983, Folio edn, 1989.

Sartre, Jean-Paul, *La Transcendance de l'ego*, Paris: Librairie philosophique J.Vrin, 1988; originally published in *Recherches philosophiques* 6 (1936).

*La Nausée*, Paris: Gallimard, 1938; 1968 edn.

*L'Imaginaire*, Paris: Gallimard, 1940; 1962 edn.

*L'Etre et le néant*, Paris: Gallimard, 1943; édition 'tel' 1995.

*L'Age de raison*, Paris: Gallimard, 1945; Folio, 1993.

*Réflexions sur la question juive*, Paris: Gallimard, 1946; Folio, 1995.

*Huis clos* in *Théâtre I*, Paris: Gallimard, 1947.

*Les Mains sales*, Paris: Gallimard, 1948; London: Methuen, 1963.

*Qu'est-ce que la littérature?* Paris: Gallimard, 1948; Folio, 1985.

*Le Diable et le bon dieu*, Paris: Gallimard, 1951.

*Les Mots*, Paris: Gallimard, 1964; Folio, 1990.

*Plaidoyer pour les intellectuels*, Paris: Gallimard, 1972; Gallimard 'Idées' 1980.

*Situations IX*, Paris: Gallimard, 1972.

*Situations X, politique et autobiographie*, Paris: Gallimard, 1976.

*Les Carnets de la drôle de guerre, 1939–40*, Paris: Gallimard, 1983.

*Lettres au Castor et à quelques autres, tome I: 1926–39, tome II: 1940–63*, Paris: Gallimard, 1983.

Schacht, Richard, *Classical Modern Philosophers: Descartes to Kant*, London: Routledge, 1984.

Scriven, Michael, *Paul Nizan: Communist Novelist*, Basingstoke and London: Macmillan, 1988.

Siegel, Liliane, *La Clandestine*, Paris: Maren Sell, 1988.

Simons, Judy, *Rosamond Lehmann*, Basingstoke and London: Macmillan, 1992.

Sirinelli, Jean-François, *Génération intellectuelle. Khâgneux et normaliens dans l'entre-deux guerres*, Paris: Fayard, 1988.

*Intellectuels et passions françaises: manifestes et pétitions au vingtième siècle*, Paris: Fayard, 1990.

Smith, Sidonie and Watson, Julia (eds.) *De/Colonizing the Subject: The Politics of Gender in Women's Autobiography*, Minneapolis: University of Minnesota Press, 1992.

Smith, Sidonie, *Subjectivity, Identity and the Body: Women's Autobiographical Practices in the Twentieth Century*, Bloomington and Indianapolis: Indiana University Press, 1993.

Sontag, Susan, *On Photography*, Harmondsworth: Penguin, 1979.

Soper, Kate, 'Forget Foucault?' in 'Michel Foucault: J'Accuse', *New Formations* 25 (1995), 21–7.

Southern, David W., *Gunnar Myrdal and Black-White Relations, The Use and Abuse of An American Dilemma, 1944–69*, Baton Rouge and London: Louisiana State University Press, 1987.

Spurling, Laurie, *Phenomenology and the Social World, The Philosophy of Merleau-Ponty and its Relation to the Social Sciences*, London: Routledge, 1977.

Stanley, Liz, *The Auto/biographical I*, Manchester University Press, 1992.

Stanton, Domna C., 'Autogynography: Is the Subject Different?' in Domna C. Stanton (ed.) *The Female Autograph*, University of Chicago Press, 1984, pp. 3–20.

Stein, Gertrude, *The Autobiography of Alice B.Toklas*, Bodley Head, 1933, Harmondsworth: Penguin, 1983.

*Everybody's Autobiography*, 1938, London: Virago, 1985.

Sturrock, John, *The Language of Autobiography*, Cambridge University Press, 1993.

Tambling, Jeremy, *Confession: Sexuality, Sin, The Subject*, Manchester University Press, 1990.

Taylor, John, 'Psychasthenia in *La Nausée*', *Sartre Studies International* 1–2 (1995), 77–93.

Thacker, Andrew, 'Foucault's Aesthetics of Existence' in *Radical Philosophy*, No.63, 1993, 13–21.

Todd, Olivier, *Un fils rebelle*, Paris: Grasset, 1981.

Todorov, Tzvetan, *Genres in Discourse*, trans. Catherine Porter, Cambridge University Press, 1990.

Van Casselaer, Catherine, *Lot's Wife, Lesbian Paris 1890–1914*, Liverpool: Janus Press, 1986.

Warnock, Mary, *Existentialism*, Oxford University Press, 1970.

*Memory*, London: Faber, 1987.

Weatherby, W.J., 'The Life and Hard Times of Nelson Algren', *Sunday Times*, 17 May 1981.

Weeks, Jeffrey, *Sexuality and its Discontents, Meanings, Myths and Modern Sexualities*, London: Routledge, 1985.

Weintraub, Karl, *The Value of the Individual: Self and Circumstance in Autobiography*, Chicago and London: University of Chicago Press, 1978.

Whitford, Margaret, 'Merleau-Ponty's Critique of Sartre's Philosophy: An Interpretative Account', *French Studies* 33 (1979), 305–18.

'Luce Irigaray and the Female Imaginary: Speaking as a Woman', *Radical Philosophy* 43 (1986), 2–8.

'The Feminist Philosopher: A Contradiction in Terms?' *Women: a Cultural Review* 3 (1992), 111–20.

Williams, David, *Jean-Jacques Rousseau: Rêveries du promeneur solitaire*, London: Grant and Cutler, 1984.

Wittig, Monique, *Le Corps Lesbien*, Paris: Minuit, 1973.

*The Straight Mind and Other Essays*, Hemel Hempstead: Harvester, 1992.

Woolf, Virginia, 'Modern Fiction' in *The Common Reader*, First Series, London: The Hogarth Press, 1948, pp. 184–95.

'A Sketch of the Past' in *Moments of Being*, St. Albans: Triad/Panther, 1978, pp. 71–159.

*Mrs Dalloway*, St. Albans: Triad/Panther, 1978.

*A Room of One's Own*, St. Albans: Granada, 1983.

*Orlando*, London: Granada, 1984.

*The Complete Shorter Fiction*, (ed.) Susan Dick, London: Hogarth Press, 1985.

Wright, Elizabeth, (ed.) *Feminism and Psychoanalysis: A Critical Dictionary*, Oxford: Blackwell, 1992.

Wright, Richard, *Native Son*, New York: Harper and Brothers, 1940; New York: Harper Perrenial, 1993.
  *Black Boy*, New York: Harper Brothers, 1945; London: Pan Books, 1993.
  *The Outsider*, New York: Harper Brothers, 1953; New York: Harper Perennial, 1993.
  *American Hunger*, New York: Harper and Row, 1977.


FILMOGRAPHY

'Simone de Beauvoir', réalisé par Dodo Humphreys, Balfour Films, London, 1976, 39 mins.
'Sartre par lui-même', réalisé par Alexandre Astruc et Michel Contat, Sodaperaga, Institut national de l'audiovisuel, 1976, 180 mins.
'Simone de Beauvoir', un film de Josée Dayan et Malka Ribowska, réalisé par Josée Dayan, La Société française de productions, MK2 Pierre Films, 1978, 60 mins.
'Shoah', réalisé par Claude Lanzmann, 1985, 566 mins.
'Hommage de Kate Millett à Simone de Beauvoir', réalisé par Anne Faisandier, 1986, 11 mins.
'Daughters of De Beauvoir', directed by Imogen Sutton, Arts Council of Great Britain, 1989, 60 mins.

# Index

Book titles in French are indexed alphabetically ignoring the article. SdB = Simone de Beauvoir. The headwords refer to her and her writings except where otherwise specified.

# CAMBRIDGE STUDIES IN FRENCH